A Practical Guide to Working with Sex Offenders

of related interest

Changing Offending Behaviour
A Handbook of Practical Exercises and Photocopiable
Resources for Promoting Positive Change
Clark Baim and Lydia Guthrie
Foreword by Fergus McNeill
ISBN 978 1 84905 511 6
eISBN 978 0 85700 928 9

**A Community-Based Approach to the
Reduction of Sexual Reoffending**
Circles of Support and Accountability
Stephen Hanvey, Terry Philpot and Chris Wilson
ISBN 978 1 84905 198 9
eISBN 978 0 85700 423 9

Violence, Restorative Justice, and Forgiveness
Dyadic Forgiveness and Energy Shifts in Restorative Justice Dialogue
Marilyn Armour and Mark Umbreit
ISBN 978 1 78592 795 9
eISBN 978 1 78450 795 4

The Child's World, Third Edition
The Essential Guide to Assessing Vulnerable
Children, Young People and their Families
Edited by Jan Horwath and Dendy Platt
ISBN 978 1 78592 116 2
eISBN 978 1 78450 382 6

A Practical Guide to Working with Sex Offenders

Diane Wills and Andrew Wills

Jessica Kingsley Publishers
London and Philadelphia

First published in Great Britain in 2021 by Jessica Kingsley Publishers

An Hachette Company

1

Copyright © Diane Wills and Andrew Wills 2021

Front cover image source: pexels.com.

A CIP catalogue record for this title is available from the
British Library and the Library of Congress

ISBN 978 1 78592 506 1
eISBN 978 1 78450 892 0

Printed and bound in Great Britain by Clays Ltd

Jessica Kingsley Publishers' policy is to use papers that are natural, renewable and recyclable products and made from wood grown in sustainable forests. The logging and manufacturing processes are expected to conform to the environmental regulations of the country of origin.

Jessica Kingsley Publishers
73 Collier Street
London N1 9BE, UK

www.jkp.com

Contents

Introduction

This book is about working with those people who perpetrate sexually harmful behaviours. Acknowledging the very serious impact on those who are affected by this behaviour, the book is not about 'victims' – that is a different book. It is difficult to strike a balance in content and use of language professionally and more generally. Whilst the title of this book uses the term 'sex offenders', the use of language throughout attempts to avoid the term where appropriate, and there are several reasons for this.

Using the term 'sex offender' strictly means that a person has been found to be guilty by a Court of illegal sexually abusive immoral behaviour. Without entering too deeply into the philosophy of law, it is possible to suggest that the law is underwritten by a common base of principles of the community that constitutes 'institutional morality' (after Ronald Dworkin, 1931–2013, cited in Gillespie & Weare, 2019, p.11). The term 'sex offender' does not cover all those who have harmed or are suspected of harming somebody. Therefore in Chapter 4 we use the phrase 'people who sexually harm others' because this is a broader term that includes all those who have been found guilty of a sexually harmful behaviour in a Criminal Court, and includes situations where it is accepted that harm has occurred or is likely to occur but where no person has been found guilty of a crime (see also Chapter 7).

What is more, by naming or labelling a person a 'sex offender', the person is identified primarily by the worst 'bad' thing that they have done. Recognizing that harming another person sexually is 'a very bad thing', identifying the person *solely* by their harmful behaviour is not helpful when trying to work effectively with them to reduce future risk of harm (see Chapter 9).

The next point raised by language is whether to call the person who has been harmed a 'victim' or a 'survivor'. Bearing in mind that not all people survive the extremes of sexual violence, identifying a person as a victim also has a number of connotations. Identifying a person solely by the worst thing that has happened to them is again perhaps not entirely helpful; the person is more than just 'a victim'. Whilst we have tried, where appropriate, to avoid the term 'victim', we have inevitably had to use it, as there is no entirely suitable alternative.

Sex and sexual behaviour is a complex phenomenon that is hard to define in its totality. Sex is generally socially ubiquitous, even in its absence. 'Deviant' abusive sex adds a layer of complexity, particularly in the use of language – it is a moving social landscape that has undergone very significant changes in social expression. Some social expressions used in the past would not be acceptable now, and some contemporary social expressions would have been decidedly judged immoral in the past – there are substantial examples all around us. Undertaking this work requires us to consider our own standpoint on sex and sexuality, including an understanding of our own sexual interests, experiences and behaviour that can be an uncomfortable process but necessary for an effective reflective practitioner. It is also reflexive because when we think reflectively about sexual behaviour, our thoughts about sex tend to change.

Talking about sex is uncomfortable, but paradoxically it is ubiquitous. Herschel Prins (1980), a founding voice of forensic psychiatry, raises some fundamentally insightful issues, such as whether sex offenders should be treated as a separate identifiable group of people different from all others; that (in 1980 at least) there were as many claims of spurious as well as genuine expertise as to causes of sexual harmful behaviour; and that this is an intensely emotive topic. He concludes, from a psychodynamic perspective, that 'successful management treatment may lie within the person offering it' and that it is necessary to be 'aware of one's own sexual "blind-spots"' (1980, p.213). Hence the initial chapters in this current

8

book make reference to work by cultural anthropologists Bronisław Malinowski (1884–1942) and Margaret Mead (1901–1978), as well as sexologists Alfred Kinsey, Clellan Ford, Frank Beach, William Masters and Virginia Johnson, which suggest that sexual behaviour is culturally located. It raises questions about ideas of what is normal, abnormal, dysfunctional or deviant sexual behaviours. The focus of Prins's writing about sexual behaviour and sexual offending (1980, pp.213–262) is on behaviour that 'the law holds to be coercive, exploitive, degrading, or an affront to public decency' (p.217). Having been described as contemporary 'folk devils' (West, 1996), the common issue is whether those who harm others are offenders, deviants or even patients, and that 'sexual offending and sex offenders cannot be seen in isolation from sexual behaviour in general' (Prins, 1980, p.213).

Legal jurisdictions around the world have different criteria as to what is categorized as a sex offence, and the definition of sex offender is not necessarily the same everywhere. Here we are concerned with the UK, but we acknowledge the disparities over what is defined as sexually offensive (Terry, 2017).

Understanding and working effectively with the complex behaviours of those who sexually abuse others is difficult to unravel, and cannot be totally understood. Forensic analysis by investigative services sufficient for the needs of criminal justice agencies to determine guilt or otherwise leads to appropriate punishment, control and sanctions. Whilst criminal justice processes can uncover and describe the 'what', understanding the 'why' of deeper reasons for abuse is often partial and contingent, perhaps also insufficient and enigmatic.

As part of a burgeoning academic industry, although it can be highly emotive and professionally and personally challenging, by focusing on 'the offender' we aim to explore the fundamental cause of harm.

CHAPTER 1

A Brief History of Sex

It is no surprise that sex has a modern social history and that the understanding of sex has changed and continues to change over time. As with much historicism, Dabhoiwala (2013), for example, begins a factual history of modern sex in England on the very specific date of 10 March 1612, describing the punishment of two unmarried people found to have had sex out of wedlock and punished by the Westminster Court to whipping and expulsion from the city. Whilst clearly sex has been around before 1612, it is the historical modern legacy and its impact on contemporary ideas of sex that concern us today.

At various times in history and over differing cultural contexts, an ideal of human sexuality has been promoted, in particular the mores of sexual restraint that under the influence of the church has only been largely allowable within marriage, and between a man and a woman. Despite harsh punishments for behaviour outside of moral social codes, the social history of sex contains many contradictions and paradoxes. What mostly men have expected most other people to do and not to do, and what those men actually do themselves, is not necessarily the same. Deep-rooted double standards abound throughout, not least in the social and personal desexualization of women in the 19th and 20th centuries, and the expectation of their general sexual passivity within normative social marital bounds as the apogee of respectability. The modernist approach to sex is a general 'hetero-normative' hegemonic socio-political desire to impose normative sexual behaviours and attitudes and to eradicate those behaviours that do not comply with this version of sexuality.

This raises the difficult issue of social power and powerlessness, but also of the social construct of sexuality and sex abuse that affects some of our deepest intimate thoughts and feelings, and our fears, not least that part of our own understanding of our emotional sexual selves.

Bailey and colleagues (2016) describe the socio-political debate on sexuality, saying that there are strong feelings and opinions on each side of an unresolved and often poorly articulated debate, particularly in considering issues surrounding homosexuality. Much of the relative rates between heterosexual and homosexual populations, namely those who are sexually aroused to either a different or the same biological sex or both, appear to be unchanging over time and place. Such preferences appear to emerge at an early age and range from extreme to more subtle behaviours. The various sides of the debate either believe that sexuality is dependent on inherent genetic causes, or is the result of social influences, but no causal theory has, to date, emerged scientifically. The issues tend to be under-researched and under-articulated, in that sexuality is not a matter of personal choice and it is not socially contagious, although tolerance may facilitate a personal expression of sexuality.

SEXUAL BEHAVIOUR

Sexual abuse is behaviour that is morally, ethically and legally abhorrent. It is harmful to victims, exercised by those who have power. It is a human betrayal of trust and compassion. It takes many forms and takes place in many different contexts for many different reasons.

The precedent route to sexual abuse is complex. It can take diverse paths, travel at different speeds and in different settings, with different people and behaviours. Despite a number of established theories and models (see, for example, Andrews & Bonta, 1994; Finkelhor, 1984; Hall & Hirschman, 1992; Marshall & Barbaree, 1990), and despite the desire to construct a generally comprehensive explanation, no theory is entirely sufficient for all types, categories, contexts and examples of sexual abuse (Ward & Sorbello, 2003).

There are considerable unknowns in forensically understanding the route to sexual abusive behaviour, and there are challenges in being able to cognitively and emotionally understand and come to terms with what is considered to be a particularly socially reviled behaviour.

BIOLOGY

Sex is 'nearly universal in the biological world' (Luo, 2016, p.377), but why it exists biologically has not been entirely resolved. There are biological evolutionary advantages for sexual reproduction as opposed to asexual reproduction, with genetic mutations and adaptions leading to the greater chance of a species adapting to its environment and hence surviving, but whilst it is a fact that there are two human biological sexes as opposed to gender, this has some puzzling features (Ridley, 2004, p.342).

For example, in asking the fundamental question as to why there are two biological sexes, not one, or three, or none, is not easily answered. Human behaviours are unique in many ways and cannot be fully understood unless we think about evolutionary history and technical evolutionary explanations, including how early cellular life originated on Earth and then diversified (Rhen & Crews, 2007). Eukaryotic cells have a bounded membrane (eukaryotes) within which there is genetic material that can reproduce either asexually, where one cell in effect divides into two genetically identical cells, or sexually, whereby each of the sex cells (gametes) recombines individual DNA through fertilization, copying chromosomes from each parent. Human diploid cells contain 23 pairs of chromosomes that combine through ova and sperm to fuse together to form 46 chromosomes. This allows genetic mixing between two individuals, and the creation of genetically diverse offspring. Some of these offspring cope and adapt better and some worse with their changing environment, and as a result, some are more successful than others. The successful ones in turn reproduce, and the less successful ones reproduce less, leading to the adaption of the species as a whole.

The history of evolutionary biology has been vastly influenced by

Charles Darwin's 1859 publication of *On the Origin of Species* (quoted in Ridley, 2004, pp.7–9). In the early half of the 20th century, this has subsequently become enmeshed with theories associated with Mendelism (Gregor Mendel, 1822–1884), genetics and theories of heredity. Evolution is linked to the process of sexual reproduction and to miniscule variations from generation to generation that provide adaptions and advantages for species (Ridley, 2004). Despite some doubt as to whether binary sex is necessary for adaption and survival, the evolutionary theory of natural selection suggests that human beings are the remote descendants of one-cell organisms that have an inherent instinctive desire to survive and reproduce. At its simplest, this is a 'beautifully simple and easily understood idea' (Ridley, 2004, p.4), and we are programmed to do just that without any other purpose. Dawkins (1976) suggested that the gene is naturally pre-programmed to replicate itself without any conscious choice, and this instinct is then translated into various genetic survival strategies and behaviours.

Such behaviour includes the human desire for sex, conventionally described as a Freudian 'sex drive' or libido. Many, but not all, people are sexually motivated. For Sigmund Freud (1856–1939), classically the sex drive is contained within the unconscious id, and develops over time, during infancy to adulthood. For Carl Jung (1875–1961), the libido is the energy of striving and desire. Sexual behaviour and desire 'is a vast, complex, and provocative topic' (Bear, Connors & Paradiso, 2016, p.587), and the functional anatomical view of neuro-anatomy provides a description of three components within the human body: the *secretory hypothalamus, autonomic nervous system* and *diffuse modulatory systems of the brain.*

Within the brain significant activation by sexually arousing stimuli takes place in the pre-frontal cortex, also involving the amygdala and hypothalamus. Within the limbic system, neurotransmitters such as dopamine and serotonin are especially relevant. Having a number of functions, dopamine inhibits the release of prolactin from the pituitary gland, suppressing a hormone that dampens sexual functioning. Serotonin has particular effects compared to dopamine, but the complex relationship between serotonin, dopamine and other neurotransmitters is generally uncertain (Grubin & Mason, 2007).

The hypothalamus exerts a powerful influence over the body via the pituitary gland. Situated immediately below the brain, it 'communicates' with the body through the release of neurohormones regulating various complex bodily functions that are necessary at different times, not least, for example, the effect of testosterone, oxytocin and vasopressin. Testosterone, produced from the testes, is linked to male sexuality, but also, to an extent, to female sexuality. Having a range of functions, it relates to male spontaneous sexual interest (Grubin & Mason, 2007) and sexual motivation, arousal and performance (McKenna, 1999). Oxytocin is associated with both social bonding during sex, and is intimately involved in childbirth, and vasopressin regulates the balance of blood volume and salt concentration.

The relevance of understanding the biological mechanisms to sexual 'deviance' should neither be over-emphasized nor ignored (Grubin & Mason, 2007). Whilst open to challenge from socio-political perspectives, the medical model is useful in exposing errors and presumptions. As a functional physical description of biological processes, it is relatively free of moral judgements of 'right or wrong'. For example, 'sexual attractions to prepubescent children is, in essence, a form of sexual orientation' (Berlin, 2014, p.404).

Those body parts usually associated with sex – the penis, vagina, breasts and various other parts implicated sexually – are in some ways the outward visceral parts of the sexual being, but it is the brain and its various parts that control the way people sexually behave through the cycle of sexual arousal, plateau, orgasm and resolution (Bear et al., 2016). During sexual development, as the human body grows, the hypothalamus in the brain causes the anterior pituitary gland to secrete two important gonadotropins, the luteinizing hormone (LH) and follicle-stimulating hormone (FSH). In a circuitry system, the hypothalamus becomes stimulated to release a substance (gonadotropin-releasing hormone, GnRH) that causes the pituitary gland to release hormones that circulate in the blood. LH and FSH perform different key roles in male and female fertility, but the control of sexual organs in both males and females is similar.

Physical sexual maturation occurs at puberty. The release of the sex hormones of testosterone in males and estradiol in females is implicated in the development of the maturation of secondary sex characteristics. The interactive nature between the gonads and brain continues in adulthood to maintain and activate sexual behaviour, and has implications during adult development for differences in male-form and female-form brains (Luo, 2016, pp.396–397).

During adult sexual behaviour, sexual arousal causes changes in the female labia and clitoris and the male penis. Stimulation of the mechanoreceptors in these body parts can itself cause changes associated with blood engorgement. Eventually, through various mechanisms, the male achieves orgasm accompanied by neural activity, but 'it is a complete mystery how patterns of neural activity [then] evoke feelings' (Bear *et al.*, 2016, pp.585–589). In mammalian species, there are various mating strategies of polygyny, where males mate with many females, polyandry, where females mate with many men, and monogamy, where an individual mates with only one partner at a time, sometimes for the duration of a lifetime. In humans, the implications for love and bonding are not entirely understood (Bear *et al.*, 2016, pp.590–595).

The relationship between brain activity, conscious and unconscious feelings and emotions is subject to complex theories and research (see Bear *et al.*, 2016), but the question arises as to whether neuro-anatomy or evolutionary theories of sexual behaviour have any relevance for sexual abuse. It is clear from evidence of brain injury, mental disorder and disease affecting the frontal lobes (Grubin & Mason, 2007) that brain activity obviously affects how people think and behave sexually, but the relationship between the brain, social behaviour and emotions is not always entirely clear.

SEX, SEXOLOGY AND SEXUALITY

Freud was clearly influenced by sexology. Sexologists claim that it is possible to discover the underlying scientific understanding of sexuality, or natural laws. Sexology has several key ideas such as that humans are born with a biological sexual nature, that sex is a basic powerful human driver, as is the need to eat or sleep, and that heterosexuality is the natural order of things. Sexology has been linked with various social projects such as strengthening and creating healthy populations, engendering racial purity or strengthening the social institutions of marriage. However, whilst sexologists may argue that the purpose of sex and the underlying sex drive is predominantly linked to the desire to procreate, Freud considered that sex was at the core of the psychological self and the sex drive was linked predominantly to pleasure, which then leads to social conflicts derived from a sense of respectability and self-control (Seidman, 2011). Pleasure is contingent on numerous factors and emotional meanings ascribed to pleasure, but whilst endlessly discussed, it is not universally defined and explained, according to James (2011). Sexuality is conceived as a 'bundle of social phenomena that shape erotic life: laws, religion and values, beliefs, ideologies, the social organisation of reproduction, family life, identities, domestic arrangements, diseases, violence and love – everything we evoke when we speak of the sexuality of a culture' (Weeks, 2005, p.19).

Within the idea of 'normal' sexuality is the idea of sexual promiscuity. Whilst it is socially normal to find a mate with whom to establish a long-term relationship and have progeny, within the animal kingdom at least, it is reckoned that, for some animals, promiscuity has evolutionary advantages. Males and females will seek to mate with as many partners as possible, displaying instinctive, pre-programmed sexual deceit and dishonesty, navigating group social processes including the 'policing' of monogamous sexual relationships (Cooke, 2019).

Bridging biological evolutionary theories and anatomical processes, there are some obvious but controversial theories of sexual assault, in particular an evolutionary theory of the offence of rape (Thornhill & Palmer, 2000), but they have been subsequently challenged (Ward & Siegert (1), 2002). Rape is portrayed as either a behaviour that increases reproductive success and an opportunity for genetic inheritance, or contrastingly as an acquired distortion of social beliefs of sexuality, women and relationships. On the one hand, rape is seen as a mechanism of genetic determinism, or as a behaviour that is fundamentally socially determined. Somewhere in between is the issue of attitudes – whether attitudes determine behaviour and how behaviour influences attitudes, and so on (Maio, Haddock & Verplanken, 2019).

Female sexuality, across races and class, has historically been associated with male ownership of property, extending to the concept of a child as the property of the father. This is a complex area to investigate through historical Court records, such as from the 18th century, which indicate an underlying historical misogyny or 'heavy prejudice against women' that existed in the legal process from accusation to conviction, and that many convictions failed because they 'were frequently seen to falter as a consequence of the legal definition of rape' (Walker, 2013, p.140). As Walker says, 'Flattening the history of rape into an unchanging phenomena...or overstating the differences between past societies and our own... potentially impedes our understanding of the past and present in ways that may perpetuate the very injustices that inform our commitment to studying rape's history' (2013, p.142).

The concept of rape as anything other than an abhorrent expression of abusive power is extremely challenging. Human beings are essentially part of the animal biological world, and within this view of sexual assault, male rape behaviour is thought of as an evolutionary adaption. Female adaptions focus on selection from a range of mates and choosing those that have higher status, access to greater resources and greater caring propensities that will ensure the survival of their offspring. The desire of males for sex and to have a range of sexual partners helps ensure a better chance of reproduction by fertilizing a greater number of females. Females, on the other hand, choose multiple partners in order to increase the chance of fertilization.

Sex, sexual assault, sexual violence, rape, pornography, capitalism, class, patriarchy, gender, political power, oppression, ethnicity and feminism are linked in an intersectional relationship that is difficult to objectively and factually disentangle. Whilst located within the dominant capitalist society (in the UK and other Western societies) of buying and selling, the complex relationship between the impact of a neoliberal market economy and sexual abuse is difficult to exactly determine. Although sexual abuse may have associated economic factors, it takes place under all social conditions, and it is possible to claim that these are very separate issues. The dominant economic ethos of contemporary Western and Westernized societies involves market forces of demand and supply. It is fair to say that we live within an increasingly constructed sexualized society in which sexual material is ubiquitous (Attwood, 2009; Gill, 2012). Sexual abuse takes place against such a background. Sex and sexual imagery is on a scaled spectrum of social behaviours and demand is linked to supply, some of which is legal and presumed to be non-abusive, some of which is illegal and highly abusive (see, for example, The COPINE Project: Quayle, 2008). The international buying and selling of human beings as sexual goods past and present is an obvious example of a mostly hidden abusive aspect of market forces of supply and demand, with about a third of all instances of current illegal human trafficking involving sexual exploitation (Home Office, 2016). Customer demand and supply drive pornography, abduction and trafficking of people for sexual prostitution (both men and women of all ages), the trading of abusive images of children and the digital distribution of abusive images. Sex and sexual abuse is a financially lucrative and marketable commodity. Further, if sex and sexual imagery is paid for, the market then suggests that the buyer has some entitlement to have what they have paid for. In this context, sex is a marketized salacious commodity (Campbell & O'Neill, 2006; Lobert, 2017; Weitzer, 2010). A sense of entitlement is not uncommon in sexual abuse, but it is clear that sexual abuse as a distortion or literal perversion of values is likely to exist under any socio-economic regime or ethical framework.

From a feminist perspective, the assumption that much of sexual assault is conducted by men against women locates it within a patriarchal society that exercises control over sex and women. The 1970s feminist movement emphasized that sexual violence is an instrumental patriarchal lever of control within sexual politics (Brownmiller, 1975; Donat & D'Emilio, 1997; Millet, 1970). The threat of stranger rape has been used over time to attempt to control the behaviour of women and to reinforce cultural hegemony about the morals of women. Such an example could be that women 'should not' be out alone late at night in case they are attacked. This is a common example of a moral judgement placing the responsibility of being assaulted with the victim. Compounding this is the design of most towns and cities, with poor lighting, the use of subways and footbridges etc., designed and built without women in mind, contributing to the feeling of fear and isolation that might be experienced. Added to this is the rise of television dramas featuring rape and/or sexual murder as the central theme.

This ultimate lever of control need not be 'actual' rape but may be the threat or symbolic institutionalized behaviours and attitudes of the acting out of sexual violence within the gendered public spheres of politics, law, normative cultural attitudes, mores within society generally and within personal relationships. Bryson (2016) challenges what she says is the popular myth that most victims of rape know their attacker (p.175), pointing to the prevalence of rape and the sexual abuse of women and children within warfare by 'normal' men who would not consider rape acceptable within their own civilian societies. Our view is that the vast majority of women are said to experience sexual assault at some time during their lives, and it is the fear of assault and intimidation that is central to the domination and subordination of women, which, in the late 20th century, some feminist literature would say encourages women to seek the protection of one man against all other men, to the subsequent benefit of men and the subjugation of women. Dworkin (1983) and MacKinnon (1989) have argued that pornography is a symptom and cause of hatred of women, that male power is eroticized, that female oppression is sexually arousing for men, and that the consciousness of this has led to the politicization of pornography (Bryson, 2016, pp.175–177). In this analysis, rape is therefore a clear socio-political patriarchal crime.

SEX AND GENDER

Although human beings as a species reproduce sexually, and as an essentialist biological approach 'having sex' between the two biological sexes of male and female is the principal mechanism of reproduction, the relationship between sex, sexuality and gender is more complex. As a contested concept, gender is a complex and varied arrangement between people that encompasses reproduction, cultural and socio-political divisions of femininity and masculinity (Bradley, 2012). It denotes traditional but currently changing social definitions of social sexual roles related and rooted in an historical dominant hegemonic male view of what is natural, where heterosexuality is defined as normal and other sexual behaviours considered deviant (Marchbank & Letherby, 2007, pp.252–256).

Furthermore, there is some considerable evidence that rape was, in the past, seen as an issue of race, and that only respectable white women in colonial settings (for example, in 19th-century South Africa) could be considered to have been the victim of rape, that non-white women were not seen as subject to the same jurisprudence, and that there is a considerable silence about white owners and overseers who, it is suggested, often enforced sexual entitlement on black women as workers, indented servants, colonial slaves and ex-slaves, that 'black' was closely aligned to barbarous, unrestrained sexual instincts for both males and females, and that licentious sexuality was determined by race (Scully, 1995).

The definition of gender is a relatively novel concept that differs from person to person, from culture to culture, and within differing socio-political contexts. At the same time it is a 'lived experience' (Bradley, 2012, p.4). Whilst having a considerable history of usage, not least in grammatical classifications (such as male and female nouns in Latin, French and other languages), it is a relatively novel concept that differs from person to person, from culture to culture, and within differing contexts.

Gender is closely linked to cultural identity. Many people may define themselves as either male or female, but many may have multiplicities of gender identity, and in a complex contemporary society people can define themselves both by communal affiliation, for instance by saying that they are male or female, but they may also belong to other collective identities such as heterosexual, homosexual, bisexual or asexual, or have multiple socio-cultural identities (Josselson & Harway, 2012).

Modern gender roles were re-examined, questioned and altered in the 20th century by referencing other times and places (see, for example, Margaret Mead's (1901–1978) studies of South Sea cultures). It has been recognized that the cultural conventionalization of biological sex roles, and the social limits placed on these, sometimes artificially, by the cultural institutions of school, work and occupations and home, disguises and can distort the differences between people and their sense of gendered maleness or femaleness.

Gender has clear socio-economic implications. Whilst pre-capitalist occupations have been socially gendered, this has been displaced by 'economic sex' (Illich, 1983, chapter 11), and whilst women engage more now in formal work occupations than in the past, they are paid less and under-recognized in terms of their necessary involvement in a capitalist economy as a subsidiary workforce generally economically reliant on their male spousal primary source of family income that contributed to cheaper production costs. Recent reporting on similar economic discrimination based on gender makes it clear that, in 2018, a person's monetary reward continues to be an issue of economic status significantly defined and disadvantaged by gender (BBC News (4), 2018). The gender pay gap, sexism and violence against women continues, and although there may be specific issues relating to national cultures, there is a common realization of globalized discrimination in gender roles, pay and opportunity across the Western world (BBC News (5), 2018; International Women's Day, 2018; World Economic Forum, 2017). Growing awareness by women of women's contemporary socio-economic status is developing the realization that there are perspectives, ways of thinking and behaviour that are distinct from the predominant male perspective.

As a kaleidoscopic social construct (Spade & Valentine, 2014), gender is a socially determined and predominantly traditionally binary concept of either male or female despite the anatomical ambiguity of those born with 'intersexual' characteristics because of chromosomal, gonad, genital or hormonal features of anatomy. Being 'born with indeterminate sexual organs indeed problematizes a binary understanding of sex and gender' (Preves, 2014, p.32) that has had a tendency in the past to be more medicalized and 'corrected' through treatment and surgery. The binary nature of sex and gender is cultural, with some groups of people describing more than two gender variants (Nanda, 2014). There is evidence that people become gendered through reflexive social processes, of 'how we are gendered and how we do gender' (Holmes, 2007, p.173). Questions arise as to whether bodies have a 'natural' state that indicates gender, that this is then acted out, or questioned, changed and influenced through social influences and the lived experience.

Much has been said about the politicization of gender, particularly within the context of suffragist/suffragette history in the UK, and the demand that women be given the same democratic rights as men both historically and as a result of the historical legacy in contemporary life. This is more than just votes for women; it reflects a much wider legacy of male privilege, inequalities and discriminatory institutionalized social structures, of private and public patriarchy, and hetero-normative gendering, based on the underlying idea of a binary approach to sexual identity (Holmes, 2007). It is based on the historicism of maleness as a complete perfect gender, and femaleness as an incomplete and less perfect gender that lacks the male physical attributes of external genitalia (Laqueur, 1990). Thomas Laqueur's historicist idea of a social and cultural 'one sex model' of gender, that female gender was a variation of the single male gender, which is supposed to have been predominant from classical times up to 1700, has been criticized for an over-simplification based on limited historical sources, that the historical issue of intentions, agency and female agency in particular are illusive, and that some gender-based historical constructions that may influence how contemporary gender is constructed are questionable if not over-simplified and exaggerated (Ingram, 2017, pp.29, 32). In this account, this developed into a two-sex model and a modernist understanding and acceptance of scientific 'fact', but with an incomplete understanding of the biological functioning of, for example, chromosomes and hormones (see Holmes, 2007, pp.22–24).

The history of sexuality tends to be far wider than just the act of sex, with wide-ranging implications for humanity in a changing historical social context (Toulalan & Fisher, 2013). The consciousness of biological sex has historically been seen as the determination of gender and sexuality, but likewise it is the consciousness of the lived experience of gender that has influenced sexuality. Sexuality has, at various times, been understood in different ways because of the emerging understandings of the human body and the social context of this understanding. Historical writings on sex in the modern era have been transformed since the 1970s (Crawford, 2013), particularly under the influence of Foucault (1976) and Laqueur (1990), with women's studies investigating the history of the sexuality of women, as virgins, wives, nuns and prostitutes, among other categorizations. The period 1500–1750 ushered in new ideas in art and science, culture and politics, about the body, forms of social control and sexual anxieties within the institutional structures of the church, the state and the family, and within emerging science from Renaissance times. This had an impact on aspects of sexuality such as the changing conceptualization of rape and the pre-eminent example of sexual assault, the reconfiguration of women's bodies, anatomical differences, phallocentricism and new socio-sexual identities.

Gendered knowledge about sexuality has historically passed through various iterations, with 'men of learning' professing privileged expert knowledge whilst certain occupations such as midwives had a lower status but more practical understanding assigned to a lesser status that was not formally recognized as knowledge. The gendering of scientific knowledge has extended in the past to medical practice, but this, in turn, has led to restrictions on the mores and behaviours of medical practitioners, and ideas of propriety in the viewing and touching of other people's bodies. The increasing knowledge of the biological mechanisms of men and women's bodies and fertility has led to the conceptualization of purely sex-as-reproductive destinies, but the socio-political control of the knowledge of sex has determined the knowledge of sexuality and its legitimacy.

CHAPTER 2

Sex and Sexuality

Whilst sex, sexuality and gender are clearly linked, they are also distinct. Obviously, sex is and has been associated with reproduction, and this emphasis on reproduction has socially influenced previous concepts of sexuality. Additionally, much of the previous textual knowledge of sexuality has been informed by Eurocentrism, particularly the effects of colonial contact with non-European cultures that has influenced ideas as to the comparative cultural status of sexuality and a tendency to make morally privileged judgements on other non-European non-white people and their behaviour as less civilized and bestial. The legacy of racism within language to describe sexuality continues.

SEX, LOVE, POWER AND SEXUALITY

In addition to the distinction between sex and sexuality, we might add the idea of love. Love has and has had an ambiguous association, if not some dissociation, with the act of sex and procreation (Onfray, 2015, p.61). Theories of love and sex are as problematic as the concept of sex, gender and sexuality, and whilst there are evolutionary, behavioural and neural theories (Weis, 2006, quoted in Sternberg & Weis, 2006), the evolutionary theories of love promote the genetic survival or the survival of personal, family and tribal genes through reproduction. The narrow evolutionary biological function of emotional investment for men and women tends to differ. Within this view, females require stable environmental circumstances from inception to birth and on into their early years, to ensure the survival of their offspring, and males functionally wish to disseminate their genes as much as possible (Kendrick, 2006). Contemporary society clearly associates love with familial bonds through long-term relationships, although the term 'love' encompasses a range of emotional states including the classical categories of love: *eros*, from which we derive the word erotic; *storge*, the love of family and friends; *agape*, often associated with the unconditional spiritual love of humanity; and *philia*, or the love of warm friendship, from which we derive the word 'paedophilia'. The articulation of the relationship between love, sex, sexuality and gender is perplexing. There are multiple examples of poetry, stories and lyrics that seek to articulate how each of us feels about the powerful relationship between these concepts.

Michel Foucault's work *The Will to Knowledge* (1976) has been a significant influence on the conceptualization of sexuality. The carefully confined legacy of Victorian sexuality has strongly associated sex in the language of reproduction when everything else about sexuality was vague, silenced and sanitized. The sexually liberating influences that have occurred since Foucault have not entirely freed society of Victorian-like perspectives, and the issue of sex and sexuality remains socially, politically and culturally complex.

In the Victorian age sexuality was repressed and placed into a separate bounded arena of the brothel and that of fallen women. The medicalization of sex and the placing of sex other than for reproduction into the discourse of the strange and unusual 'othered' behaviours banished sex as 'fruitless pleasures' (Foucault, 1976, p.36) into the realms of perversion, abomination, moral corruption and mental illness. These 'othered' non-reproductive sexual behaviours were subject to strict moral constraints and laws, both within marriage and without, relegating non-productive sex within marriage as illegitimate. Vaginal sex was approved of for the purpose of begetting children, but non-vaginal sex was disapproved of. What was seen as the predominantly male behaviour of the immature vice of masturbation was relegated to the unnatural, to be controlled and repressed through a host of mechanisms both practical and medical, behaviours that were seen as a dangerous slippery slope to degeneracy and sickness. Female masturbation was mostly relegated to the distasteful and unmentionable.

To speak of the repression of sex is to delineate sex as 'a discourse'. The relationship between power and repression, and the power of sexual prohibition, questions whether the examination of sexual repression is in itself a contributory repressive factor (see Foucault, 1976, p.10). Contemporaneously, sex is ubiquitous, powerful, titillating and powerfully attractive.

Over a matter of a few days in February 2018, four separate different kinds of sexual news items appeared on the mainstream BBC News website:

Barry Bennell was sentenced to 31 years' imprisonment for the sexual abuse of multiple boy victims whilst he was acting as a football coach. He was described by the sentencing judge as 'the devil incarnate' and 'sheer evil'. (BBC News (2), 2018)

Matthew Falder was sentenced to 32 years for being what was described by the sentencing judge as 'A "warped and sadistic" paedophile...,"an internet highwayman" with a "lust to control"'. (BBC News (1), 2018)

Emily Maitlis, a news reporter for the serious mainstream television news magazine, reported that the male stage sex-show, the Chippendales, are not objectified sex objects. (Maitlis, 2018)

A copy of a Georgian sex manual published in 1720 named as *Aristotle's Masterpiece* was to be sold at auction, containing what is humorously seen to be naive titillation. (BBC News (3), 2018)

These examples and many others show a view of sex from very different standpoints, of the way that sex is contradictorily constructed in disparate and contradictory ways. Despite serious underlying implications for the objectification of both men and women, a photograph of a smiling Chippendale performer is in extreme contrast to the sexual abuse of children. It is challenging that a Georgian sex manual, seen as historical and naively amusing male paternalism, is set alongside an account of an offender described as 'devilish'. Sexuality attracts, revolts, horrifies and amuses all at the same time. It has the power to liberate and repress, that some constructions of sex are okay but that others are decidedly not. Some social portrayals of the constructions of sex and sexuality are acceptable and legitimized, whilst others are very decidedly not.

The history of sexuality is a reflexive account encompassing a fluidity of understandings of multiple discourses on society and culture that has changed and is continuously changing. The construct of sexuality in different contexts, cultures and subcultures at different times and places is diverse and variable.

As Foucault's examination of the historicism of the prison and the asylum demonstrates how the ideas of the prisoner and the mental patient are constructed, so the historicism of sexuality has constructed a sense of our sexual selves, desire and sexual shame (Boyarin & Castelli, 2001; Foucault, 1976). Sexual shame and shaming, the rights and wrongs of sex and sexuality, is predicated on the construction of power within socially constructed relationships. For Christian morality this was predominantly a male gendered issue, although not exclusively, of the crime of 'the seductress' who morally corrupted 'the seducer'. It was not the male fault of 'the rebellious will in the penis that moves without its "owner"', according to St Augustine of Hippo (Boyarin & Castelli, 2001, p.361), but the fault lies with the person who is penetrated by the penis, and there is, to some extent, some suggestion that this legacy permeates contemporary male attitudes. The historical distorted myth that a woman in particular cannot be raped without at least some level of consent, and the distorted myth that women secretly harbour rape fantasies, still appears to ill-inform that women victims are in part to blame for sexual enticement. Rape myths and the distortions of sexuality continue, according to many sources (see, for example, IDAS, 2018).

The historical legacy of discriminatory moral judgements on heterosexual and non-heterosexual behaviours abound, conflating moral responsibility with concepts of blame, enticement and disease. Conflation of contamination, disease, sexuality and moral judgement have been seen in the criminalization of HIV positive individuals in legal but ultra-conservative jurisdictions such as in Texas and elsewhere (De Orio, 2017). Sexual behaviours and sexuality have been seen as socially harmful and consequently subject to punitive attitudes, including the indefinite incarceration of people for treatment. The criminalization of gay and lesbian sexual relationships, and the criminalization of sodomy up until the later years of the 20th century in Western societies (De Orio, 2017), have only gradually been displaced with the associated view that being gay is morally corrupt and in some instances related to the term 'sexual psychopath' (George, 2015). The recent example of rugby player Gareth Thomas illustrates the continued impact of the social stigma of being gay and having HIV (Brown, 2019).

In all of this, it is clear that sex and sexuality is socially constructed, and defined differently in different contexts and different places, sometimes with multiple contradictory meanings. As such, the history of sexuality can be a reflection of the changing nature of society and of sexuality, 'from sex and desire to intimacy and relationships' (Weeks, 2005, p.201). Changing the lens through which sexuality can be viewed involves changing both the nature of the lens as well as seeing differently. The Foucauldian lens is not a matter of inventing a morality but 'to invent "practices of freedom" that eschew the models of domination and subordination, sin and confession, natural and perverse' (Weeks, 2005, p.200). Sexual identity is diverse, consisting of multiple constructed narratives, and personal identities have contradictory multiple social belongings.

The distinction between sex, sexuality, love and gender, whilst used variously within the broad biological, social, cultural, psychological, political and feminist literature, is complex, and can be extended to intersectional issues of age, class and ethnicity. It is notable that despite the fluidity of the concepts of sex and gender, there are multiple examples at both the individual and macro level of gendered institutionalization. Girls and boys learn gendered sexual attitudes and behaviours within families, through friends, schools, clubs, media, and consumer goods of clothes and toys.

It can be socially determining, providing unconscious messages for girls and women through the Disneyfication of gendered sexual relationships and the gendering of emotions. Boys and men are potentially encouraged to feel sexual and emotional entitlement, and girls and women to be held responsible and shamed.

Sometimes objectified and pathologized through medicalization, there is a range of sexual behaviours or paraphilias included in the copyrighted materials in the standardized American Psychiatric Association's *Diagnostic and Statistical Manual of Mental Disorders* (DSM), of which there are a number of editions. Considered to be outside of the 'normal' parameters of sexual behaviour, there are some specific criteria for inclusion (APA, 2013). For example, there is the term 'sex addiction', which is not generally recognized as an addiction by the NHS in the UK. It appears in the International Classification of Diseases (ICD-11) as an impulsive mental or behavioural disorder characterized by an inability to control intense and repeated sexual urges, which become a central focus in a person's life that is potentially harmful.

Definitions of compulsive sexual behaviour as an addiction and diagnostic indicators are not entirely clear (Kraus *et al.*, 2016). Other conditions and disorders may involve high interest in and preoccupation with sex, such as during periods in adolescence, or mental disorders such as manic episodes of bipolar disorder, etc. Both the prevalence and diagnosis of sexual addiction is controversial, associated not just with behaviour but also with a preoccupation with sexual thoughts and sexual imagery. Visual sexual imagery and salacious written or printed material can be described as pornographic, again problematic to exactly define socially.

THE PORTRAYAL OF SEX

The social context of sexual behaviours is heavily influenced by the portrayal of sex, and the increasingly intensive nature of the digital age that is accelerating the rate, density and saturation of communication within mass media and personal interaction through social media. The portrayal of sex covers a spectrum of imagery from explicitly pornographic to socially accepted legal sexual imagery, and that with indirect sexual content. What is acceptable or unacceptable is both personally and societally located within a place, time and context – each of us has a view. Just as sex and sexuality is complex, so is the portrayal of sex, adding a level of social reflexivity in that what we see sexually portrayed influences how we think and feel about sex, and what we think and feel influences the way in which we define the acceptable boundaries of sexual imagery, and subsequently what is acceptable sexual behaviour.

The control of images of sexuality have been subject to different sections of society, with art and frescos tending to be limited to the upper classes and their servants, whilst the lower classes had their bawdy songs and stories. The advent of printing technologies, and the emergence of sophisticated technologies in contemporary times, has increased the accessibility of sexual images, changing ideas about erotica, and in turn has affected behaviours and sexuality. The invention of the term 'pornography' was not generally used until the 19th century, and became more widespread in the 20th (Moulton, 2013). Naked imagery has been evidenced as far back to the beginnings of human pre-history. During the medieval period and into the modern era, naked imagery became associated with moral behaviour, and sexuality and eroticism became problematically associated with each other. The depiction and context of some forms of nakedness appears to have been originally produced and controlled by different sections of society for historically ill-defined erotic purposes of the social elites. Much of the sophisticated fine art and frescos tended to be limited to those who could afford it. The lower classes had their songs and stories described as bawdy or lewd low culture, both visual and literary, and were more ephemeral, disposable and less well documented. The advent of printing technologies, and the emergence of sophisticated digital technologies in contemporary times, increased the accessibility of sexual images, changing ideas about erotica. The term 'pornography' was not generally used until the 19th century (Hunt, 1996), becoming more widespread in the 20th (Moulton, 2013). Whilst erotic sexual imagery abounds before

31

this time, it cannot be defined as 'pornography' since the term did not exist.

The definition of pornography can be ambiguous. There are examples of explicit depictions of sex within fine art such as J.M.W. Turner's explicit sexual drawings (Warrell, 2012), the explicit medieval drawings by Leonardo Da Vinci (Da Vinci, circa 1492), and Boucher's clearly erotic 'Venus Playing with Two Doves' (Boucher, circa 1754), and many other examples in classical and modern times (see Hughes, 2019). Edouard Manet's painting 'Olympia' (Manet, 1863) deliberately evokes ambiguity, and social and sexual controversy. What is pornographic is open to judgement, both the intent of the person who makes the image and the purpose of the person who views it. An explicit image of sexual parts in medical literature would not usually be considered pornographic. There have been debates in the past as to the legitimacy of liberationist sex manuals such as *The Joy of Sex* (Comfort, 1972). This avoided the use of photographic imagery and attempted to use drawings instead in order to distinguish it from the purely pornographic. The debate has moved on with the development of technology and the ability to produce pseudo-images, covered by UK law (Protection of Children Act 1978 (as amended); Section 160, Criminal Justice Act 1988). Much of what defines pornography relies on what is legally permissible and what is not, but it is generally accepted that pornography, either as a visual image(s) or in writing, is the depiction of sexual behaviours for sexual gratification or to stimulate sexual arousal. There are a number of relativist terms, including erotic and obscene, so whilst material might be erotic, it need not be obscene, and what is obscene may not be erotic but have the opposite effect and elicit disgust.

The definition of 'obscene' has tended to be seen as self-evident and culturally and socially normative, that is, what most people would consider to be 'wrong'. In the UK 'obscene' has tended to fall within the scope of legalistic definitions based on prior historical common law that saw and currently sees obscene publications as being corrupting, depraved and morally perverting and poisonous (Vagrancy Act 1824; Obscene Publications Acts 1857, 1959, 1964;

Children and Young Persons (Harmful Publications) Act 1955; Protection of Children Act 1978; Civic Government (Scotland) Act 1982; Criminal Justice and Immigration Act 2008).

The law on obscenity does not restrict itself to sexual images but includes such things as the portrayal of dismemberment, torture and activities involving 'perversion'. UK government guidance includes a definition of decency 'which ordinary right-thinking members of the public would set. The "recognized standards of propriety" are outlined in *R v. Stamford 1972*', and the Crown Prosecution Service (CPS) states that the issue of obscene is a changing standard according to the standards of the time, and must be decided by a jury without the assistance of expert advice (CPS (4), 2019).

Context and intent is everything, such as having the intention to corrupt a child, which is defined in the Sexual Offences Act 2003 as a person under the age of 18, as distinct from the age of sexual consent (see Chapter 4). Historically, the influence of Britishness on global concepts of obscenity gives a sense of what is morally acceptable and 'hygienic', appropriately regulated and controlled through social, political and cultural technologies (Heath, 2010). Pornography remains a global driving force within media technological developments such as photography and film. It is a significant economic global enterprise and tells us much about how society thinks about gender, sexuality and relationships (Jenkins, 2004). Whilst some imagery is generally acceptable and mainstream, other images are considered to be generally unacceptable to a mainstream audience, especially if they show children who may then become morally corrupted and corrupt by seeing such imagery. This is despite the fact that seeing domesticated farm animals mate with each other is now subsumed into mainstream televised wildlife programmes. It is significant that we speak about animals 'mating' whilst pornography contains images of people 'having sex'. The exercise of Foucauldian (Foucault, 1976; see also Boyarin & Castelli, 2001; Weeks, 2005) discursive power is emphasized in some feminist anti-pornography writing (Segal, 2004), seeing that pornography creates objectified images, is predominantly for the consumption of men, and is a virtual violent assault on women and the rights of women.

Controversy arises about the fact that what is sexually arousing for one person is not necessarily sexually arousing for another, and what may be used by one person for sexual excitement may be seen as entirely non-sexual for another. In some instances, some people experience sexual arousal by the most obscure images or even merely just the thought of the image, described in a range of unusual and sometimes very specific paraphilias, as seen in extreme pornography (Alexandros & Akrivos, 2017). This cognitive imagining has considerable practical, ethical and legalistic controversies, not least the role of the state in intervening in the lives of private individuals (see Wolfenden, 1957). It is likely that a person who has a strong sexual interest in children may find what are 'innocent' images of children sexually arousing. This is not illegal – it is behaviour that is sexually harmful to another that is illegal. It is not illegal for a person to masturbate in total privacy to any imagery or fantasy, but this has implications for treatment, intervention and risk management.

A classification of abusive images of children was constructed by the Combating Paedophile Information Networks in Europe (COPINE) Project based in Dublin, Eire, attributed to Taylor, Holland and Quayle (2001; Taylor & Quayle, 2003) originally as a research tool to investigate the types and levels of the seriousness of the images. It has subsequently become adapted in modified form for use in a number of legal jurisdictions to indicate the seriousness of internet-related offending (Merdian *et al.*, 2011). The COPINE scale consists of a description of types of offending in 10 levels, ranging from 'indicative' or non-erotic imagery including family photographs to 'sadistic or bestiality' including images of a child tied up, physically abused and in pain, or sexual behaviour involving animals. At level 2 (nudist) and level 3 (erotica), the imagery is of naked or semi-naked children in what might usually be considered appropriate settings, such as on a beach sunbathing, or in catalogues containing children's underwear, and at level 4 (posing), level 5 (erotic posing) and level 6 (explicit erotic posing) there is an explicit sexualized element, either deliberately or unknowingly taken. Levels 7–9 describe images of sexual touching or masturbation, involving sexual activity with an adult, and grossly obscene pictures of sexual assault. A number of issues arise, however, in that the COPINE scale applies some normative reasoning about what constitutes 'obscene' (see above).

Feminists and post-feminist writers and campaigners have alluded to pornography as an adjunct to discriminatory male sexual privilege and female repression. Others discuss women as consumers of pornography. Attwood (2018) makes a distinction between men who tend to use pornography as an 'expression of arousal' and women who use it as a 'means to arousal' (p.56). Attwood notes the development of 'female-friendly' or 'feminist' pornography from the 1980s as a cultural revolution.

The term 'child pornography' is no longer used, with the language now more accurately reflecting what is actually going on, that is, child sexual abuse. There are some deeply ambiguous messages conveyed about how images of children can be used. Some images are unequivocally abusive, or may be seen as sensitive by some and innocent by others, and sometimes there is a split between generational or cultural views. Images of children are not infrequently used to sell products, sometimes appropriately, sometimes less so. Using imagery is, of course, related to adult projection of both sexual and non-sexual idealizations and fantasies about childhood onto children, and not based within the child's view of social reality (Schor, 2014).

Pornography is closely associated with sexual fantasy, and sexual fantasy is closely associated with sexual behaviour in that the thought of sexual behaviour precedes and motivates the behaviour itself. For some sexual offenders who view indecent images of children, it is the voyeurism itself that is arousing and not necessarily the thought of acting themselves. For others, there may be a combination of using indecent images as well as committing contact offences. Some will view a combination of legal and illegal images. The swapping and selling of illegal images of children is routine commercial business for some abusers, selling or exchanging images that others want, and is part of their pattern of abuse. Acknowledging that it is difficult to establish any approximate figure because of the deliberately hidden nature of and the sensitivity of researching the subject online, reporting in the HuffPost, Carr (2012) says that the British police estimate that 56,000 people are involved in peer-to-peer child abuse image exchange networks in the UK. This is likely to be a gross under-estimate that has subsequently increased but is unfortunately too common.

Chapter 3

Theories of Sexual Offending

WHY DO THEY DO IT?

Why people abuse and sexually harm others and what to do about it has long been debated and researched. This raises considerable contested issues that perhaps for many practitioners cannot be entirely resolved. In the words of one highly experienced and knowledgeable specialist practitioner, 'at the end of the day, we still do not know anything' (anonymous professional, August 2019). Virtually all theories, whilst having strong explanatory and some predictive qualities, are still theories; even the most essential and great monolithic scientific theories such as the Theory of Evolution (after Charles Darwin) are still only theories (Self, 2019). Social theories tend to fare worse for their predictability.

Considerable research evidence has been accumulated that provides some insight into working with people who sexually abuse others. Such is the diversity of those who abuse that not all theories apply to all abusers and their circumstances and motivations. The overwhelming fact is that abusers are not a homogeneous group of people. They are individually distinguished by personal factors, which includes social identity such as age, gender, socio-economic status, level of education, race, ethnicity, disability (including hidden disabilities) and socio-cultural beliefs; sexuality and personal circumstances, including their family background; their upbringing and social background, which includes adverse experiences in childhood and adult life; and by redemptive factors of the abuser taking responsibility for the harm they have caused and doing everything to avoid future harm.

The dilemma in dealing with abusers is the uncertain relationship between theory and practice, the relationship between cause and effect, and problematic questions about approaches based on research evidence. Theories of sexual offending have tended to approach the topic with a high degree of positivist scientificism as a particular strand and approach to theory, establishing the predominance of the high status of experts. This has a tendency to select and subjugate some understandings in preference to others, 'trapping' the abuser in a dominant narrative of 'the un-redeemable abuser' condemned forever to be labelled predominantly and solely as 'a dangerous sex offender', devoid of other redemptive characteristics as a person. Abusers are not singular personal constructions but are complex people with multiplicities of potential constructions. Psychiatry, psychology and other psychotherapies create discourses based on a substantial mass of sophisticated theories and research that shape how this knowledge is constructed (Furlong, 2008). The uncertainties of the contemporary complexity of social realities indicate that theory does not have all the answers.

Acknowledging that the reasons why people sexually abuse others involves uncertainty, there are obvious limitations to knowledge and research. Most theories are derived from research based on convicted 'sexual offenders', and there is much that remains uncertain about aspects of personal sexuality and sexual behaviours. Duggan and Dennis (2014) make a pointed criticism of the evaluations of treatment outcomes, basically pointing out that treatment should be based on the best evidence from research trials, particularly randomized control trials (RCTs), often described as the 'gold standard' approach to 'scientific' research, and that few RCTs have been conducted because of being able to overcome the difficulties of conducting such research. This raises issues about what kind of things we do not know, such as the behaviours of those who are not 'caught' and known about, and whether what we know can be applied to all situations. The social setting of social interventions and social work in particular is complex (Hood, 2018), and works within uncertain settings where there is sometimes sufficient evidence to suspect but insufficient evidence to prove sexual abuse beyond reasonable doubt in a Criminal Court or even on the balance of probability in a Civil Court. As pointed out by Kilpatrick, Veronen and Best (1985), and acknowledged by McClurg and Craissati (1999), those who have been convicted of sex offences have long been known to represent only the 'tip of the iceberg' (p.22).

Whilst not purely a novelty of the late 20th century, since the 1890s treatment of those named as sexual offenders or sexual psychopaths has a longer history of psychodynamic intervention (Lang, Damousi & Lewis, 2017). The medical model of sexual offending provided the initial framework by which sexual offending was interpreted and understood through the work of people such as Richard von Krafft-Ebing. *Psychopathia Sexualis*, originally published in German in 1886, and translated into English in 1892 (von Krafft-Ebing & Chaddock, 1892), is said to be the earliest medicalized attempt at a scientific understanding of sexual deviance. It created an influential perspective on how we interpret such behaviour (Ward, 2014). A similarly influential early text was *Studies in the Psychology of Sex* by Havelock Ellis published in 1895. Deliberately published with a title in Latin to try to ensure that the general public had restricted access to what was considered material unsuitable for general consumption, it described, medicalized and labelled sexual behaviour outside of marriage and for other than reproductive purposes as a 'perversion'. The limited open public acknowledgement of what sexual behaviours were common between people in the population calls into question definitions of what 'normal' or 'abnormal' sexual behaviour is. Controversially shocking to the conservative public of Middle America, little was generally known about the nature and general prevalence of private sexual behaviours and habits until after the post-Second World War Kinsey reports (Kinsey, Pomeroy & Martin, 1948; Kinsey *et al.*, 1953).

Sigmund Freud (1856–1939), widely acknowledged as the founder of psychoanalysis, developed a range of theories between the 1890s and 1930s that formed the basis of psychodynamic theory, including the structural model of personality consisting of three interworking parts – the id, the ego and the superego – and the five stages of psychosexual development – the oral, anal, phallic, latency and genital. People could be cured of psychopathology through making conscious their unconscious thoughts and motivations and thereby gaining personal understanding. Psychodynamic theories explain personality through the acknowledgement of conscious and unconscious forces, desires and beliefs. Childhood experiences are commonly held to be significant in shaping character and personality and are evident in attachment theory. Hammer and Glueck (1957), for example, developed a psychodynamic approach to understanding the sexual offending of 200 offenders in Sing Sing Correctional Facility in the USA. The mechanism of sexual offending was suggested as male offenders seeking a substitute for sex with women via the underlying four-stage psychodynamic process of: '(1) as a reaction to massive Oedipal entanglements, castration fear or feelings and fear of approaching mature females psychosexually; (2) interpersonal inhibitions of schizoid to schizophrenic proportions; (3) weak ego-strength and lack of adequate control of impulses; and (4) concrete orientation and minimal capacity for sublimation' (Hammer & Glueck, 1957, p.325). In the light of almost 60 years' 'progress', the research may be substantially revised in a number of ways today.

Costopoulos and Juni (2018, p.57) theorize that 'childhood trauma is the source of adult sexual violence' through a complex mechanism whereby early sexual or violent childhood leads to adults who subsequently act out through 'an adaptive behaviour (psychological) complex and a retroactive amelioration of pain and anxiety' (p.74). In this account, sexually aggressive behaviour is the result of an ambivalence of aggressive and erotic yearnings, self-reparative compensatory behaviour, an inability or unwillingness to understand or empathize with others, and an inability to exercise impulse control.

Psychodynamic theories clearly remain highly influential in the way in which practice is pursued through psychotherapeutic methods (Gunst, 2012; Willemsen et al., 2016) enabling effective processes of engagement and delivery supporting personal change, reducing defensiveness, and encouraging engagement with the worker that seeks to generate deeper levels of cathartic self-reflection, instilling personal hope. The main criticism of psychodynamic theories is that they are not empirically based and have therefore fallen somewhat out of favour in terms of their use within correctional services. Such approaches are clinically based and time-consuming and not necessarily in tune with the organizational scaling-up of the almost industrial processing of high numbers of those convicted of sex offences through correctional institutions. Psychotherapy tends to be used for a small number of people in high secure therapeutic communities, and it is not based on more recent research evidence, even though a considerable number of men have been studied over a number of years in the past (see, for example, Hammer & Glueck, 1957).

Theories about sexually abusive behaviour have developed over time and become increasingly sophisticated. Social learning and behavioural theories focus on sexually harmful acts being learned behaviour that is then reinforced by socio-cultural influences. The main limitations of this approach are about it not being able to explain why some people with this type of learned behaviour go on to commit sexual harm while others do not. Evolutionary theories propose that human behaviour has evolved over millions of years, adapting as necessary. Within this context, coercive sexual behaviour is viewed as a reproductive strategy, as it is within the wider animal kingdom. These theories are widely seen as limited (Travis, 2003). Cognitive-behavioural theories put forward the idea that our thinking and beliefs influence our behaviour. The focus is on deficits in thoughts and beliefs, such as about how much harm has been caused by the sexual act, the perpetrator's sense of entitlement about sex, beliefs about women or children and sex, and blaming the victim for the act occurring.

Biological theories have been posited that have considered brain abnormalities (see, for example, Aigner et al., 2000), hormonal imbalances (Hucker & Bain, 1990), genetic defects (Harrison, Clayton-Smith & Bailey, 2001) as well as intellectual disability (Murray et al., 2001). These theories are not currently considered to be empirically strong without a great deal more research.

Feminist theory puts forward a structural gendered perspective in that men are behaving in accordance with their conditioning and a culture that perpetuates the subjugation of and violence against women and children. There are limitations to this theory, not least because women are also capable of perpetrating sexual harm.

Addiction theories of sexual offending offer a comparison between perpetrators of sexual harm and others who experience addictive behaviour, such as alcoholism (Herman, 1990). This theory focuses on the role of fantasy in sexual offending, with fantasy increasing in frequency and severity, so that the perpetrator feels compelled to commit an act of sexual harm (MacCulloch *et al.*, 1983).

Theological theory (Keenan, 2012) suggests that the tradition of 'splitting' the body and spirit has become institutionalized. It is suggested that a complex array of conditions – about sexuality, emotion and gender – of sexual abuse takes place, which is then compounded by 'institutional grooming' (McAlinden, 2011).

From the 1980s to the present, comprehensive explanations have been attempted, more detailed descriptions of specific single factors, rich descriptions of the offending process and relapse prevention, and more specific situational factors respectively (Ward, 2014; Ward & Beech, 2017). The wish to find the elusive 'cure' and a move towards the need for a coordinated multi-disciplinary approach in both policy and practice has moved through a process of stepped changes and continuous development. So far 'a one-size-fits-all' approach or a 'magic bullet' is yet to appear, and nor is it likely to appear despite the increase in interest, the burgeoning number of cases researched and the number coming to the attention of the Courts, as well as the number of people in prison. The result is more questions than answers. So, for example, there is a wealth of academic and professional knowledge about child sex abuse that has appeared since the 1970s (Itzin, 2000), but no 'solution' to the problem of addressing individuals who sexually harm others has been found. The standardization of a common set of practical approaches to addressing all types of abusive behaviour tends to be elusive. The march of knowledge accumulated through and built on research is necessarily fundamentally informative, but over time specific descriptions of causality and theories can, according to Ward and Beech (2017), become moribund and formulaic, and organizationally 'stale'.

TREATMENT

Theories associated with sexual offending have influenced how we think about and work with sexual offenders – this is the evidence that underpins effective 'treatment'. Not all approaches have shown an effective outcome. For example, many of the sex offender programmes in the UK and US were originally designed to have a strong element of encouraging greater victim empathy by the perpetrator. This was a 'hot topic' for practitioners, with many believing that encouraging victim empathy was a significant factor in treatment effect.

Empathy is difficult to define (Blackburn, 2000; Polaschek, 2003), both as a state or trait and as an outcome further broken down into potentially intertwined cognitive empathy and affective empathy (after Galdstein, 1983, cited in Polaschek, 2003, p.173). The measurement of empathy tends to be transparent – for instance, in asking a perpetrator if they feel sorry for their victim, knowing that they are more likely to be viewed positively if they answer 'yes', the likely answer is indeed 'yes'. Identifying behaviours associated with feeling empathic is problematic since 'feeling' is an internal state that can only be reported by the respondent. Being able to accurately identify the difference between 'a thought' and 'a feeling' is often encouraged prior to practical programme exercises that seek to encourage and enhance a sense of victim empathy. This is perhaps not easy, but having made some distinction between 'thought', 'feeling' and 'behaviour', programmes may then use a progressive intervention of using victim statements and factual descriptions of offending, and then ask a perpetrator in a group to imaginatively role-play the victim of an offence, or write or video-record an imagined account as a victim (see Polaschek, 2003, p.181).

This was subsequently researched and found to be less significant with regard to recidivism (Hanson & Bussière, 1996, 1998). This was later revised again to say that rather than trying to elicit empathy for past victims, eliciting greater levels of the five identified constituent elements of a more sophisticated model of empathy is more effective, 'the ability to have an emotional response, perspective-taking ability, compassion and respect, absence of certain situational factors, ability to manage personal distress' (Barnett & Mann, 2013, p.234). Smallbone and Cale (in press), looking at 88 prisoners, conclude that there is a relationship between lower levels of empathy and violent offending, and lesser incidence of low levels of empathy and sexual offending, but that criminal versatility is a common indicator used in risk assessment. The conclusion by Barnett and Mann (2013) is that by building empathic capacity and practising these in real-life situations, this is helpful in avoiding creating future victims. This illustrates that evidence-based approaches are far from easily operationalized, and that much of *how* the evidence is used and applied in practice is as important as what the research evidence is said to be. Our clinical experience suggests that emphasis on victim empathy can be a barrier in treatment for developing greater insight about themselves and their ability to make progress.

The additional feature of how research evidence is operationalized and translated into effective intervention is the organizational culture and 'way of doing things'. The culture of professions and organizations has an impact on this relationship. Organizational culture and professional leadership has a profound effect on 'how things are done around here' (Deal & Kennedy, 1982), and it is symbolic and tacit shared understandings that create meaning, vision, cohesion and 'orientation' (Alvesson, 2002, p.13). Professional background can influence perspectives on what constitutes good practice and effective outcomes. Interprofessional differences are suggested as influential in achieving effectiveness (Morgan *et al.*, 2012). A host of professional disciplines has influenced the way in which effective interventions have been applied using a variety of approaches that have changed over time. Much of the original, and in some cases poorly evidenced and informed, attempts at 'treatment' came through criminal justice agencies that did their best in the absence of research evidence, and to the discomfort of some 'traditional' probation officers who were de-skilled and unable to access training. As a result, practitioners began to develop a systematic approach to managing sex offenders, of which there are some notable pioneers, such as probation officer Ray Wyre (1951–2008) (see Marriot, 2008), as well as many others who are unnamed.

Founded in 1991, the National Organisation for the Treatment of Offenders (NOTA) grew from a regional network of probation officers and other colleagues in the North West of England to encompass the UK and influence professional practice internationally. This grew into a collective sense of understanding and purpose within the professional community of people working with those who perpetrate harmful sexual abuse. These practitioners have a palpable sense of professional alliances, as well some differences, reflected in professional cultures and the way in which the impact of activities is interpreted and collectively understood. Cultural changes have taken place within NOTA arising from the inclusion of new generations of practitioners from other disciplines alongside widespread organizational cultural changes within criminal justice services such as probation and the prison service, where forensic psychology has dominated sex offender treatment. These organizational changes have influenced the professional culture of how interventions have been and are carried out.

Theories about the cause and causality of sexual offending are problematic (Ward & Beech, 2017). Very broadly, these are generally either biological, psychological, socio-cultural or a combination, namely a bio-psycho-socio-cultural approach, which has become increasingly favoured. Single theoretical approaches appear to be insufficient to explain behaviour, and it is accepted that there are multiple factors within sexual abuse, for example the sexual abuse of a child (Beech & Ward, 2004), and the wider acceptance that offending behaviour is the product of more than one single cause (Agnew, 2013). Integrative pluralism is the preferred tendency to theoretical approaches about sexual offending. This method is able to accommodate the historical and structural elements of offending behaviour, and crucially includes the dimension of someone exerting agency, seeking to make connections between the different types of causes (Ward, 2014). Ward and Beech (2017) consider that it is better to think about 'causal fields' rather than 'a specific cause' (p.45). In working with an individual, all of their personal, social and cultural factors (Thompson, 2005) should be considered, influenced by social systems thinking and Bronfenbrenner's ecological model (1979).

Accredited programmes of intervention with the aim of reducing sexual abuse are underpinned by evidence-based theory, a model of change, a mode of delivery and a tight regimen of ensuring that the intended intervention is delivered according to the design. Each offender should meet strict eligibility criteria for each specific programme. However, what is significant is that accredited sex offender programmes were designed using available expert research and theory in order to address those factors that are thought to contribute to offending. The disappointing impact of sex offender treatment calls into question the underlying thinking and application of the theory of sexually harmful behaviours. The Sex Offender Treatment Programmes (SOTPs) were well constructed and implemented, following the principles of 'what works' or effective practice (Priestley & McGuire, 1985). The battery of research and theories drew on an extensive list of theories and approaches that include child and human developmental, sexual developmental, cognitive, positive psychological and behavioural theories, and theories about current social, cognitive, emotional and behaviour deficits including aspects of empathy for others, self-regulation and control (Allam, 2001; Faux, 2001; Mandeville-Norden, Beech & Hayes, 2008).

Previous 'core' and 'extended' SOTPs within prison and Community Sex Offender Groupwork Programmes (CSOGPs) based on a suite of theories centred mostly on a cognitive-behavioural approach showed only modest positive treatment outcomes. Mews, Di Bella and Purver (2017) undertook a study of core SOTPs in UK prisons: 2562 convicted sex offenders undertook a programme over 13+ years up to 2012 and were matched with 13,219 sex offenders in a comparison group using 87 matching factors. This found:

More treated sex offenders committed at least one sexual reoffence (excluding breach) during the follow-up period when compared with the matched comparison offenders (10.0% compared with 8.0%).

[and]

More treated sex offenders committed at least one child image reoffence during the follow-up period when compared with the matched comparison offenders (4.4% compared with 2.9%). (Mews *et al.*, 2017, p.3)

Citing other similar research, the study concluded that there was little or no change in sexual and non-sexual re-offending, with some caveats that perhaps the true effect of treatment could not be detected; that there may be a number of significant variables; and that the poor outcomes could not be attributed conclusively to treatment design or poor implementation, etc. (see Chapter 8). Care should be taken in reaching this conclusion and any implications, not least that the rate of recorded sexual offending is low, as re-offending rates are notoriously difficult to assess (see Chapter 6).

Theories of desistance have subsequently overtaken those previous theories based on cognitive-behavioural approaches. Desistance theory in sexual offending is viewed as a non-linear process moving away from a deficit model towards a strengths-based approach aligned with approaches in other professions (DH, 2017; Saleeby, 2013). Like other types of crime, perpetrators of sexual harm are likely to stop offending at some point. Desistance theory looks to expedite that process as far as possible. Particular stages in life have been found to be significant in the desistance process of general offenders (Sampson & Laub, 2003), and have been identified as including ageing, marriage, prison, education, cognitive transformation, spirituality, fear of assault or death, sickness and incapacitation, employment and military service. This has developed into a suggested integrated theory of desistance (Göbbels, Ward & Willis, 2012). This presumes that well-designed programmes reduce re-offending, but that there is an independent process of desistance that sees most offenders naturally stop offending.

Increasing age, entering into a long-term intimate relationship, social support, employment, imprisonment, increasing education, as well as internal processes of cognitive change and the impact of the high expectations of others for change, separation from offending associates, spirituality, anxiety about being assaulted, illness and military service have all been associated with desistance (Laws & Ward, 2011, cited in Göbbels *et al.*, 2012, p.453). Much of this replicates the general theme of life course approaches to the theory of crime and criminality that have been developed and tested over time to show that certain influences have an effect on 'delinquents' eventually stopping offending (Sampson & Laub, 2003) and experiencing personal transformation.

It is suggested that this transformative process comes in four dynamic phases (Göbbels *et al.*, 2012), the first of which is the 'initial decisive moment or momentum', not uncommon to ideas surrounding desistance from addictive substances. This is triggered by a significant positive or negative event and acts as a catalyst, and is similar to Prochaska and DiClimente's (1982) contemplation phase in the cycle of change (see below). This important stage is only available if the offender is cognitively and emotionally open to the possibility of change, enhanced, perhaps, by a consciousness-raising process. Life events that trigger a novel emotional and cognitive state of readiness for change are personally meaningful to each individual; at times a life event may or may not trigger a turning point, and instead be a possible trigger to confirm and deepen the persistence of existing patterns of behaviour. An enabling approach with offenders at this stage encourages deeper self-reflection and self-evaluation. As individuals with personal agency, people are likely to change if the context in which they find themselves coincides and is consonant with their social circumstances and the way that others perceive and treat them, sometimes referred to as the 'Pygmalion effect' (Laws & Ward, 2011), after George Bernard Shaw's play 'Pygmalion' (1931), based on a classical tradition of personal transformative change.

The next phase of the desistance process replicates Prochaska and DiClimente's (1982) 'preparation and action stage' that presumes that there are two principal social states, the world of the antisocial and the 'normal' benign pro-social world, and that a person who offends is in the former and can desire and actively move into the latter. It is a particular traditional view of crime that persists in many criminal justice agencies, not least within the traditions of placing an offender on probation, in that an offender may and can wish to 'turn their lives around' through a sense of supportive personal agency. The psychic effort of investing in change through developing personal insight and sustaining this is substantial and has considerable complexity.

This is followed by the third phase, 're-entry' from prison back into the community, as both a stressful event and a process that requires sufficient continued and sustained social support and possible family reintegration, requiring that the offender re-identifies themselves as a non-offender, which is reinforced pro-socially by others. This is more than avoidance of offending but incorporates psychological sustained maintenance of prior changes, including treatment effects and building on a 'Good Lives Plan' (GLP) (Prochaska & DiClimente, 1982, p.458) constructed in the preceding phase. The hope is that the offender is able to use, adapt and develop further their GLP and eliminate their criminogenic needs. This may be seen as a controversial aim if theories of endogenous sexual arousal are deeply embedded within the brain; however, the need to have a sufficient supportive plan that allows the offender to gain a 'Primary Goods Package' (Prochaska & DiClimente, 1982, p.459) that includes those pro-social factors of housing, employment, education, friendships (including romantic relationships), leisure activities, good health, etc. is not necessarily easy to obtain in the face of limited resources and potential community resistance. For those offenders whose backgrounds were in some ways socially limited, with precarious social circumstances of poor accommodation, employment, personal relationships, etc., this may be a novel situation, and the continuing stigma of being a 'dangerous sex offender' may act against the creation of a new personal non-offending personal schema.

Finally, the last stage of the desistance process is 'normalcy or reintegration' (Prochaska & DiClimente, 1982, p.460), implicitly encompassing a sense of redemption and real change over time, a factor that Göbbels *et al.* (2012) emphasizes as requiring a considerable period of support to become 'a non-offender (i.e. exhibiting the same risk of offending as a person, who was never apprehended for a criminal offense)' (p.461). The Integrated Theory of Desistance from Sexual Offending (ITDSO) was, according to the authors, 'a first attempt to construct a comprehensive theory of sex offender desistance and is not intended to be the last or definitive word' (Göbbels *et al.*, 2012, p.461); it had some deeply embedded assumptions, but nevertheless was important, alluding strongly to many complex pivotal factors in the journey from sexual offence to continued non-offending and hence potential future victim safety.

The 'Good Lives Model' (Ward & Brown, 2004) suggests a lifestyle that a person would reasonably aspire to seek. This includes having a well-balanced and generally pleasurable lifestyle of both rewarding paid employment and enjoyable leisure activities, happily living within a community relatively free from stress, feeling good about oneself and having some close meaningful intimate relationships. Added to this might be the more generalized idea of some sense of spirituality and a sense of a personally creative lifestyle as well as good health. The theory posits that perpetrators of sexual harm go about seeking these primary goods in a way that is harmful. It encourages practitioners to assist offenders in learning different and less harmful ways to achieve these goals.

Put simply, this appears to be an acknowledgement of the need to approach each offender as an individual. Policy development through the 1990s meant that there was a desire to put large numbers of offenders through accredited programmes. There has always been much criticism of the 'one-size-fits-all' approach. The integrative pluralistic approach recognizes that there is likely to be a range of factors that might be biological or physiological, social, environmental, cultural or situational that combine in an idiosyncratic way for each individual who goes on to perpetrate sexually harmful behaviour.

Even among these different theoretical disciplines there is an array of different approaches depending on the preferences of the researcher and the context of research. In the early 1990s, the political direction compelled agencies to only adopt research that was 'evidence-based'. This has come to be interpreted to mean a largely positivistic approach that utilizes large amounts of quantitative data in order to establish meaning and extract statistically significant relationships between factors related to re-offending. This approach has been the policy direction and led to the mainstay of assessment and treatment over the last 20 years. Because of its claims to be 'scientific', this approach has been favoured by the most recent administrations as, to a limited extent, it can be said to be proven 'effective' or not. The limitations of this tend to be that the data can only be generalized to an offender population with similar characteristics rather than individualized to particular perpetrators. It also largely relies on reconviction data, which is not necessarily an accurate reflection of the true nature of sexual harm.

Qualitative data can provide a rich quality of information but tends to be from much smaller sample sizes, and its findings are therefore not able to be generalized to a larger population. It also relies heavily on the interpretations and meanings ascribed by the particular researcher, and inherently holds some bias.

There are considerable limitations to each approach, and a great deal of time and energy is spent by researchers trying to protect future victims by discovering the aetiology of sexual offending and 'what works' in its assessment and treatment. The uncomfortable truth of this appears to be that we only know what is effective with some people some of the time; what motivates each perpetrator in the commission of each act of sexual harm is likely to be a combination of factors that are idiosyncratic to that individual.

For the purpose of this book, it is sufficient to say that no single theory is fully satisfactory. The world is complex, and the reason why a person harms another sexually is simultaneously sometimes simple in terms of the act of *what was done* and sometimes complicated in terms of *why it was done*. This can perhaps only be understood on an individualized level, involving awareness of the integration of theory, research and professional skill, the *what* and the *how* in order to understand the *why* of the past and the *what next* of the future.

Having an awareness of theory associated with sexual harm is, of course, extremely important in developing an effective knowledge base from which to practise. As with all other areas of practice, workers have a tendency to favour one theory over another, based on their personal and professional values. This can have the effect of skewing perspective and allowing generalizations to guide thinking instead of seeing the person as an individual with their own set of particular influences and factors that may have contributed to this harmful behaviour.

CHAPTER 4

People Who Sexually Harm Others

TYPOLOGIES

Differentiating between types and categorizing offenders is part of the criminal justice system. We are constantly trying to make sense of ourselves and of others, and in this context there is a particularly laudable effort in attempting to understand the factors that contribute to someone committing harmful acts that devastate lives. If we understand the commonalities between certain offenders, we can then attempt to implement interventions that aim to inhibit or ameliorate further harm. Large-scale research does find trends and patterns that are consistent with particular groups of offenders, and this categorization allows for mechanisms such as assessment tools and certain approaches to intervention. Because of the wide differences and heterogeneity between people who sexually harm others, whilst inevitable that people are placed into 'types', it is both helpful and potentially not helpful to use typologies.

As said previously, people who sexually abuse others are difficult to put into categories, although much of the literature based on specific research samples does have a tendency to do this. The nature of undertaking research, the need to have specific samples and the reduction of variable factors has a tendency to place people in one category or another. When working with individuals, this can enhance thinking errors, and lead people to think that because a person has been categorized as a particular type of abuser with an identified type of victim in the past, they will not abuse another category of victim. That is, for example, that a child abuser will not abuse an adult, or that a male perpetrator who has perpetrated abuse against a female will not, in the future, go on to abuse a male. The obverse of this is to presume that a person who has perpetrated harm to one category of victim will always be at risk of abusing absolutely anyone! Neither of these presumptions are obviously necessarily true in all cases, but are dependent on a number of factors such as the social identity of the abuser, age and gender, situation and context, relationship to victim, opportunity, triggers to arousal, nature of arousal and sexuality, disinhibiting factors, thoughts and feelings, self-regulation and control factors, etc. The opposite to specialism is criminal versatility, namely having a wide range of interests in both sexual and non-sexual behaviours. A person who commits sexual offences and is also criminally versatile in other ways is likely to be considered at increased risk of further sexual offending.

We know that people who sexually abuse others are not a homogeneous group – the diversity of types of abuse and situations are about as wide as anybody can imagine. No matter how unwelcome and unwanted the thought, if you can imagine it in your worst waking nightmare, it is true that somebody somewhere has had the same thought but has turned the thought into action – they have thought it and done it! Such thoughts and behaviours can be challenging, but do not necessarily have to lead to a sense of hopelessness or nihilism. Somewhere between a sense of absolute pessimism and a false optimism and over-confidence is a sense of realism and a coming to terms with the nature of abuse and how it affects how we think, feel and behave as professionals (see Chapters 8 and 9).

Sometimes referred to in the literature as cross-over offenders, the debate is problematic as to whether a person previously convicted of a specific type of sexual offence will commit a sexual offence against a different kind of victim, or if those who sexually harm others tend to be specialists with highly defined preferred types of victims. For example, if someone has abused a child who is well known to them, are they at risk of abusing a 'stranger' child? This is a difficult question to answer. Williams *et al.* (2016) found considerable variation within the literature on cross-over offenders, but within their small sample of 110 men who had offended against children, the re-offending rate was about 7 per cent and the cross-over rate from known to stranger victim was 1 per cent, although abusers who met the 'victim' through someone known to the offender, such as a work colleague, friend or even a family member, were more likely to re-offend against a stranger child compared to other categories of a known child. The greatest risk was in cases where the offender first offended at a young age. Klebin *et al.* (2012) found that previous studies were unclear as to whether subsequent victims were the same gender and age range and had the same victim–perpetrator relationship. As an aside, although uncommon, Abel (1999) noted that those who commit sexual acts on animals are among the most deviant and indiscriminate of sexual offenders and with the most 'cross-over' in terms of victim types (Wilcox, Foss & Donathy, 2005).

As a useful overview of the types of adult sexual offender with whom it is most likely a professional might come into contact, they might broadly be distinguished as:

- child sexual abusers
- adult rapists
- sexual murderers
- non-contact offenders.

The specific diagnostic guidelines and definitions within the various editions of the *Diagnostic and Statistical Manuals* (DSM) produced in the US and influenced by inter-disciplinary politics, increasing involvement of the US government, the health insurance industry, and pharma (Mayes & Horwitz, 2005), produced some significant effects in the way in which complexities of mental health were categorized, understood and addressed. Things tend to become problematic when it comes to understanding the presenting individual who may not neatly fit into any of the boxes. So although having the knowledge about types of sexual offender is, of course, useful, it can be less so when general knowledge or stereotyped information is applied to a person without taking individual circumstances, responsivity factors and other idiosyncrasies into consideration. This chapter therefore outlines what might be described as 'typologies', but with a caveat that people who commit sexual offences, similarly to others, are subject to the vagaries of life that can lead people to behave unpredictably and 'not to type' in certain circumstances.

People who abuse children tend to create most concern. Interest in this type of offender has increased significantly in recent decades, with particular attention paid to high-profile offenders, including a somewhat controversial interest in investigating and prosecuting historical crimes of sexual violence.

There is a wealth of research into all facets of the lives of child sexual abusers in a bid to understand the different sociological and psychological aspects of this group of people. In broad terms, child sexual abusers can be categorized into those who have a strong sexual preference for children and those whose sexual interests are broader but who might opportunistically offend against a child for a number of different reasons.

There is some evidence to say that sexual abuse is a mental disorder, such as the inclusion of paraphilia including pedophilia (US spelling) and other illegal behaviours in the DSM-III (APA, 1980). Some behaviours are considered normative and some are considered abnormal and of clinical significance. These issues within psychiatry have been explored in the specialist press (see Sorrentino, 2016), and there is a discussion as to whether paraphilia is a persistent sexual orientation, or not, that arises during childhood.

OFFENDING AGAINST CHILDREN

The word 'paedophile' has become a ubiquitous term largely due to media portrayals of cases of sexual abuse. The DSM-5 gives specific criteria for being included within this category (see APA, 2013).

This sexual attraction may be directed towards children exclusively or the individual may have a sexual interest in adults as well as children, and may be attracted to girls or boys. It is generally assumed that males with paedophilic disorder begin to feel sexual attraction towards children around the time of puberty, which is consistent with our practice experience. Many men with whom we have worked stated that they had been aware of their sexual attraction from an early age and generally hoped it would pass and subsequently feel distraught when it does not. Some men sought advice prior to offending, usually by going to a GP initially, and sometimes they are referred onto counselling but to little effect. In our experience most men just keep quiet, with a subsequent decline in their mental health, and in some cases they go on to commit a devastating act of harm (APA, 2013).

Those who have a strong sexual preference for children are more likely to have an equally compelling inclination towards male or female children, although this is not always the case. Additionally, some will be opportunistic and offend against a child who happens to be present, regardless of their gender. Pre-pubescent children share similarities in their bodily shapes and it is this childlike physical appearance that can be of sexual interest. Because of these similarities, an individual may mistake a boy for a girl (or vice versa) because of factors such as hair and clothing.

Other specific factors might include those who offend within or outside of the family, or both. Research into these kinds of preferences is used within accredited risk assessment tools linked to recidivism and/or perceived dangerousness, but these should only be used as a general indicator and not applied to any particular individual.

Not all people who commit sexually harmful behaviour present a risk to children, however. Some will present a risk of sexual harm to some children in some specific circumstances that may not be generalized to all children. Some men who have no history of sexual offending may present a risk of sexual harm to children in some circumstances. This is a complex problem that requires considerable analysis and reflection.

Child sexual exploitation is defined as:

> ...a form of child sexual abuse...where an individual or group takes advantage of an imbalance of power, to manipulate or deceive a child or young person under the age of eighteen into sexual activity

(a) in exchange for something the victim needs or wants, and/or (b) for the financial advantage or increased status of the perpetrator or facilitator. (DfE, 2017)

It can take place in person or online. It is a complex issue that may include other aspects, such as links to serious and organized crime, human trafficking, gang culture or modern slavery. When working with individual perpetrators it is useful to make sense of whether child abuse is the dominant feature of the criminal behaviour or whether child abuse in itself is just one part of more general nefarious activity that might have other important meanings for the perpetrator.

A limited study by Cockbain, Brayley and Sullivan (2013) reveals that people involved in groups perpetrating child sexual exploitation showed that offenders have multiple group affiliations with four key themes – a pathway to group involvement, establishing a group identity, resources derived from group involvement, and evolution of the group – indicating that belonging to a group is a powerful influence on the thoughts and actions of the perpetrators. Intervention needs to be adapted in these circumstances to take account of other factors that may be important for the individual.

Hebephilia is often misrepresented as paedophilia. Hebephilia is a sexual preference for adolescents usually aged between 11 and 14. It is different from a sexual attraction to younger children and is not the same as being attracted to adults, although it is, of course, a crime to engage in sexual activity with a person below the legal age of consent. There is some controversy as to whether it is a specific sexual interest in its own right. Controversy centres round whether being attracted to adolescents is 'deviant' or displays normative sexual attraction (Prentky & Barbaree, 2011). Some more recent research suggests that hebephilia is a specific sexual interest and should be deemed as being so when working with individuals (Stephens & Seto, 2015, 2016). Young people who are developing emotionally and physically are beginning to become interested and curious in sex as part of normal maturation and human development, and clinical experience indicates that this is then a factor that attracts sexual interest from adults. For some people the combination of emerging maturity, the lack of perceived potential emotional threat and the absence of problems within adult relationships mean that teenagers are particularly vulnerable. The adults in these circumstances can falsely attribute mature decision-making and the ability to give fully informed consent by young people. They fail to consider the emotional and psychological immaturity of teenagers and their ability to make impactful decisions. Children of all ages have a natural tendency to seek approval through compliance with adult demands, making them vulnerable.

There is a growing controversial body of academic research that supports the idea of child sexual preference being an inherent innate sexual orientation. Problematic for those who experience this, it is not a reason not to exercise control and is not an excuse for illegal abusive sexual behaviour.

The rise of social media has allowed for 'non-offending paedophiles' to anonymously have a presence, a voice, and to contribute to the debate and discussion about treatment and prevention as the equivalent of a 'service user group'. They widely use the phrase 'minor attracted person' (MAP) to describe themselves. The online group Virtuous Paedophiles offers support and guidance to individuals with a sexual attraction to children with a view to preventing abuse occurring. In the 1970s, a highly controversial group called the Paedophile Information Exchange (PIE) campaigned for 'children's sexuality' including reducing the age of sexual consent to 14 and supporting adults in legal difficulties as a result of having underage sexual 'partners'. It was affiliated to the National Council for Civil Liberties (now 'Liberty'). Highly controversial, it openly held conferences and forums with the aim of normalizing sexual contact with children. Unhelpfully, it appeared to try to conflate its cause with homosexuality and the general trend towards more liberal attitudes. The group was eventually disbanded in 1984 as a reflection of changing moral relativism.

In 2018, NOTA set up a prevention committee that aims to promote research and practice related to the prevention of sexual abuse (NOTA (1), n.d.). Survivor groups are also beginning to have a coordinated voice and influence over policy developments.

People who make, possess, download and view indecent images of children have caused great public concern and anger in recent years with the increased availability and access to abusive imagery. The nature of the internet has provided degrees of anonymity for those who are motivated to access indecent images of children, despite considerable efforts by enforcement agencies to counter the 'dark web'. Many professionals who are working with these offenders are very concerned about the potential for these offenders to 'cross over' into direct contact offending.

Greater access to the internet has clearly shown increasing access to indecent images of children, which is an increasingly profitable international market and is linked to globalized organized crime. Consumers of online illegal imagery tend to be younger and better educated with less of a general offending background when compared to contact offenders, but with an assumed greater level of self-control and greater barriers to behaviours to acting on sexually deviant interests (Babchishin, Hanson & Hermann, 2011). A diagnosis of pedophilia (US spelling) or antisocial personality traits appears to increase the risk of a contact offence. Those who have a history of contact offending appear to have an increased risk of committing another contact offence if they have accessed illegal images of children, but for those whose only offending is internet offences, the risk is low (Franke & Graf, 2016), and this appears to be supported by some other studies where it is suggested that there may be a distinct subgroup of sexual offenders who pose a low risk (Seto, Hanson & Babchishin, 2011). Endrass and Rosseger (2010), who explored 231 internet offenders over six years, conclude that the majority of those found to have used illegal imagery had not committed a contact offence, and that the use of child pornography alone did not present as a risk factor for those who had not previously committed a sexual contact offence.

A somewhat disturbing evolution of the sex industry is that of sex dolls. Although they have been around for some time, their level of sophistication has increased alongside technological advances. Maras and Shapiro (2017) describe current sex dolls as being made from flesh-like silicone whose orifices are designed to create suction. They also describe some dolls being designed to cater to deviant tastes, for example one named 'Frigid Farrah' that encourages its users to rape the doll. Another is 'Young Yoko', described as 'barely 18'. Even more disturbingly are the dolls created to be realistic representations of pre-pubescent children with anatomically correct genitalia. They can be designed to appeal to the preferences of their users with facial expressions including happiness, anger, fright, etc., and are apparently designed as 'an alternative to offending' (Maras & Shapiro, 2017). It is currently not illegal to possess such a doll in England and Wales, but the CPS is taking steps to address this gap in the law. The first criminal case involving a child sex doll occurred in 2017 after a man purchased one online and it was imported into the UK. He was prosecuted under the Customs and Excise Management Act 1979 and sentenced to two years and eight months' imprisonment. The CPS has now published guidelines (CPS, 2019 (3)), and although there is no offence of 'possession' of a childlike sex doll, prosecutions can occur in relation to obscene articles under the Customs and Consolidation Act 1876 or the Customs and Excise Management Act 1979, the Obscene Publications Act 1959 and the Postal Services Act 2000. To date, the UK Border Force has seized 230 childlike sex dolls since 2016 (CPS, 2019 (3)). Even when individuals are found guilty of such offences, the sentences are unlikely to be of sufficient length for perpetrators to undergo any kind of 'treatment' programme. Nevertheless, when working with such individuals, establishing whether there is a sexual interest in children is important to any subsequent intervention or case management.

Other kinds of non-contact offenders might include indecent exposers and voyeurs, including those who take sexually intrusive images under a person's clothing without them knowing, referred to as 'upskirting', and usually involving the use of a mobile phone. Although some of these offences can be harmful in themselves to victims, professionals are usually most concerned with the possibility of 'cross-over', and there is some relevant research about this (for more information see Chapter 8).

SEXUAL VIOLENCE

Rape is a serious specific offence, if not the most serious of sexual offences (see Chapter 7), defined in law as forced penetration without consent by a penis of the vagina, anus or mouth on either a male or female. Because it is done without consent it is often imagined as an inherently violent offence, sometimes with additional violence or the threat of violence, and sometimes coercion, although this is not always the case. It should be borne in mind that each case has to be examined and perhaps presented to a Court to test the legality, evidence and specific circumstances, particularly over contentious issues of consent. If consent is withheld and there is penetration, it may generally constitute rape according to the specific circumstances. There are situations where consent has been given to some things but not others, such as consent to have sex when using a condom – if a person then agrees but fails to use a condom, it is open to challenge in law whether full consent has been given, and this may constitute rape. The issue of being able to give consent is a particular issue. If a person is drunk or affected by drugs, is cognitively impaired, or does not have the mental capacity to give consent under the Mental Capacity Act 2005 in England, consent cannot be presumed. A young person who gets drunk on a night out and gets into bed with another person 'to sleep it off' who then thinks that this implies consent is again open to legal challenge and the possibility that this may constitute rape, although it may not have involved explicit violence and coercion.

Rape can occur within a domestic relationship as part of a pattern of intimate partner violence. The definition of domestic abuse and what this consists of has undergone revisions in recent years, both in the public understanding and legal understanding – domestic abuse law in the UK is governed by different acts in different jurisdictions. It is defined across government as an incident of controlling, coercive or threatening behaviour, violence or abuse between those aged over 16, regardless of gender or sexuality. It can be psychological, physical, sexual, financial or emotional abuse (CPS, n.d.), and it encompasses honour-based violence and forced marriage. A person may be forced into marriage and be made to have sex – this may be a situation where full consent has not been given despite a person being pressurized to do so, for example by the victim's family. Again, it would be up to a Court to consider the evidence and the circumstances. At present a range of legislation is applicable to domestic abuse, but there are proposals to update the legislation in keeping with a better social and political awareness of the issues.

Most rape is often perpetrated by a person known to the victim. This has become known colloquially as 'date rape', but occurs under a range of circumstances and in a variety of contexts. This is sometimes viewed less seriously than 'stranger rape' as there is an erroneous belief that it is less traumatic for the victim or that the victim may bear some responsibility in some way. In truth, not only has the victim been intimately assaulted, but the perpetrator has also likely breached a pre-established level of trust, leading to extremely serious emotional and psychological consequences for the victim. Motivators for this type of offence vary considerably from a planned premeditated attack to, controversially, a person who completely and catastrophically misunderstands the concept of gaining active consent. If a person lacks the capacity to give consent, perhaps because they were intoxicated, it cannot be assumed that consent can or has been given. Without consent, it is generally the case that this then constitutes rape.

Rape by a stranger is more unusual but is featured more in the media, crime fiction, drama and popularist consciousness. Reliance on this type of violence as a form of entertainment and to watch a woman in fear for her life raises questions of systemic misogyny. The fear of sexual violence is an aspect of the social control of women, and its manifestation can be seen in how spaces in cities and towns are thought about and planned, including the use of pedestrian underpasses, footbridges, lighting and public transport. This type of attack may include the threat or use of additional violence in order to secure compliance or to increase sexual arousal. Some men who commit this type of offence have a particular sexual interest in the use of violence and humiliation as part of the arousal process; others use additional violence or threats of violence only as a way of ensuring victim compliance.

There are many 'rape myths' that perpetuate contemporary nuanced false awareness within the criminal justice system and beyond that influence how rape is recognized and dealt with. Perhaps the strongest myth is that when women say 'no', they really mean 'yes', and that consent can be implied because of circumstances. The use of substances is often an issue that is linked to sexual offending and used by offenders in order to minimize responsibility.

Some substances can cause symptoms similar to mental illness, and in some circumstances the perpetrator may not present a sexual risk other than when substances are consumed. More often substances are used as part of the offending process, in order to disinhibit the usual internal obstacles to offending, and may form part of a ritual associated with the offending act. Substances do not cause sexual offending and a perpetrator is still likely to pose some risk of offending even when sober. There are substances that also facilitate rape if a perpetrator gives them to a victim, rendering the victim unable to consent to sexual activity.

Most recorded rape is perpetrated by men against women. Although men also rape other men, recorded figures for this are lower. About 75,000 sexual assaults on men occur annually in the UK, and about 9000 men are the victims of rape, although only about a third come to the attention of the police. The UK government created the Male Rape Support Fund to tackle the taboo subject of male victims of rape (Gov.uk., 2014). Women can perpetrate the serious offence of sexual assault by unlawful penetration (Section 2, Sexual Offences Act 2003). Rape is also recognized as being used as a weapon of war, of which there is a considerable history, such as the wholesale unrestrained vengeful multiple gang rape of the civilian population of women in 1945 in Budapest, and the use of rape as a weapon of war (Beevor, 2014, (online) loc. 13304, 13387; Copelon, 1995; UN Human Rights Office of the Commissioner, n.d.).

FEMALE PERPETRATORS

There tends to be a lack of data on female sex offenders, partly because of the low numbers of females convicted, but not necessarily reflecting the general prevalence. Women appear to be treated more leniently than men in these situations – they are less likely to be arrested and convicted, and are likely to receive shorter sentences (Sandler & Freeman, 2011). Wijkman (2011) studied all female sex offenders in the Netherlands between 1994 and 2005 and distinguished between generalists (who also commit other serious non-sexual offences), specialists (who commit mainly sex offences) and once-only offenders. She found that there is no such thing as a 'typical' female offender.

It is estimated that women are responsible for approximately 4–5 per cent of sexual offences (Cortoni, Hanson & Coache, 2010), although the true extent is likely to be much higher, given that it is significantly under-reported (Clements, Dawson & Das Nair, 2014). It has been argued that social constructions of gender have led to a 'culture of denial' (Denov, 2001) failing to acknowledge the volume of sexual harm perpetrated by women. Sandler and Freeman (2009), in their study of the relative sentencing of male and female sex offenders, found an inherent bias in what is considered to be a male paternalistic chivalric response in some cases, and a harsher penalty for those offenders seen as outside the boundary of traditional female social role expectations, of caring rather than hurting children. Single notorious cases, such as that of Vanessa George who offended against children whilst working as a nursery assistant, receive particular notoriety as well as public and political vilification perceived as justified within local communities (PlymouthLive, 2019).

Some women perpetrate sexual abuse alongside male perpetrators, who are usually their partners. This seems to be deemed more understandable as it might occur within the context of an abusive and coercive framework. Existing literature, such as that from Gannon and Rose (2008), suggests that in this situation the abuse tends to occur within the family and the women tend to have low socio-economic status and few educational qualifications. What professionals and the public seem less ready to acknowledge is that women might sexually abuse on their own with similar motives to their male counterparts. Findings from a study by Darling, Hackett and Jamie (2018) challenged these stereotypical notions as well as the well-worn titillation of female teachers engaging in sexual contact with willing teenage boys. These women offended alone, had no criminal histories and were established professionals who would appear to understand the conventional boundaries of relationships between adults and children. The victims were most likely to be male and in their mid-teenage years. These female perpetrators were similar to their male counterparts in that some predisposing factors were found to be similar, for example relationship problems, low self-esteem, loneliness, etc., and they appeared to be seeking intimacy and solace from the abuse. They were dissimilar to traditional notions of male offenders in that they did not appear to be 'predatory' and seeking to work with children due to their sexual interest; rather, they began to engage in sexually abusive behaviour once within that environment. Within this study, a large proportion of the women were either formal or informal 'mentors' to the children they abused. The difficulties for addressing women perpetrators are compounded by their comparatively small conviction population, in that there are often insufficient numbers for similar treatment options to men. The largely positivistic and 'evidence-based' approach to assessment and treatment requires a large enough population to apply accepted research methods.

STALKING

Stalking is an offence under the Stalking Protection Act 2019. Whilst the definition of stalking is unclear, it is generally considered to include intentional repeated unwelcome behaviour that causes fear, upset and annoyance (Scottish Government, 2002). Researchers have attempted to categorize sub-types of 'stalker', such as, for example, Holmes (1998), who differentiates between types of stalkers. These may be variously where a personal relationship has ended and an ex-partner obsessively and dangerously pursues, tracks and follows the other; or those who are sexually motivated or who obsessively desire to enter into a personal relationship. Stalkers may identify victims who have a public profile such as celebrities or be motivated by political views and extreme behaviours. Power is clearly related to stalking behaviours either within a domestically abusive setting and an obsessive wish to exert control. Making threats to kill or being motivated to carry out and plan sexual assault can clearly increase the level of risk to the victim.

MENTAL ILLNESS

In practice, most people with 'atypical' sexual interests would not be considered to have a mental disorder. Care should be taken over clinical and legal distinctions of terminology and the relationship between a diagnosis of mental illness or mental disorder and sexually abusive behaviour. Major mental illness is about a substantial impairment of cognition, affect or behaviour. It is important to establish what the link is, if at all, between the mental illness and the offending behaviour (Garrett, 2017). It is possible that a person with acute mental illness might act in a way that is harmful to others, including sexually abusive behaviour due to making impulsive or irrational decisions. In these circumstances, this does not necessarily mean that they have unhealthy sexual interests when they are not unwell. For a person who has unhealthy sexual interests, their risk of offending may increase if they become acutely mentally ill. Douglas and Hart (1996) suggest that there may be a particularly strong relationship between violence and psychosis or mania, although Wallace *et al.* (1998) say that the risk of someone who has a major mental illness committing a serious offence is small.

People with a psychopathic personality disorder may have traits that have a causal association with violence including sexual violence, which might include lack of empathy, sensation-seeking and impulsivity (Krug *et al.*, 2002). There is a limited association between re-offending and sexual violence in people with psychopathy (Hare's *Psychopathy Checklist – Revised* (PCL-R), 1991, 2003, 2016; WHO, 2016, codes F60–62), although when sexual violence does occur, it tends to be more severe, diverse, with greater use of weapons and with more tendency to target strangers (Barbaree *et al.*, 2001; Hanson & Harris, 2000b).

Sexual murder arises intermittently and has an impact on public consciousness and fascination. Despite its rarity, it features a great deal in popular fiction and drama. Cases that do occur receive notoriety for many years. Violence in sexual offending can serve a number of functions such as an individual being motivated by anger and expressing this physically, seeking to silence the victim, or as an aid to arousal. Some individuals kill by accident; for others it is an intentional act, possibly including the use of gratuitous violence. The sexual element of murder is not necessarily always obvious as it may not always involve overtly sexual acts but can nonetheless be sexually motivated. In reviewing stranger sexual murderers, Greenall and Wright (2019) suggest that the act can be a way of seeking intimacy for some and to objectify the victim for others. Because of the relatively low numbers involved, it is difficult to identify common characteristics. Some of the research that does exist cites a distinguishing characteristic of sexual murderers as being lonelier than those who rape but do not kill (Grubin, 1994).

HARMFUL SEXUAL BEHAVIOUR BY YOUNG PEOPLE

Working with harmful sexual behaviour perpetrated by children and adolescents is an area of specialism in itself, and is generally managed within social work and youth offending teams. The policy and procedure for children who display sexually harmful behaviour has developed over recent years, with an emphasis that children are not the same as adult perpetrators, require a different approach and understanding, and should not be treated as just 'little' sex offenders, using the same approaches and theories as with adults. Many, if not most, children display harmful sexual behaviours within a family with all the implications for family practice (Hutton & Whyte, 2006; Stevens et al., 2013, cited in Smith et al., 2014).

Reviewed by Smith et al. (2014), much local policy, process and approach has been found to be inconsistent, with poor under-developed practice, the indications and opportunities for early intervention missed, and poor multi-agency communication and coordination, and that based on inspections over 20 years apart, little progress was being made in developing the need for treatment of and intervention with children who display harmful sexual behaviours up until the Criminal Justice Joint Inspection in 2013. Scotland has a welfare-oriented Children's Hearings approach (Children's Hearings Scotland, 2019), favourably compared with the more criminal justice approaches in other parts of the UK. In England the development of multi-agency young offender teams (YOTs) has been under the policy guidance of a centralized Youth Justice Board established in 1998 (Bateman, 2017; Bateman & Neal, 2014) but subsequently with a reduced role and 'virtually abolished' by the UK Coalition government in 2010 (Pickford, 2012, p.93), and influenced by the successful Multi-Agency Public Protection Arrangements (MAPPAs; see Chapter 6), designed principally for the management of dangerous adults in the community. There are clearly some contradictory issues when managing and intervening with children who are seen as being 'in need' rather than a criminal justice system that has a tendency to punish and treat as well as rehabilitate. This has implications as to whether children and families social work or criminal justice services should take precedence when working with children and young people who sexually harm others, and potentially divert away from criminal justice processes, restorative approaches or child protection measures. In practice this remains deeply ambiguous, treating the child as a perpetrator to be punished or as a child in need, or both.

Smith *et al.* (2014) reviewed developments in approaches using key themes from an earlier 2003 study by Masson and Hackett (2003) examining denial and minimization, differences and similarities to other young offenders, the management of young people, terminology and categorization, and assessment and intervention. Their conclusion was that there is 'continuing cause for concern' (Masson & Hackett, 2003, p.227), regarding Working Together guidance (DfE, 2013), and whilst there is greater understanding of the complexities and diversity of young people who display sexually harmful behaviour, there is inconsistent rigour and assessment in agencies applying this in practice, with some major differences between the separate national jurisdictions within the UK. There is also a continuing trend towards the criminalization of troubled and vulnerable young people (Smith *et al.*, 2014).

Young people (aged under 18) represent between a fifth and a third of all sexually harmful perpetrators (Hackett, 2004), bearing in mind uncertainty regarding the level of disclosure and probable under-reporting. Many children and young people who abuse within their family do so against their siblings, with a smaller notable proportion perpetrating harmful behaviour in both the family and the community. It appears that most young people who are sexually abusive start to display sexually abusive behaviour within their family and then progress to the community outside of their family, and those who abused in both their family and the community are likely to have started to abuse at an earlier age and experienced adverse childhood experiences themselves. Those whose behaviour was motivated by factors within family relationships, such as jealousy, were unlikely to abuse outside their family in the community and may be referred to as a sub-group of 'sibling abusers' and are the most common type of intrafamilial abusers, mostly by older boys against younger sisters, which is many times more prevalent than parent–child abuse. Much of the popular concern is about abusive parents, although a possible explanation for this is the great discomfort that the issue raises, explained away as being part of experimental sexual development which is seen as non-abusive but which may have serious and harmful consequences (Yates, Allardyce & MacQueen, 2012).

Many of the approaches to addressing harmful sexual behaviour involve interventions that emphasize taking personal responsibility for the abuse, the preconditions of that abuse, increasing victim empathy, promoting normative healthy sexual attitudes and constructing personal abuse prevention strategies as well as addressing general antisocial behaviour, enhancing social skills and aggression replacement therapy. Again, however, the theme of inconsistency of approach appears not to be uncommon, including, perhaps, social interventions that do not specifically address sexual behaviours and provide support at the pivotal stage of disclosure (Kjellgren, 2019). McCrory's (2010) manual for addressing adolescents who display harmful sexual behaviours, as well as providing specific activities, stresses the need for individualized case formulation based on a range of approaches of cognitive-behavioural therapy, psychodynamic approaches, attachment-orientated and metacognitive theories, as well as the GLM and positive psychology. Lloyd (2019) locates both the harmful behaviour and the response to that behaviour within an environmental contextual approach rather than focusing on the risks and vulnerabilities of the individual child. Recognizing that the discovery of harmful sexual behaviour is inconsistent across agencies and specific settings, the usual response is to refer onwards to social work or via criminal justice agencies. Whilst traditional approaches to harmful sexual behaviour may suggest a cognitive-behavioural approach, and a focus of reducing future risk, Lloyd suggests that multi-systemic therapy (quoted in Henggeler *et al.*, 2009) can address the ecological aspect of the young person, as well as adapting the GLM to address future needs, but rather than focusing on individual behaviours, it is suggested that multiple activities are required involving all those in the person's life. The current practice of 'referring on' to another agency in some way avoids addressing the contextual space in which the behaviour has occurred and its significance. What is needed is a 'whole school approach' of examining and adapting school policies, cultures, physical space and the curriculum, working with staff and parents, and recognizing how the school fits systemically into the wider safeguarding policies and processes.

Acknowledging that the young person is an individual with unique circumstances is clearly essential. An individualized approach appears to be productive but with preparation and post-treatment follow-up and support. Much sexually problematic behaviour may be placed within the ideas broadly associated with human development and life course theory (Sampson & Laub, 2003). Adolescence is clearly a period of substantial transition. Changes in a young person's life can evolve into socially adaptive or maladaptive patterns of behaviour. The aftermath of the abuse can be perpetuated for the abuser as personal guilt, regret, suicidal thoughts and community stigma and will have a significant impact on family relationships (Kjellgren, 2019, p.126).

Sexual offending in adolescence is more common than some might think. Some young people will go on to become adult sexual offenders while others will not, and therein lies the difficulty with assessment. Vizard (2013) concludes that 16.5 per cent of 11- to 17-year-olds have experienced sexual abuse by either an adult or a child, and that almost 60 per cent of contact sexual abuse is carried out by a child.

OLDER PEOPLE

As well as children being the victims of sexual abuse, bearing in mind the considerable increase in the number of people who are living longer (over the age of 65) and that the older age group is set to increase globally (ONS, 2018; UN, n.d.), the older population is vulnerable to sexual abuse. Those who are the least able to protect themselves and the least able to report sexual assault are particularly vulnerable such as those in residential care settings, where carers have easy intimate access to those with a physical, cognitive or communicative disability. Whilst the term 'gerontophile' has been attributed to von Krafft-Ebing (see von Krafft-Ebing & Chaddock, 1892), later referred to as 'gerontophilia', this tends to be a strongly taboo subject even amongst those involved in caring for the older population and who need to be aware of the potential risks (Iversen, Kilvik & Malmedal, 2015a). Research in this area tends to be limited and is a generally under-recognized problem; online sources including those from North America provide some information about potential identification of abuse such as physical symptoms of injury, signs of trauma and agitation, etc., exacerbated by potential social isolation (Burgess *et al.*, 2007; Nursing Home Abuse Center, n.d.; WHO, 2016). Both men and women have been found to be victims. While both men and women have been found to be victims, unsurprisingly perpetrators appear to be mostly men, and while the abuse is generally carried out by staff, other residents in residential settings can also be perpetrators (Iversen, Kilvik & Malmedal, 2015b). Whilst there is some considerable uncertainty as to the motivation and triggers for the sexual abuse of older people, teenagers and men across other age categories upto their 50s and 60s appear to have committed such offences, most being unrelated to the victim, and where opportunism or pervasive anger was present (Burgess *et al.*, 2007), although Burgess and colleagues strongly counsel against attempting to create an overly deterministic typology of elder abuse.

CHAPTER 5

Theories of Risk

THE RISK SOCIETY

Much of the concern about sexual abuse is about 'risk'. The word 'risk' is interpreted in several ways, sometimes meaning dangerousness, as in 'risky', but usually referring to the probability of a negative harmful event. Despite its common usage, there is sometimes an assumption that we have a common shared understanding of what we mean by 'risk'. Kemshall (2010) refers to contradictory 'risk rationalities' translated into organizational policy and practice.

Representing a shift in thinking about the nature of society (Beck, 1992; Giddens, 1990), the term 'risk society' has been used generally since the publication of Giddens' and Beck's writing in the 1990s. Ulrich Beck's (1992) *Risk Society*, originally published in German in 1986, has been a seminal text focusing on two interacting themes of modernization and risk. The 'risk society' is a challenge to a sense of social certainty and 'a culture of scientism' (Lash & Wynne, 1992, p.2). Early modernism has led towards the dubious suggestion that there is a singular answer to problems of risk and that it is possible to be able to predict the future with certainty given enough expertise and sufficient information.

Despite its apparent universality, risk is a continuously shifting discontinuous construction, not as a fixed idea, but constituted from the social, organizational and cultural world that we inhabit. The 'risk society' is recursive, reflexive, self-confrontational and philosophically sceptical of a fixed idea of social reality, a moving reflection of concerns rooted in a particular temporal, organizational and cultural context, simultaneously set in a social world of needs, rights and social justice. Whereas a postmodernist view of the social world is one of multiplicities of competing relativist and discontinuous view of social reality: 'There is no stable social world to know, but knowledge of that world contributes to its unstable or mutable character' (Giddens, 1990, p.45). The nature of social reality is itself reflexively sociologized in a way that has no parallel in the natural sciences.

Assessing risk through a calculation of chance and based on probability is far from the whole story. Michael Blastland and David Spiegelhalter, respectively a broadcaster specializing in a popular BBC radio programme based on statistics ('More or Less', BBC Radio 4, 2018) and the Winton Professor for the Public Understanding of Risk (The Statistical Laboratory, Centre for Mathematical Sciences, University of Cambridge), in their book *The Norm Chronicles* (2013), define probability as 'magical, a brilliant concept. It yokes together our two world-views, the two faces of risk: the orderly view of whole populations...and the maze of stories' (Blastland & Spiegelhalter, 2013, p.10). However, it makes the point that risk is dynamic, in that it does not stand still, because the world and the counting of numbers continually changes. This leads to the somewhat controversial view that there is no fixed view of probability, and if it is uncertain and not fixed at all, that for reasonable day-to-day purposes probability does not exist (Blastland & Spiegelhalter, 2013).

The nature of the contemporary world of the 'risk society' is one of disorientation, resulting from a sense that 'many of us have of being caught up in a universe of events we do not fully understand, and which seems in large part outside of our control' (Giddens, 1990, pp.2–3). The mix of issues surrounding 'risk', its definition and operationalization, has developed in scale, intensity and diversity throughout the 'noughties' (2000–2009) and beyond.

The concept of risk has a considerable modern historical legacy but has not always been understood in the same way as today. From the 1700s onwards, appraising risk has become increasingly universal in decision-making, crossing boundaries of commerce, gambling, medicine, disease and crime, and at all levels, from daily mundane decisions to critical and far-reaching implications. The key socio-economic factor of neoliberalism cannot be entirely ignored – it is a context in which much of the Western world is embedded. The relationships between neoliberalism, markets, economics, financial industries and 'risk' ideologies are linked. The combination of rationalism, trade, commerce, gambling and applied mathematics gave rise to a new social order (Duménil & Lévy, 2005), difficult to define (Saad-Filho & Johnston, 2005), and crossing a wide range of social, political and economic phenomena.

PROBABILITY

Attempting to bring degrees of certainty to the process of how to assess future probability, particularly the fear of future harmful events, is associated with Antoine Arnauld (1612–1694) and Daniel Bernoulli (1700–1782), credited with the original idea that risk is not just about the mathematical calculation of a probability of an event occurring, but is also about the values that people assign to an event. This social dimension to risk appraisal leads to the view that risk assessment is not just a matter of 'calculating the odds', but that it also assigns a value to the impact of the event. Whilst risk might be seen as the superior scientific calculative preserve of mathematicians, it is also a cultural construct (Douglas, 1992). In practice, there is no single entirely satisfactory definition of risk – it is associated with different meanings within different moving reflections of concerns and 'panics' rooted in a particular temporal, organizational and cultural context, set in a social world obsessed with danger from disease, environmental disaster, political conflict, abuse, crime and lifestyle hazards (Furedi, 1997).

The probability of an event falls somewhere between two poles of the certainty that something will happen or that it will not happen. Jacob Bernoulli (1655–1705) is credited with realizing that probability is concerned with degrees of certainty, and that certainty is of two kinds, subjective and objective. Often assumed to be purely an objective value-free calculation, dependent on well-established techniques of calculation of frequency of events, the calculation of physical occurrences can be said to be objectively likely or unlikely.

But the calculation of probability rests on the relative totality of knowing all that is to be known, and certainty or uncertainty of information. Choice and lack of absolute guarantee of information, particularly within the social world, leads to degrees of relativism and the idea that probability can be said to have both elements of objective certainty and subjective uncertainty.

The over-reliance on a procedural statistically based actuarial approach has considerable dangers, not least in applying it simplistically to sexually abusive behaviours. Most perpetrators will not be high risk in all situations and in all settings with all victims of abuse all of the time, and perhaps more worryingly, not all of those deemed to be low risk will be low risk in all settings all of the time. Even those in the past who were considered the most unlikely of individuals have been found to have perpetrated harmful abusive behaviours, who, in hindsight, were suddenly transformed from being seen as 'no risk' to a situation of 'I knew something wasn't right all along'. After the event, based on the same facts, a clarity of insight arises that was not quite so obvious beforehand, as in the well-publicized examples of Operation Yewtree that investigated the historical abuse perpetrated by the radio and DJ celebrity Jimmy Savile (Gray & Watt, 2013). The phrase 'hiding in plain sight' (Gray & Watt, 2013, p.6) has been used to describe some of the reasons why a substantial number of abusive incidents took place and were not widely recognized for what they were. A powerful perceptual bias and preconception overcame the well-founded (small) number of allegations of abuse.

If an approved risk assessment tool had been applied, would Jimmy Savile have been identified as a high-risk sexual abuser? Would an alternative approach have been any more effective at uncovering the risk, such as applying professional judgement? This basic dilemma continues to confound two competing approaches to risk assessment (Hart, Laws & Kropp, 2003).

It is conjectural that an experienced practitioner can spot danger-ous attitudes and behaviours purely on the basis of professional experience. Linked to the much-vaunted and publicized idea of 10,000 hours of experience (Carter, 2014; Ericsson, Krampe & Tesch-Romer, 1993), this builds an extra layer of professional insight.

An experienced practitioner may be able to spot almost imperceptible indicators compared to a less experienced practitioner, although this can be deceptive. The difference between being able to make accurate judgements based on experience and perceptual bias is difficult to unravel.

PERCEPTUAL BIAS, LIKELIHOOD AND COMPLEXITY THINKING

The appreciation of perceptual bias within professional decision-making is not new. The way in which risk assessment is biased by individual practitioners has been previously linked to a process of 'framing', or an a priori structuring of perceptual frameworks (see Strachan & Tallant, 1997). This is associated with the desire to minimize the effects of bias as a source of error. But it is useful to make a distinction between bias and error. Whilst error is simply a mistake or oversight, bias is more fundamental, inevitable and has a clear link to professional decision-making processes. A fuller consideration of processes and biases has the potential to provide some additional insights into the problem of when those people formally assessed as low risk then seriously re-offend catastrophically, and the process of risk identification and assessment generally.

Intuitive professional judgement has largely been given lesser significance than standardized tests based on well-founded research of significant numbers of proven abusers, identifying common factors that are then constructed into well-established risk assessment tools (see Chapter 6). It is not just risk assessment that is affected by professional expertise but also the application of critical thinking skills (see Chapter 9).

Many assessments of probability are necessarily qualitative and cannot be represented by numbers. The adding up of the number of significant factors that then concludes with a level of risk described either numerically or as a probabilistic category from low to very high without insight is a problematic social determinism that ignores issues of human subjectivity, contextuality, culture, personal volition, cognitive processes and personal agency.

Technical rationality tends to reflect a deterministic view of the social world occupying the high ground overlooking the messy confused swamp of real-world settings that militates against an entirely rational structured analysis of all that there is to be known (Schön, 1987, p.3, cited in Hood, 2018, p.12).

On the one hand, probability is statistical and numerically calculated through ratios; on the other, it is epistemological and dependent on 'reasonable degrees of belief in propositions quite devoid of statistical background' (Hacking, 1975, p.12). The emergence of probability in Pascal's time (Blaise Pascal, 1623–1662) was 'essentially dual' (Hacking, 1975, p.10), and remains so, and today we are left with different approaches to probability. There is the kind of probability that relates to physical phenomena, such as tossing a coin and calculating the frequency of heads and tails, and whilst it cannot be said for sure that the next toss will come up either heads or tails, it can be said that there is a likelihood that the number of heads and tails will be equal over a long enough run, and that each toss of the coin is objectively independent of knowledge of the previous toss (named by Keynes as the principle of 'indifference'; 1921, reprinted in 1973). Placing the coin in one hand and asking a person to guess introduces degrees of 'knowing' and an interactive quality that requires a different kind of assessment of probability. The coin may be in one hand or the other and has the same statistical chance as tossing the coin, but this kind of calculation of probability is not independent of subjective knowledge. Predicting which hand also involves what is in the mind of the person hiding the coin and assessments based on what has previously happened.

Importantly, the emergence of probability is intrinsically linked to the development of inductive scientific reasoning, based on the expectation that events from the past will give rise to an expectation of events happening in the future. 'The natural man is disposed to the opinion that probability is essentially connected with the inductions of experience and…the laws of causation and of the uniformity of nature' (Keynes, 1921 [1973], p.86). But it is reasonable to remember, despite considerable assumptions to the contrary, that inductive reasoning remains philosophically unresolved.

The link between the observation of the past and the guarantee that the past will be replicated in the future remains open to question, and the doubts raised by the philosopher of the Scottish Enlightenment David Hume (1711–1776) is often overlooked, leaving assumptions of causal connection between successive individual events over time philosophically open to question. As Keynes says, 'Hume, in fact, points out that, while it is true that past experience gives rise to a psychological anticipation of some events rather than of others, no ground has been given for the validity of this superior anticipation' (1921 [1973], p.88), and within modernist thought at least, Hume's case against induction has never been improved on. Inductive logic makes an assumptive leap that remains philosophically open to challenge. Whilst there may be strong evidence based on the frequency of association between events, so that event A has often tended to happen in the past in conjunction with factor B, this may be an associative relationship, not necessarily a proven causal relationship, and there may be degrees of uncertainty that this association will happen in the future. The mantra that 'the best predictor of future behaviour is past behaviour' has been widely used in practice (see, for example, Prins, 1980), and is influential in much of criminal justice risk assessment tools and processes.

This book is not about the complexities of calculating probability, as there are substantial texts available that go into considerable detail.

Risk assessment tools that are based on a well-founded calculation of probability are used extensively in the assessment of the risk of sexual abuse. Knowing that winning the lottery is so extremely unlikely or that a farmer's Land Rover will fall through the roof of your holiday cottage in rural Cornwall onto your bed (it happened in 1999: see Mathews, 2018) is so extremely unlikely that it is reasonable to say that for all practical purposes it will not happen, but people still buy lottery tickets, and obsess about unlikely dangers that they hear about on the news.

Knowing that there is a group of people who are 'most at risk' of causing sexual harm does not mean that each one of these people will definitely offend. If it is calculated numerically using a risk assessment tool that the chance is 65 per cent, this does not mean that each person will offend 65 per cent of the time, or only commit 65 per cent of a single offence. It means that it is likely that 65 out of a group of 100 people are likely to offend. It does not predict which individual person will offend and which person will not, only that they are part of a group or statistical cohort.

If a group of 100 people each bought a single raffle ticket and there were 65 prizes, as long as the random picking of winning tickets was fair, it means that a random 35 per cent of people will not win a prize. It becomes more complicated if a person has more than one raffle ticket, or if the raffle tickets are replaced with each person assigned a single number, that there are 100 numbered balls in a jar, and after each draw the ball is put back in the jar. If a person 'holds' more than one number and each ball is replaced after each draw, the issue of the chance of each ball winning becomes more complicated.

Assessing risk through a calculation of chance and based on probability is far from the whole story. Probability is commonly expressed as a percentage, or one chance out of a 100/1000/10,000, or one chance out of a million. A calculative approach to risk is a matter of probabilities but not certainties that occur on a particular occasion, and range from the highly improbable to that which is very likely. Philosophically, prediction about the future must always be unproven because the evidence is yet to appear, but instead, future events and hence risk can be based on the best available knowledge of today and degrees of probability (Hume, 1711–1776). The fact that an event has always happened in the past is no philosophical guarantee that it will happen in similar circumstances in the future – very small variations in circumstances can result in big changes in outcome. The evidence is *presumed* to be available at some future time but is not yet available because the event has not yet happened. It may be reasonable to make a presumption about certain events that can be predicted from previous experience, but it is not a philosophical certainty.

Knowing if a particular person is at risk of abusing is dependent on individual factors, including the 'when, where and who'. For all intents and purposes, there is never 'no risk'; instead it might be 'unlikely' or 'improbable' or that 'risk is assessed as low'!

Complexity thinking in social settings is recognized as distinctly different from the modelling of complex systems within the natural sciences. What people do and how they do it influences how it is perceived, defined and interpreted, which then influences how that person subsequently behaves. Social problems and social solutions are socially constructed, and the relationship between social actor and social systems is interactive and changeable (Hood, 2016, 2018).

'Risk-thinking' is a reflexive term, knowing how risk is conceptualized within *the risk society*. It is thinking about the relationship between risk and probability, social uncertainty, belief, ways of thinking and how organizational cultures and practitioners operationalize risk.

Risk incorporates how we think and feel, from the entirely irrational to the purely calculative. It acknowledges that we live within a complex post-modern professional context of social uncertainty. It essentially encompasses safeguarding, but also acknowledges the wider traditional social purpose and practice of improving people's lives (Munro & Hubbard, 2011). This can be achieved through re-integrative and rehabilitative approaches promoted through relationship-based practice with those who perpetrate harmful sexual abuse and those who suffer from its effects.

When it comes to dealing with sexual abuse, despite the desire for some certainty, there are major challenges in definitely 'knowing' because of the uncertainties of human behaviour. Risks are socially created within a social reality that is fluid, changeable, emotionally fearful and uncertain to such an extent that it is unlikely that we can know all risks and hazards with certainty, but must remain forever sceptical and contingent on what we currently know or do not know about sexual offending and how this is applied in specific circumstances.

This is the case for assessing the chance of a person committing a sexual offence – the chance of a person who demonstrates particular characteristics can be reasonably calculated statistically, but there is no certainty. For example, there are a host of well-founded statistical tools that can be used to calculate whether a person is high or low risk. RM2000 (Thornton, 2007) is a well-established and highly respectable statistical tool that can calculate a categorization of risk of sexual (and violent) offence taking place based on nine statistically significant factors. This results in an accurate classification of the offender as falling with a statistical group of potential offenders who are labelled as very high, high, medium or low risk. Over a 15-year period, 78 per cent of those in the very high category were found to have committed a sexual offence compared to 10 per cent of those classified as low risk. This leaves 12 per cent of the very high category who do not offend, and one in ten in the low classification who do. A risk assessor may wish to say that a person is low risk or very high risk, but may be unlucky to find that a particular low-risk offender commits a sexual offence, and the unlucky very high risk classified offender does not, but whose liberty has been legally restricted as a result of the classification, with all the implications for professional practice. Risk assessment is a risky business!

DEFENSIVE, DEFENSIBLE, PRECAUTIONARY PRINCIPLE AND FALSE POSITIVES

In critical areas of social practice it has been suggested that legislative powers have come to underpin the assumption that risk is related to a broadening concept of the possibility of less than optimal conditions and omissions, for example in child protection: '"Risk"...is used loosely and widely to denote a range of negative outcomes for children, parents, society, professionals and organisations' (Daniel, 2010, p.235). Risk has become defined more broadly than just the calculation of a feared event, but associated with a broadening of the concept that encompasses a 'broadening of the range of adversities that are identified as likely to impact on children's optimal development' rather than 'a system...to deal with more narrowly defined incidences of maltreatment' (Daniel, 2010, p.238). Risk assessment has had a tendency to focus on a deficit model, although more recently the importance of protective factors has been included. Assessment incorporates the broad definition of risk as:

> The social calculation of probability of the occurrence of a feared event.

But also:

> The social calculation of probability of the occurrence of a desired event.

Working with those who are particularly vulnerable to sexual abuse leads to organizationally 'risk-averse' defensive practice, by inflicting decisions that seek to unrealistically eliminate risk altogether through risk-aversive governance and practice (Webb, 2006, pp.66–67, 73–74), and at the same time inflicting restrictions that have a negative impact on both the potential but perhaps unlikely abuser and victim, for example, by deciding that the presence of any possible risk no matter how unlikely is intolerable, or too risky, on the basis of the precautionary principle.

The precautionary principle has been applied to environmental and health hazards such as in the principles declared in the UN 1992 Rio Declaration on Environment and Development (UNCED, 1992). This suggests that if an action results in a potentially catastrophic environmental health impact, then do not do it. For example, in applying a pesticide to crops, if it results in a better crop yield but an unacceptable number of deaths (if such a thing is acceptable), then it is better not to use the pesticide despite the benefits to food production. According to Aven (2011), the precautionary principle applies when there is some *scientific* uncertainty. The basis of scientific uncertainty may be that the probability of an event cannot be calculated and is hence scientifically uncertain, or that if it were to happen, then the impact is likely to be immense, and therefore any action that might precipitate the harmful outcome should be avoided. Aven (2011) suggests that the precautionary principle should be linked to situations when an accurate model of prediction cannot be established. Boyer-Kassem (2017) disputes Peterson's alternative claim (2006) that the precautionary principle is either coherent or incoherent. In practice the test is generally that of what may appear to be reasonable.

How should this precautionary principle be applied to the risk of sexual abuse? The emotional impact of hearing about rare and extreme cases can affect decision-making. When there are strong uncertainties for sexual abuse, it appears to be reasonable to try to eliminate all risks. Many practitioners intuitively feel that this is the best course of action to take. For example, if a parent has accessed illegal sexual imagery of children and lives with a child, it is perhaps the intuitive response to ensure that the parent has no contact with the child. It is our view that a risk assessment should take place that will inform the decisions in the best interests of the child.

It is impossible to avoid the fact that 'risk' is an epistemic idea and that it is organizationally linked and culturally embedded. Risk is a moving reflection of contemporary concerns and practice and is set within a moving landscape of contemporary uncertainty, and the best we can do is to continuously strive to establish some level of certainty based on probability. In dealing with people, practice is not good at intuitively dealing with probabilities (Munro, 2011, p.58). If the influence of the 'risk society' has had a tendency to bolster proceduralism and the 'new managerialism', antithetically, practice wisdom, emotional intelligence and intuitive thinking has had a tendency to create a retrenchment towards and defence of a value-based practice paradigm. Munro and Hubbard (2011) outline a methodology that encourages more collaborative working and greater critical reflective practice.

Knowing how often something has occurred provides a simple calculation of frequency, such as, for example, how many and how often children are known to be sexually abused. A simple search online reveals that the NSPCC estimates that:

- 58,000 children were identified as needing protection in the UK in 2016 (NSPCC, 2018)

- there were 37,778 offences recorded against a child under 16 in England in 2015/16 (Bentley *et al.*, 2017)
- this represents 36.6 child sexual offences per 10,000 children (Bentley *et al.*, 2017, p.29).

Caution must be taken in generalizing statistics including that sexual offending goes largely unreported. From these figures it is inferred that the risk of sexual abuse to all children is statistically low – this may be considered to be the baseline. It has to be said that the impact of abuse is considerable and lifelong.

The evidence base that informs risk assessment is largely based on identifying the common characteristics of groups of similar people. Within that group are people who will abuse again and some who will not abuse again. Distinguishing between those who will and those who will not is problematic.

Risk assessment tools are based on a relatively small number of significant known cases that are then presumed to be typical of all other unknown cases, and this is a problematic assumption. Not only is it a matter of the perennial problem of representative sampling, it is also a problem for rare cases that do not arise in quite the same way on each occasion, simply because they are rare. Within a group of those known to have caused past sexual harm, there is a sub-group where there is the likelihood of those who will do so again, and this leaves a proportion of the group who will not, but it is the best we have as a baseline indicator. We presume that the person we are assessing is within the group of those who are known to have caused sexual harm who will again cause harm at a particular rate.

This is generally known as 'the problem of false positives', a concept that has entered widely across a considerable number of fields, representing some predictive assessment or test that shows a positive result when in fact it results in a negative outcome. It has become common to be simply illustrated in a 2 x 2 matrix, as shown below. When it is applied to risk assessment, it shows that an assessment may falsely give an indication of risk of an event when the event never happens. There are several issues that can arise, such as a binary decision of either there is a risk or there is no risk, rather than a probabilistic prediction of comparative degree, such as high, medium or low, but never entirely a 'no'.

	Predictive test	
	Positive result that the event will occur	Negative result that the event will not occur
Event occurs as predicted	A True positive prediction	B False negative prediction
Event does not occur	C False positive prediction	D True negative prediction

Applying this to those who cause sexual harm:

Box A: It was predicted that the person was going to cause sexual harm and then they did; this is a true *positive* prediction.

Box B: It was predicted that a person would *not* cause sexual harm, but then they did; this is a false *negative* prediction.

Box C: It was predicted that a person would cause sexual harm but did not; this is a false *positive* prediction.

Box D: It was predicted that a person would not cause sexual harm and actually did not; this is a true *negative* prediction.

A number of obvious issues arise from this. If a practitioner says that a person will not harm another person but then does so, the practitioner is likely to be blamed for getting it wrong. If the practitioner says that a person will harm another person but then no harm takes place, the practitioner is likely to be blamed for being over-zealous and for putting in place over-restrictive controls and conditions that may themselves be harmful. If the practitioner had taken no action at all, there is no way of knowing whether this would have resulted in a harmful event.

PRIOR ASSUMPTIONS AND BAYESIAN INFERENCE

Combined with the problems of an over-reliance on actuarial approaches, the emotionality involved in making judgements and bias in decision-making, risk assessment becomes highly problematic. There are some approaches that attempt to address some of the difficulties. For example, Bayesian inference would take into account some of the predisposing judgements on developing a defensible argument. Thomas Bayes (1701–1761) was a Presbyterian minister who thought about probability and applying statistics to the issue of cause and effect, possibly influenced by the philosopher of the Scottish Enlightenment David Hume (1711–1776), who emphasized that cause and effect can be discovered by experience, but that ultimately we can only assume that one thing will lead to another on the basis that it is only probable. So in our case here, it is probable that if a potential sex offender is sexually aroused by the sight of a child, and that other pre-conditions are in place such as opportunity, overcoming their own internal inhibition to abuse, and overcoming the child's resistance to abuse, if the opportunity arises then it is probable, but not certain, that sexual abuse will take place (see Chapter 8). The problem is one of the predictability of complex phenomena. Bearing in mind the 'modest' predictive power of risk assessment instruments (Gottfredson & Gottfredson, 1994), actuarial risk assessment tools necessarily use a few statistically significant associative factors, not necessarily causal factors, to calculate future risk. Most predictive risk assessment tools utilize the concept of frequentism or classical inference, that because something has occurred frequently in the past it is likely to occur in the future. In an uncertain world where not all factors are known, Bayesian approaches can help by 'allowing us to go from an effect back to its cause' (Lambert, 2018, p.12).

If we assume some prior knowledge of a cause of an event, then we have a prior belief based on what we know. When we then acquire new data or information, that prior belief is modified.

This leads to the construction of a formula (see below) – there is no need to be a statistical expert to understand the point being made, but if the reader wishes to know more, this can be found in Lambert (2018).

Take the following example:

Brian and Mary have been married for 14 years. They both work in semi-professional occupations, and live in a quiet residential area of town in a semi-detached house. Both are entirely law-abiding in their attitudes and behaviours. They have a 13-year-old daughter and a 10-year-old son. Early one morning the police arrive and knock loudly on the door. Brian is arrested for downloading illegal images from the internet, of abusive sexual images of children, traced from his use of a credit card payment. Brian is taken away, and then the social worker visits.

Brian is convicted. Mary tells the social worker that family separation is having a fundamental effect on the happiness of all involved, that Brian has a strong history of caring in an entirely appropriate way for his children and other children within their close-knit family network, that there has never been anything but love and affection evidenced. The social worker gathers further information from the school, GP, police and relatives that confirms this account.

The social worker has to assess the risk of future harm to Brian and Mary's children. The social worker thinks about this and applies a Bayesian-like approach using the following steps:

Step 1: *Prior probability* of harm to the children: on past evidence alone, the social worker assigns a low 4 per cent probability (likelihood) of Brian being a potential abuser of his children. This is called 'x' in the formula below.

Step 2: Calculating the probability of Brian being a contact child abuser based on the new evidence, the social worker finds from the research that only about 2 per cent of offenders who have only downloaded indecent images of children subsequently commit a contact offence (Seto, Hanson & Babchishin, 2010), but because the data is not entirely clear when applied to this case, the social worker decides that *the absence of evidence is not evidence of absence*, and therefore errs on the side of the extreme precautionary principle (above). They rate this as 50 per cent, or basically a matter of chance, and call this 'y'.

Step 3: The social worker estimates that the chance of Brian not being a contact sex offender based on what they have established is 5 per cent. They call this 'z'.

Step 4: The social worker applies the Bayes statistical formula of:

$$\frac{xy}{xy + z(1-x)}$$

This produces a *posterior probability* of a 29 per cent chance of Brian committing a contact sexual offence.

The chance that Brian 'maybe will, maybe won't' commit a contact sexual offence based on this calculation is lower than the 50/50 guess, even without applying the calculation. Is this sufficient to say he should never have contact with his children, or does it lead to a decision that he may have contact under certain conditions and understandings, such as never having sole responsibility for children at times and situations of high risk, for example late evenings or in closed rooms when no other responsible adult is present? Or do you say that any risk is too high to be allowed, even though there is roughly a two-thirds chance of Brian not carrying out a contact offence?

The prior assumption of risk is highly influential in the final risk assessment, and this needs to be checked out in some detail and reflected on (see Chapter 9). Going back to the problem of false positives, is it better to assume that an innocent person is blameful rather than assume that a dangerous person is safe? The problem becomes a matter of scale and a matter of how we rate harm.

So, for example, if there is 20 per cent risk of allowing something that will lead to a catastrophic event, such as allowing a convicted child sex offender to have access to children, is that acceptable? Most people would say no, but if the risk is much lower, at 0.02 per cent, at a very much higher price of keeping the offender under constant surveillance, would that be acceptable? If there is a 20 per cent risk of a person sexually exposing themselves to another adult, would it be acceptable to allow them to have unrestricted freedom in the community? This goes back to the issue of balancing impact with likelihood, and the value we place on events.

It relates to how people arrive at making some initial judgement that then influences all subsequent revised judgements, as illustrated by Kahneman (2011) in his overview of earlier research (Kahneman & Tversky, 1982; Tversky & Kahneman, 1973) and the various sources of bias.

People tend to make a rapid decision when faced with a decision or problem. The *representative heuristic* (Tversky & Kahneman, 1973) says that whilst previous experience is useful in making decisions quickly, it can also lead to errors, so that when faced with a problem involving dangerousness, people tend to fall back on making a decision based on the most obvious or salient features last time they faced a similar problem. Less salient features tend to be discounted.

If the risk assessor more easily identifies and imagines certain types of case, those easily accessed and vividly brought to mind are thought to have significance, for example reading and being aware of high-profile news items in the popular press (e.g. McTague, 2014). This is the *availability heuristic*. So, for example, people who cause sexual harm are erroneously more readily described in the popular press as random strangers who grab children from the streets, and therefore a risk assessor may erroneously consider that risk to children is greater from strangers than from family members, and downgrade the danger for girls or boys from a potentially dangerous family member because they are not a random stranger.

The *affect heuristic* is the way in which our feelings or emotions automatically distort our decision-making, such as judging a person on first impressions as seeming to be somebody who either does *not* appear to be a person who causes sexual harm, or who at first sight looks like what they presume *is* a person who causes sexual harm, whatever that may be. All subsequent information is then interpreted in this light. So, for example, a well presented articulate individual who in the assessor's mind 'doesn't look like a person who might cause sexual harm' is given greater credibility of denial than a person who is evasive and not articulate. The emotional response to what we experience is rapid and automatic, affecting how we feel about a particular risk (Slovic & Peters, 2006), and how threatening that risk may appear to be.

To know the probability of a potential event of sexual harm we must combine a calculation of the risk of the potential perpetrator with a calculation of the vulnerability of the potential victim. Research on the characteristics of victims of sexual harm has tended to be overlooked in favour of the 'risk factors' presented by the potential abuser, but this represents only part of the story.

The message is 'never stop assessing', revising, learning and applying different frameworks of understanding. Whilst there are a considerable number of risk assessment tools and approaches available to practitioners, there remain contrasting approaches that on the one hand tend to take the view that the science of risk can be fully determined and on the other that risk must be viewed uncertainly as applied in the uncertain 'real world' (Lash & Wynne, 1992). Sexual abuse is, by its very nature, set within social settings, and at the heart of sexual abuse is the uncertainty of knowledge about sex and sexuality (see Chapter 1).

CHAPTER 6

Assessing the Risk of Those Who Cause Sexual Harm

ORGANIZATIONAL DEFENSIVE AND PROFESSIONAL DEFENSIBLE DECISION-MAKING

Despite its apparent universality, risk is constituted as a shifting social construction (as discussed in Chapter 5). With sexual abuse, risk assessment tends to place greater emphasis on social control and defensiveness, and emphasizes a particular ethical, moral and value standpoint that should be balanced with compassion and care (Stanford, 2008, p.218).

Risk assessment tends to deal with categories, that certain groups are more or less risky than others. Categories are guided by similarity, but not all people within categories are guaranteed to share all the same similarities. The predictive quality of using categorization is probable but not guaranteed.

The risk of categorization is that this will influence some of the presumptions we make. Most 'sex offenders' are adult males, but there are a significant number who are formally under the age of 18 and legally a child (according to the Children Act 1989), and a significant number are women. Would we presume that a male stranger presents a greater likelihood of sexual abuse to a child than the risk presented by a person under the age of 18 or a woman? On the basis of an overall baseline to calculate environmental risk, this may be reasonable, but on the basis of not checking things out, it may not.

Friendship and Beech (2005) produced an overview that indicated that the re-offending rate, as indicated by reconviction rates, that is, those who were caught and successfully prosecuted, was about 5 per cent over four years for the UK, and about 11–13 per cent over the same time frame within the international literature. These figures need to be treated with caution since for some offences the conviction rate for some types of cases appearing in Court is extremely low, for example for rape. The timespan of measuring the reconviction rate must also be thought about, as there is some indication that the reconviction rate perhaps increases when taken over a longer timespan.

Risk assessment should be a shared responsibility between agencies. Each agency has a different remit, targets, priorities and cultures. Each views each case through a different lens, with a differing perspective. There is an assumption that the task of managing the perpetrator is the sole responsibility of criminal justice agencies such as the police, probation or prison service. Our view is that other agencies can contribute to this task. A distinction should be made between 'defensible' and 'organizationally defensive' practice that has become embedded over several decades, more recently in the *Munro Review* (2011) and highlighted by Whittaker and Havard (2016). Defensive practice is a reactive professional and organizationally fear-based decision that aims to protect reputation from criticism on the basis of what is precautionary and expedient, 'just in case'.

The difference is inherent in the use of words. A professionally defensible decision is one for which it is possible to give a rational and logical argument based on all that can be reasonably known about a particular situation or a case, combined with two other factors. First, that there is a stated approach to assessment that has been used, and that the approach is rational and reasonable to use in the circumstances. And second, that the person undertaking the risk assessment has some professional expertise about sexual offending, including what the comparative base rate is, what the general risk factors are thought to be, an awareness of causes and what is known generally about the probability and severity of a future repeat event. The greater the breadth and depth of understanding (Chapter 3), using all known information, and the greater their critical thinking skills (Chapter 9), then generally the greater the expertise of the assessment. Whilst an assessment can err towards either a defensible or a defensive decision, the best can incorporate elements of both.

There is no absolute ironclad guarantee of either a totally defensible decision or of being able to ensure that no future harmful behaviour will ever take place. The optimum approach is to combine both expert *defensible* and organizationally *defensive* approaches. The mechanism for doing so is to acknowledge that no risk assessment is perfect, and to transparently acknowledge limitations. Whilst it is dangerous to assume 'no risk', it is also potentially harmful and wrong to say there is certainty of risk where no absolute certainty exists. There is the risk that the risk assessment is wrong, the 'risk of risk', or that 'risk thinking is a risky business'.

There is a tendency that most serious re-offending takes place in cases where the risk assessment has been 'properly' carried out using approved risk assessment tools and the risk has been deemed 'low' (Wills, 2008). Risk assessors are likely to take risk-averse decisions with a potentially high impact/high seriousness case, and be more risk-taking with a low impact/low seriousness case. An over-reliance on the accuracy of risk assessment tools can lead to the risk assessor adopting a greater (false) pragmatic sense of certainty. If the risk of a further serious offence is assessed as low, when combined with a sense of false certainty based on over-reliance on risk assessment tools this may lead the risk assessor to be less vigilant to the indications that the assessed risk is inaccurate.

The message from David Kahneman (2011) might be that intuitive thinking styles should be simultaneously used with logical analytical thinking, and that we shouldn't undervalue properly evaluated and examined professional intuition over and above the more procedural approach of formal risk assessment tools with all its limitations!

USING RISK ASSESSMENT 'TOOLS'
There are a number of statistically derived tools used to predict the probability of a person known to have committed a sexual offence.

These 'risk assessment tools' identify a relatively small number of factors associated with sexual offending and then test their validity by applying them to a statistical population of offenders. The risk assessment tools tend to calculate the general probability of 'an offender' committing a sexual offence.

In order to bring some greater objectivity to risk assessment, there are several contrasting approaches, and in particular two identified by Grove and Meehl (1996) who describe what is known as the earliest attempt at creating a predictive statistically based risk assessment tool. Taking a cohort of 3000 prisoners, Burgess (1928) identified 21 factors to produce a simple actuarial predictive tool that exceeded the predictive ability of professionally subjective or clinical approaches based on decision-making by expert assessors. Providing other examples of actuarial assessment tools in a number of different contexts, Grove and Meehl (1996) concluded from over 66 years of various examples that a statistical actuarial approach is superior to professional clinical judgement. It has become standard and necessary practice to use actuarial tools within criminal justice agencies when managing a case.

Thornton's RM2000 (Thornton, 2007) is widely used by criminal justice agencies as a risk assessment tool, using nine items that are graded by a trained assessor according to a scoring protocol that produces a risk classification of low, medium, high or very high. Based on a considerable body of research and a number of prior risk assessment tools, the predictive accuracy has been assessed as far better than clinical judgement alone (Thornton, 2007). The considerable advantage of using an actuarial tool to predict future behaviour has been highlighted in the literature as far back as 1954, when Meehl claimed to have settled any dispute that a statistically derived assessment was far superior to that based purely on the judgement of the practitioner, or clinical assessment would inevitably include considerable sources of bias and error leading to the conclusion that deciding risk on purely clinical judgement alone is barely better than chance or just guessing (Meehl, 1954; see also Monahan et al., 2001). The ripostes to the claims that mechanistically applying statistical forms of assessment is far superior to purely skill-based professional clinical judgement are considerable, not least that decision-making is inextricably woven into the processes of social and criminal justice systems (Prentky, Barbaree & Janus, 2015). When there is an over-reliance on statistical forms of risk assessment, the process of proportional social justice in determining culpability, punishment and judicial social control may be reduced to applying an automatic algorithm. The use of an actuarial tool influences and generally determines the allocation of scarce resources more to those cases assessed in this way as high risk, and assigning different levels of resource to low-risk cases. High-risk cases tend to be resource multi-agency intensive oversight, probably through MAPPAs (HM Prison & Probation Service, 2012; Ministry of Justice NOMS, 2019).

Actuarial tools used administratively for the purpose of assigning greater levels of resources and for organizationally defensive reasons is an essential part of risk management within criminal justice agencies. Outside of criminal justice agencies an actuarial score may or may not be available. Holistic risk assessment by an expert with knowledge of sexual offending, and knowing the offender's particular circumstances, provides for a broader picture of factors associated with risk.

Over the last couple of decades there has been an explosion of research papers on the risk assessment of sexual offenders, and a consensus that these risk assessment tools should be evidence-based. It is confusing for practitioners to distinguish the best and latest that have developed from first-generation risk assessment tools to what may be considered third- or fourth-generation tools (Harris & Hanson, 2010). In England, the Structured Assessment of Risk & Need (SARN) is routinely used by psychology services within the prison environment, and the Probation Service uses the Active Risk Management System (ARMS) tool. These attempt to explore dynamic risk factors as well as protective factors. The STABLE-2007 and ACUTE-2007 (SA2007) (Hanson et al., 2007) was developed in Scotland and is similar to the SARN, more lately revised as STABLE-2000 that builds on previous risk assessment tools such as STATIC-99 (Hanson & Thornton, 2000) and SORAG

(Quinsey *et al.*, 1998), among others. This builds on research that associates re-offending with a specific risk factor(s). Echoing many previous authors in claiming that a structured risk assessment is better than an unstructured 'clinical' assessment, Eher *et al.* (2012) conclude that the predictive validity of STABLE-2007 is high, using sophisticated techniques of statistical analysis, and point out that there are differences between those factors that are considered to be 'static' (not changing over time) and dynamic (those that can change over time). This is a fundamental issue in that static factors are usually thought of as generally historical factors that cannot change, such as previous proven convictions for sexual and other offending, the age of onset of known offending, and whether the person has been in a long-term relationship. The exception to the list of past historical factors is that of age, which, whilst it changes over time, is considered to be a static factor. A further distinction is made as to 'stable' factors such as personality characteristics and learned behaviours that may change through intervention. Acute factors are those social environmental factors that can change relatively rapidly over time, such as personal circumstances of work, occupation, social support networks, relationships, housing, etc.

In using these structured risk assessment tools drawn from our general practice and experience, care must be taken in that:

- The assessor has been trained to use the tool and strictly applies the coding 'rules' for scoring.
- All information is reasonably known and taken into account.
- Interpretation of the 'score' is interpreted by the assessor to contribute to an holistic assessment.
- The tools are based on particular, sometimes specific (male or female, young or adult offender, etc.), relatively small research samples, often from specific jurisdictions and demographic cohorts that may include particular cultural heritage factors.
- There are some special statistical populations, for example sexual offenders with intellectual disabilities (SOIDs) (Skye *et al.*, 2017).
- The score derived from these tools is accurate for most of

any statistical cohort, but not all, and a group score is being applied to an individual.

- The score tends not to change from 'pre-treatment' to 'after treatment'.
- The circumstances and personal motivations of individual perpetrators change.

Structured risk assessment tools have changed over time, and have become more sophisticated. In all of the statistical approaches to structured risk assessment it is the issue of interrater reliability, namely that one person will come to the same 'score' on a risk assessment tool as another, depending less on the individualized clinical skill of risk assessment, that is, in turn, based on a number of hard-to-assess factors such as personal experience, knowledge and engagement skills. Some tools have a score-based outcome whilst others are more psychologically embedded in formulation, such as the Risk of Sexual Violence Protocol (RSVP). These tools require the assessor to consider circumstances that are likely to increase the risk of re-offending and those that are likely to decrease this risk. They tend to also require the assessor to consider related hypothetical scenarios to illustrate examples of an increase or decrease in risk. It must also be remembered that there are few risk assessment tools for young people and women for a number of reasons, such as diverse highly individualized factors and small samples.

There are a number of issues that should be thought about, not least that decision-making is complex, with a large number of interacting variables that can produce a non-linear, complex and causal result that is difficult to predict. Human behaviour can be a matter of arbitrary and random events or a number of small events that appear to trigger decision-making and behaviours that lead to a major event.

Gerwinn *et al.* (2018), in differentiating between those who offend against children and those who are classified as paedophiles, found that 'psychiatric comorbidities, sexual dysfunctions and adverse childhood experiences were more common among paedophiles and child sex offenders' (p.75). Biollat *et al.* (2017)

examined deviant personality characteristics in sex offenders, and found that 'neuroticism is associated with a broader range of psychological problems' in sex offenders who offend against children.

As a generalized approach, there are a number of broad areas that are useful to be cautiously explored and carefully interpreted, drawn partially from practice and from structured or semi-structured risk assessment tools (e.g. Thornton's risk domains (Thornton, 2000, 2002); Structured Assessment of Risk and Need (SARN) (NPS, 2007); RSVP (Hart *et al.*, 2003); see also Craig & Beech, 2012; Heffernan & Ward, 2017):

- Sexual interests: What are the person's dominant sexual interests and are they generally seen as 'deviant', for example sex with children or rape, etc.? Are they very preoccupied with sex generally? Also important is consideration of whether the person has healthy sexual interests that can be worked with.
- Attitudes that might support sexual offending, for example that children are not harmed by sexual contact or hostile attitudes towards women. How might these have come about?
- Family and environmental circumstances: Has the person had a range of adverse childhood experiences? What kind of family environment do they come from? What is the 'story' of their life? We find incorporating a loose chronology to be a useful way to make sense of the person and how they see themselves. It is not necessarily what has happened or not happened in their life but how they have made sense of it and what meaning they have attributed to events.
- Mental health and psychological adjustment: Has the person had any serious mental health issues or any substance misuse issues? Are there indications of any kind of personality disorder, intellectual disability or social communication difficulty? How does the person tend to deal with stress and how able are they to cope with the day-to-day challenges of life? How do they manage difficult emotions?

- Relationships: What kinds of relationship does the person tend to have? This includes intimate relationships, sexual relationships, relationships with significant caregivers, as well as those with friends, those in authority, etc.
- General criminality: Does the person tend to break boundaries generally, and how does this tend to manifest?
- Is the person likely to comply with recommendations and/ or treatment, or what support is necessary for them to get to this point?
- Anything else that seems significant.

Another way of applying theory to an individual is to interpret and adapt the five 'P's that have developed generally and broadly within approaches to risk assessment in criminal justice and social work, as a binary list of risk factors and protective factors, and in psychology (for a description of the specific detailed use, see Macneil *et al.*, 2012, p.2). Reinterpreted as a useful contextual guide, not for medical diagnosis, this has become used in general practice as:

1. Presenting Problem – Why is this person of concern and has come to the attention of professionals? For example, has someone made an allegation? Is there behaviour that is causing concern? Are children potentially at risk?
2. Predisposing Factors – In other words, what are the factors that made the person vulnerable to potentially causing sexual harm? For example, specific sexual interests, experiences of trauma, attitudes and beliefs, etc.
3. Precipitating Factor – What are the precipitating factors, or what were the triggers to the particular offending behaviour that is of concern? For example, has there been a breakdown in relationships, employment or other kinds of destabilising events?
4. Perpetuating Factors – What could keep the problem going? This might be about situational factors such as access to a child or it could be about problematic issues with substance use, not engaging in intervention, etc.

5. Protective Factors – As with all the other factors, these will be different for each individual – for example, being in a relationship or in employment are often considered to be protective, but not for everyone, but what are the general areas of support?

(adapted from Macneil *et al.*, 2012, p.2)

In our experience, causing sexual harm is a way of behaving that often fulfils the core needs of the perpetrator that frequently they do not understand. Focused intervention allows for greater understanding. It need not be an 'expert' in sexual offending who enables the person to begin this process; any contact that is supportive and therapeutic in style is likely to be facilitative to a person being able to make progress. Taking these steps reduces the risk of abusive behaviour that is often part of external lawful constraints applied appropriately.

CHAPTER 7

Legal Contexts

PROSECUTIONS

The number of cases of sexual harm taking place is not the same as the number of recorded convictions, and it is recognized that there is a substantial unrecorded 'dark' figure. Sexual crimes including the most serious such as rape and those such as opportunistic sexual assault in private, social and public settings are ubiquitous. All offensive sexual behaviours have a serious impact on the victims.

Duggan and Dennis (2014) point out that as few as 1 per cent of sexual offenders are prosecuted. The pathway from abusive behaviour to successful prosecution has to overcome multiple hurdles, perhaps surprisingly sometimes because of the lack of realization that an offence has happened, sometimes as a result of ignorance of such things as what constitutes consent (see below); the reporting stage, when there may be multifarious reasons for the victim not to disclose; the investigation stage and the search for evidence; and finally, the decision to prosecute.

The decision to prosecute for sexual offences, and all others, lies largely with the CPS, and involves two stages: first, the so-called merits basis, or the potential ability to achieve a conviction based on the history of all other similar cases; and second, the issue of public interest to either prosecute or not. When applying the merits-based approach, prosecutors may consider the credibility of the account of the offence rather than the credibility of the victim. The usual issues of inconsistency, lies and evidence of bad character are preceded by issues arising during the investigative stages, where there are a number of pitfalls.

The CPS provides guidance on sexual offences (CPS (1), 2019), giving the principal act under which prosecutions usually take place, namely the Sexual Offences Act 2003, which repealed the previous Sexual Offences Act 1956 and the Indecency with Children Act 1960. In 2013, following a decline in convictions for rape, the CPS introduced Rape and Serious Sexual Offences (RASSO) Units that operate regionally. The CPS now provides advice on the joint working of the CPS or police and other stakeholders at the investigative stage of proceedings and provides specialist prosecutors.

The significant change to the Sexual Offences Act 2003 was the way consent is legally established, shifting the presumption to one of no consent unless the alleged perpetrator has sufficient evidence to prove otherwise. This is a fundamental cultural change rooted within a patriarchal framework.

CONSENT

The full list of offences is given in the Appendix at the end of this book. Section 74 provides the definition of consent stating that a person consents if he (the usual convention to refer to either male or female) 'agrees by choice and has the freedom and capacity to make that choice' (Pegg & Davies, 2016, p.57). This definition is not without some legal debate, and as Pegg and Davies state, the definition of consent remains legally 'unsettled' (2016, p.71), as does the term 'capacity'. Capacity has tended to be associated with intoxication, but also refers to other people such as those with a mental disorder or impairment, or those under the age of 16.

Pegg and Davies (2016) discuss further the various legal aspects of conditional consent where, for example, a person consented on the condition that ejaculation in the person's vagina would not take place, or that a condom would be used, that there should be reasonable evidence produced to support some belief of consent that did not involve using intimidating violence and nor was the complainant unlawfully detained, asleep or drugged, etc., and there was no deception as to the nature of the carrying out of the act, through impersonation or fraudulent behaviour.

Rook and Ward (2016) provide detailed discussion on consent (as does the CPS;[1] see CPS (2), 2019). The law distinguishes the ability to give effective consent. Sections 1–4 of the Sexual Offences Act 2003 (CPS (2), 2019) require a person engaging in sex to determine that consent has been given and requires the prosecution to prove absence of consent. Other offences do not require the test of consent, but it is the act itself that has to be proved by the prosecution. A person gives consent only if they have the capacity to do so and are able to make the choice of sexual activity freely. For example, a person may give consent to sex using a condom, but if the perpetrator then deceives the other person into thinking that they are using a condom but does not do so, the law is likely to say consent has not been given, depending on the Court's decision as to the circumstances at the time in a particular case. In some instances it is for a jury to decide after it has been established that the defendant believed consent had been given, as to whether their belief was reasonable. It is for the defendant to establish that consent had been given.

SENTENCING

The CPS provides detailed guidance on sentencing,[2] and this should be referred to for information and read with care, taking into account that guidelines change over time. This is a complex area of legal expertise reflecting some of the changes of policy and political sentiment over recent years. In summary, the Criminal Justice Act 2003 introduced the legal concept of a dangerous offender, which came into force on 4 April 2005, amended by Sections 13–18 of the Criminal Justice and Immigration Act 2008 which came into force on 14 July 2008, amended by the Legal Aid, Sentencing and Punishment of Offenders Act 2012.

The conditions are that the offence must reach the seriousness threshold with an exception being that the offender has been previously convicted of a number of types of very serious offences.

---

1   See www.cps.gov.uk/legal-guidance/rape-and-sexual-offences-chapter-3-consent
2   See www.cps.gov.uk/legal-guidance/sentencing-dangerous-offenders

The Court must be satisfied that the offender has committed a specified serious offence under the extensive list of offences in Section 15 of the Criminal Justice and Immigration Act 2008 punishable for an adult with at least 10 years' imprisonment, and that there is significant risk of harm to the public, or if the maximum penalty is a discretionary life sentence and the seriousness meets the criteria for a life sentence, the Court has no discretion but to impose a life sentence, or custody for life if the perpetrator is aged 18 but under 21 years old. Previously, where the conditions for imposing a sentence of life imprisonment or equivalent had not been met, the Court was able to impose a sentence of Imprisonment for Public Protection (IPP) (Section 225 of the Criminal Justice Act 2003) commencing April 2005. Following criticisms, these were abolished in 2012 under the Legal Aid, Sentencing and Punishment of Offenders Act 2012, but a number of prisoners are still in prison under an IPP (on 6 June 2019 there were approximately 2400 prisoners on an IPP; House of Commons Library, 2019) subject to release by the Parole Board if the risk is deemed to be acceptable (see below).

Great care must be taken in specific interpretation of the law – it is beyond the scope of this text to provide guidance except for general information only. The guidance for seriousness of sexual offences can be found on the Crown Prosecution UK website (CPS (1), 2019). Dangerousness generally means that 'the court is of the opinion that there is a significant risk to members of the public of serious harm occasioned by the commission by him of further specified offences'.[3] The definition of 'significant' is a decision for the Court, but the Court of Appeal has held that 'significant' concerns more than just the possibility of re-occurrence and represents a higher threshold of future risk associated with future protection of the public. This introduces a legal contextualization of probability (or likelihood) and grave harm (impact) in that if the probability is slightly lower but the likely impact is high, this may be significant in the opinion of the Court. Taking previous examples and illustrations

---

3   See www.cps.gov.uk/legal-guidance/sentencing-dangerous-offenders

in this book, if an offender were to commit a murder, the likelihood may be low but the impact will be high, and may therefore be considered a significant future risk. Similarly, a trajectory of repeated harmful offending may represent an increasing escalation of risk that is significant, and the Court should consider all information, not just previous convictions. The police can provide information that includes details on patterns of behaviour, relevant acquittals, complaints, allegations and background intelligence using the form MG 16.

The Parole Board is an independent body that carries out risk assessments on prisoners to determine whether they can be safely released into the community. It was established in 1968 under the Criminal Justice Act 1967, and became an independent executive non-departmental public body on 1 July 1996 under the Criminal Justice and Public Order Act 1994. Its primary role is to determine whether prisoners serving indeterminate sentences and those serving certain determinate sentences for serious offences continue to represent a significant risk to the public. The main groups they are concerned with are people serving:

- life sentences and sentences of IPP, under the Crime (Sentences) Act 1997, as amended
- extended determinate sentences, under the Criminal Justice Act 2003 (as amended by the Legal Aid, Sentencing and Punishment of Offenders Act 2012)
- sentences for offenders of particular concern, including terrorists and serious child sex offenders, under the Criminal Justice and Courts Act 2015. (Parole Board, n.d.)

In addition, consideration is given to:

- the re-release of prisoners who are recalled to prison for breach of their licence conditions under the Criminal Justice Act 2003.[4]

---

4   See www.legislation.gov.uk/ukpga/2003/44/section/254/enacted

The Sexual Offences Act 2003 introduced the IPP indeterminate sentence for those whose crimes would not attract a life sentence but for whom it was deemed too dangerous to be released at the usual sentence expiry date. Such a sentence was deemed to be unlawful in 2007 by the High Court, and it was eventually abolished under the Legal Aid, Sentencing and Punishment of Offenders Act 2012. The abolition was not applied retrospectively, however, and approximately 4000 IPP offenders remain incarcerated (Strickland, 2016).

CIVIL ORDERS

The Sex Offenders Act 1997 brought in notification requirements for sexual offenders, creating the 'sex offenders' register' for those convicted of a sexual offence against adults or children after 1997. The convicted offender must register their details in person at a police station within three days of conviction or following release from prison, and failing to do so is a criminal offence. The length of time a person's name remains on the register is dependent on the sentence they received, ranging from two years to lifetime registration. Police forces began to develop a shared database to monitor registered offenders and share information via the ViSOR national database (the Dangerous Persons Database), shared with other relevant agencies such as the Probation Service.

Sexual Harm Prevention Orders (SHPOs) are sanctions available to the Court for those who have been found guilty of any of the offences listed in Schedule 3 or 5 of the Sexual Offences Act 2003, even if their offences predate this Act. The Court must be satisfied that the person presents a sexual risk of harm to the public and that an SHPO is necessary to protect against this risk. Whilst these provisions may be broad, they have to be proportionate and tailored specifically to the risk presented, as specified by the *Court of Appeal in R v. Smith and others [2011] EWCA Crim 1772*. It is a criminal offence to breach the conditions of an SHPO.

A Sexual Risk Order (SRO) is a civil order that can be sought by the police against an individual who has not been convicted, cautioned, etc. of a Schedule 3 or Schedule 5 offence but who is nevertheless thought to pose a risk of harm. An SRO may be applied for on freestanding application to the Magistrates' Court by the Chief Officer of Police or the Director General of the National Crime Agency (NCA). An SRO may be made in respect of an individual who has:

- done an act of a sexual nature, and
- as a result of which, there is reasonable cause to believe that it is necessary to make an order to protect the public from harm.

The Child Sex Offender Community Disclosure Scheme is now available in all policing areas in England and Wales. This allows people to apply to their local police area if they are concerned about someone who has contact with children. There is a strict protocol in place for the police to go through in making enquiries and disclosing information. A student examination of the scheme (McDermott, 2018) in one police area found that the majority of applicants were women, and most of the requests related to new partners or neighbours.

CHILDREN AND YOUNG PEOPLE

It is presumed that a child under the age of 13 cannot give consent, but what is usually referred to as the age of consent is 16. The age of a person relating to various sections of the law varies slightly, so it is against the law for a person in a position of trust, such as a teacher or sports coach, to have sex with a person under the age of 18.

A person under 16 cannot give consent in law. The term 'child in need' in England is generally understood to refer to Section 17(1) of the Children Act 1989, and is a general preventative duty imposed on local authorities. Under this it is a general duty:

...to safeguard and promote the welfare of children... (Section 3(a), Children Act 1989)

and:

...to promote the upbringing of such children by their families by providing a range and level of services appropriate to those children's need. (Section 3(b), Children Act 1989)

Sections 17(10) and 17(11) state:

...a child shall be taken to be in need if:

    f. he is likely to achieve or maintain, or to have the opportunity of achieving or maintaining, a reasonable standard of health or development without the provision for him of services by a local authority...

    g. his health or development is likely to be significantly impaired, without the provision for him of such services...

Sections 17(10)(c) and 17(11) deal with children who are disabled, blind, deaf or dumb, or who suffer from 'mental disorder of any kind or is substantially and permanently handicapped'.

The definitions are deliberately broad, but the term 'looked after' is specifically defined (Carr & Goosey, 2019, p.215), although often referred to in practice by those who have duty under the Act. To be 'looked after' a child is made the subject of a care order (or provided with accommodation by the local authority). It is then the duty of the local authority 'to safeguard and promote his welfare' (Section 22(3)(a), Children Act 1989).

In addition to the general duty in Section 17 of the Children Act 1989, Part 1 of Schedule 2 contains some specific duties, laid out in full in Carr and Goosey (2019, pp.221–223), but for the purpose of this book contains duties to prevent neglect and abuse and that the local authority 'shall take reasonable steps, through the provision of services under Part 3 of this Act, to prevent children within their area suffering ill treatment or neglect' (Part 1, Schedule 2, paragraph 4(1)). This includes sexual abuse (Section 31(9), Children Act 1989).

When local authorities' social work departments have 'reasonable cause to suspect that a child who lives, or is found, in their area is suffering, or is likely to suffer, significant harm' (Section 47, Children

Act 1989), the local authority has a duty to investigate, which is not to be confused with and opposed to previously being placed on a child protection register. This provision was replaced in April 2008 (Carr & Goosey, 2019, p.255).

Section 47 (Children Act 1989) governs the process of referral, investigation, case planning and preparation for application to Court for a potential care order. In 2015, only 25 per cent of all referrals led to a Section 47 enquiry, only 11 per cent led to a child protection conference, and 62,200 children became the subject of a child protection plan, but 60,400 plans were ended. In 2017, 646, 120 referrals were made, an increase of 10,500 on the previous year, and there was an increase in Section 47 enquiries of 7.6 per cent between 2016 and 2017 (Carr & Goosey, 2019, pp.255–256). As such there has been an overall increase in referrals for a number of reasons (Family Rights Group, 2018; Holt & Kelly, 2019; Hood, 2016; LGA, 2018).

MENTAL HEALTH

Police and social workers should be trained using the current guidance on interviewing children. This suggests a four-phase approach of *rapport building, free narrative, active listening strategies* and *questioning* facilitated by the use of open questioning rather than closed questioning (see Davies, Bull & Milne, 2016). Following the well-publicized miscarriages of justice in the cases of the Guildford Four and the Birmingham Six, various interviewing techniques and protocols have been introduced in investigative practice (see Oxburgh & Hynes, 2016).

Pegg and Davies (2016, p.111) cite two other relevant cases, that of *Cooper* (2009) and *Tower Hamlets LBC v. (1) TB* (by her litigation friend, the Official Solicitor) (2014). The first case was a 28-year-old woman with schizo-affective disorder, an emotionally unstable personality disorder and low IQ. Convicted under the Sexual Offences Act 2003, the defendant appealed, then in turn the Crown appealed to the House of Lords that reinstated the conviction on the basis that the victim lacked the capacity to choose to take part in the sexual activity because she held an irrational fear of the consequences if she did not take part, namely her imagined fear of the potential behaviour of the perpetrator, even though she did not object to the sexual behaviour at the time. In the second case, a married woman who had a learning disability was judged not to have the capacity to consent to have sex with her husband because she did not understand the mechanics of sex, that there were health risks including the risk of pregnancy, and that she had a choice to consent or not. Such cases indicate that it is the perpetrator, the defendant, who can be reasonably expected to know that the person concerned has a mental disorder and that, as a result, the person's capacity to choose is affected, and they may be likely to refuse to give their consent. Baroness Hale concluded that 'the prosecution "has only to prove the inability to refuse to consent rather than the complainant actually did not consent"' for conviction under Section 30 (Pegg & Davies, 2016, p.112). The prosecution has to prove that the perpetrator ought to have known that the person's ability to consent was affected by their mental disorder.

The issue of reasonably being able to know that a person has a mental disorder is an issue for care workers. A 'care worker' is defined under Section 42 of the Sexual Offences Act 2003 as a person employed in a community home, voluntary home or children's home, or who works in a hospital or a clinic, and who has regular contact with a person who is a resident and who has a mental disorder. It also covers those who are care assistants who provide services in connection with the care of the person with a mental disorder, so, for example, cleaners or providers of domestic services should also be covered by the Act, as well as volunteers. Sections 38–41 relate to sexual activity with the person with a mental disorder, causing or inciting sexual activity, sexual activity in the presence of that person, and causing that person to watch a sexual act. Whether or not the person has the capacity or not is not an issue in itself, but that the worker is caring for a person with a mental disorder despite the capacity to consent or not. However, if a care worker engages in sexual activity with a person whose capacity or ability to consent is affected by a mental disorder, the worker may be charged with the more serious offence under Section 30, with the possibility of a harsher sentence.

Adults with disabilities and illnesses are thought to be especially vulnerable as potential victims of crime, and this may additionally affect their ability to act as witnesses. The identification of vulnerability is subject to 'special measures' directions, and although there is no internationally accepted definition of 'vulnerable', it includes a person who has a mental disorder, significant impairment of intelligence and social functioning, or physical disorder or disability (Radcliffe & Gudjonsson, 2016, pp.16–17). Mild disabilities are not always immediately recognized.

Cobley (2005) has made a number of points that highlight that people with disabilities or illness are especially vulnerable to being victims of sexually abusive behaviour. We know from practice that people with disabilities may be unable to escape or get away from their abuser, especially in such settings as residential care or nursing homes where there is high level of dependency. If there are issues of cognitive capacity, reported abuse may be disbelieved and misinterpreted as something they have imagined or heard about and repeated. We are also aware of closed institutionalized attitudes and behaviours, lack of awareness, or simply that it is too uncomfortable to imagine such abuse, which makes it difficult for a full investigation to take place.

There may be some disagreement with some of these points, such as people with disabilities being vulnerable because of the *de facto* status of being in a residential setting and dependent on others, but clearly *some* institutional settings do put some people at additional risk, as seen in the case of the Winterbourne View hospital scandal (CQC, 2011), where residents were repeatedly assaulted in various ways.

Prior to the Youth Justice and Criminal Evidence Act 1999, people, including those over the age of 14, were not allowed to give evidence unless they were considered competent to take the oath in Court, and many people with disabilities were in this position. Whilst able to understand and give answers to questions, they were considered capable only if they could fully understand the proceedings and have a sufficient appreciation of the nature of telling the truth. There was an absence of provision of allowing people over 14 to give unsworn evidence, and whilst few people were deemed incompetent, it appears many were not called to give evidence because of decisions made prior to Court, such as those of the CPS. This has changed since the Youth Justice and Criminal Evidence Act 1999, allowing vulnerable people to give evidence without taking the oath.

The decision regarding 'competence' in Court may be raised by either the prosecution or defence, but is judged by the Court as having the ability to give intelligent testimony, that is, to answer questions. The standard of proof required is 'on the balance of probabilities' rather than 'beyond reasonable doubt' (Section 54(2), Youth Justice and Criminal Evidence Act 1999). Since the Youth Justice and Criminal Evidence Act 1999, determining competence should be done in the absence of the jury (Section 54(4)), and may be assisted in Court by an expert witness who is able to give their opinion rather than just factual answers to questions (Cobley, 2005). *Special measures* are mostly concerned with the means of Achieving Best Evidence in Criminal Proceedings (ABE) where children are involved, introduced in 1999 and subsequently revised in 2002, 2011 and 2013. North and Thompson (2016) highlight the issues surrounding the law and memory relating to neurological disorders such as having a learning disability or dementia, and those who have suffered a stroke, head injury or disease.

By its nature, sexual offending affects many areas of life. It therefore overlaps with many areas of legislation. Most obviously, it is managed within the jurisdiction of criminal law that has the power to sentence and pose additional restrictions on a person who has been convicted. Legislation intended to safeguard both children and adults may also be invoked. Other areas of overlap might be in domestic abuse, stalking legislation, mental health as well as other less obvious areas such as housing once a perpetrator is back in the community.

CHAPTER 8

Approaches and Debates

TREAT, CURE OR CONTROL? FROM THEORY TO PRACTICE AND FROM PRACTICE TO EFFECTIVE OUTCOMES

Historically many of the approaches to sexual offending have been to 'treat', 'cure', 'control' or change abnormal 'deviant' sexual arousal and behaviour, using various techniques, searching for evidence of effectiveness. The development of 'evidence-based practice' has been matched over the years with 'practice-based evidence' of making assumptions and seeking to find research and evaluation that supports or falsifies it. Many of the choices have had some element of expediency based on variations of bio-psycho-social-cultural-political-legal assumptions. Much policy and practice has been a muddled stop-go affair gradually moving forwards and stepping back again. Effectiveness remains an optimistic 'work in progress'.

Re-evaluations of approach have raised doubts about the effectiveness of operationalizing theory into practice. The 'what' of addressing sexually harmful behaviours is influenced substantially by some fundamental assumptions of the nature of sex and sexuality, its mechanisms, and 'how' and 'how much' should be done, to whom, when and where, and not all approaches have proved successful. As a consequence, great care must be taken in using any of the material described in this book, and never to lose a degree of intelligent professional reflection especially when assessing risk – it is not unknown for professional hubris to lead to professional nemesis, such is the uncertainty, complexity and extensive scope of issues.

There is a lack of homogeneity amongst those who sexually

abuse others, and such is the range and scope of sexually harmful behaviours, 'no one size fits all' and there are always exceptions to any rule. Competing organizational contexts since the 1990s has led to a shifting predominance of different professional organizations and disciplines, with much of the research originating from a North American context.

A BRIEF HISTORY OF INTERVENTIONS

In the UK, much of the early development of community interventions grew out of the need to work with an apparent increasing number of those convicted of sexual offences. The number of these offenders on community caseloads appeared to increase during the late 1980s, where the more traditional generation of probation officers based their approach on the long-standing 'rehabilitative ideal' (Mair, 1997) and the ethos of 'advise, assist and befriend', and found themselves challenged and de-skilled. The Probation Service was forced, politically, to change to a more functionally correctional culture rather than compassion-based practice that echoed sentiments of 'there but for the Grace of God go I' (widely attributed to John Bradford, an English Reformer, circa 1510–1555: see Mathew & Harrison, 2004). The level of expertise and knowledge required for working principally with men who were convicted of sexual offences was relatively low, triggering a number of localized 'home-grown' developments. The increasing bureaucratization of the Probation Service has caused considerable dismay amongst many practitioners who no longer feel aligned to its values.

Dating from the late 19th century, 'treating' those who commit sexual offences has a substantial history, in many instances using a behaviourist 're-conditioning' approach such as, for example, aversion therapy, the use of uncomfortable or painful negative stimuli of electric shock or nausea-inducing substances paired with showing unwanted sexual imagery.

The classical behaviourist re-conditioning approaches of the mid-20th century include the ABC model of stimulus–response that describes the linear sequence of antecedent (child)/behaviour (fantasy/masturbatory arousal/arousal) and consequence (sexual pleasure/orgasm). This model sought to re-condition the masturbatory response by means of either aversion therapy or satiation. Aversion therapy sought to bring about an automatic response to associate the stimulus with an unpleasant response. Masturbatory re-conditioning continues, despite the suggestion that there is only weak evidence of its effectiveness (Laws & Marshall, 1991). It seemed, and seems, sensible, and hence expedient. Aversion therapy put simply would involve invoking thoughts and images of a child whilst applying an unpleasant physical sensation, usually smelling salts. The theory is that when the image, the thought of child abusive behaviour, occurred, the offender would associate this not with a re-enforcing pleasurable sensation of sexual pleasure, but with unpleasant sensations. Introducing 'healthy', 'normal' sexual thoughts and associating this with masturbation sought to achieve the same effect.

Subsequently poorly evaluated, this is now largely redundant although used as a supplementary approach to other techniques. It is, however, attractive to treatment regimes in the guise of the simile of machine re-programming, much like a 'Clockwork Orange' scenario as represented by Anthony Burgess' 1962 novel of the same name and the 1971 film by Stanley Kubrick in order to 'treat' and 'cure' the offender. Added to the ABC model was the ABBC model where an 'extra' B was the belief system that allowed the offender to make sense and rationalize their abusive behaviour in a schema that involved seeing that abusive behaviour was linked to thinking errors or cognitive distortions. These cognitive distortions (see pp.124–125, 127) are beliefs such as the child would enjoy having sex with an adult, that it was a positive rewarding experience in itself, or disallowing the thought that the behaviour was abusive and harmful. Subsequently incorporated into Relapse Prevention programmes, the challenging and 'correcting' of this faulty thinking has been evaluated and shown to have poor results (in California, by Marques et al., 2005). It has now been extended to consider Contextual Behavioural Science (CBS) that speaks of 'relational learning' mediated by language and linguistic terms as a symbolic process and as verbal cognition. This suggests that human brains, unlike other mammalian brains, have a language repertoire that associates linguistic concepts with the relationship with 'actual' things, that can be incorporated into Cognitive Functional Therapy (CFT). 'The word' is not 'the actual thing' but represents and symbolizes 'the actual thing', and it is 'the word' that is associated with the experience, positive or negative. Commonly, people may have a fear of spiders, and the word 'spider' invokes anxiety and fear whilst the actual spider may not be present but is instead imagined. The word, the thought, the process of thinking about and 'the actual thing' are fused together within the mind as 'cognitive fusion'. This leads to associating both desires and fears mediated through words and language with different desirable actual things, such as 'cake' (generally considered desirable, although not to everyone) or 'spider' (generally fearful).

Within the UK Prison Service, Wormwood Scrubs and Birmingham prisons were at the epicentre of developments in treatment (Laycock, 1979), generally wed to traditional behaviour modification techniques, with some attempt at a scientific approach of results being measured using penile plethysmography (PPG) (Laycock, 1979). Approaches in the community tended towards a more holistic approach that also included improving social skills and reducing anxiety, and this developed into the Birmingham Treatment Programme (Perkins, 1982). Much of the treatment at this time was primarily aimed at child sexual abusers (Marshall & Hollin, 2015), and particular developments in treatment showed a trend towards a medicalized model of intervention, in which British psychologists followed their American counterparts (Howells, 1984).

In the broader community setting, it was generally interpreted that, with little exception, 'nothing works' (Martinson, 1974), and whilst only briefly mentioning sexual offenders, this conclusion had a far-reaching effect (Sarre, 2001). Martinson refers not only to 'treatment effect' but also to 'policy effect' in that the policy itself in its interpretation and implementation can affect treatment results. West (1996) critiqued psychological interventions and treatments available at the time as being too reliant on self-restraint and social responsibility rather than specifically targeting sexual deviance. The critique of the medical psychotherapeutic approach that relied on the expression of emotional difficulties and self-analysis was also questioned. West (1996) advocated a coordinated approach utilizing statutory and voluntary agencies that could refer for treatment at the earliest opportunity, but recognized the limitations of such an approach.

THE RISE OF EVIDENCE-BASED PRACTICE

The 1980s was a continuation of the assessment and treatment techniques that had been developed in the prison system, the use of psychometric and physiological measures and the use of 'psychological treatment' (Perkins, 1986). Cognitive-based programmes on general offending were being developed during this time, such as 'Reasoning and Rehabilitation' (Ross, Fabiano and Ewles, 1988), moving on from 'nothing works' to 'some things work' or 'what works' (McGuire, 1995), originally with a question mark. Anecdotally, probation areas were developing their own 'in-house' sex offender programmes, drawing on the growing body of awareness and literature, a dynamic time in the world of sexual offending. Ex-probation officer Ray Wyre opened the Gracewell Clinic in Birmingham in 1988, the first residential unit for sexual offenders, and helped set up the Lucy Faithfull Foundation soon afterwards (Eldridge & Wyre, 1998) as a centre for developing excellence.

In 1991, then Home Secretary Kenneth Baker announced that there would be a national strategy for sexual offenders in England and Wales for the treatment of those in prison (Marshall et al., 1998). David Thornton, as Head of the Offending Behaviour Programmes Unit within the Prison Service, was tasked with designing and implementing the first cognitive-behavioural programme for sexual offenders in custody that was widely rolled out, a choice of approach influenced by developments and new data for researchers (Marshall & Hollin, 2015).

In 1995/96, the Chief Inspector of Probation, David Ramsbotham, commissioned a review of evidence-based practice. Following this, in 1998 the government launched the Effective Practice Initiative (Chapman & Hough, 1998) requiring all local probation areas to align with 'what works principles' (Newman & Nutley, 2003). This effectively led to 'programme-ization', including for those who had committed sexual offences. The Joint Prison Probation Accreditation Panel was set up in 1999 to accredit those programmes that fit with the 'what works' criteria (Home Office (1), 1998). For sexual offenders, the Northumbria Sex Offender Programme, Thames Valley Sex Offender Programme and West Midlands Sex Offender Programme were selected (Home Office (1), 1998) based on cognitive-behavioural methodology.

A growing regional network in the North West of England, mostly based around increasingly specialized probation officers, led to the inauguration of the charity NOTA in 1991. NOTA provides a support network for professionals, and since 1991 has evolved and developed a platform for academics and practitioners in its *Journal of Sexual Aggression* and its annual conference (NOTA (2), n.d.).

Politically, this was a time of crime being high on the political agenda, in general terms. As Home Secretary in 1993, Michael Howard gave a speech to the Conservative Party conference in which he said, 'Prison works. It ensures that we are protected from murderers, muggers and rapists – and it makes many who are tempted to commit crime think twice' (Howard, 1993). With the New Labour government in 1997, the 'what matters is what works' agenda became prominent (Newman & Nutley, 2003). The rhetoric was 'tough on crime, tough on the causes of crime', which was a hard-won expedient between the political conservativism within the Labour Party under Home Secretary Jack Straw and the need to demonstrate punishing those who resist the rehabilitative process (Newburn, 2007; Reiner, 2008).

Probation was reconstituted in 2001 to the National Probation Service, indicating an emphasis on centralization (Newman & Nutley, 2003) and a dumping of the traditional organizational culture of 'advise, assist and befriend' to the organizational ideology of protection of the public and risk management, becoming the National Offender Management Service in 2004 (National Archieves, n.d.), and Her Majesty's Prison and Probation Service since 2017, subsequently reconfigured and reconfigured again following the disastrous Transforming Rehabilitation policy under Secretary of State Chris Grayling from 2013 onwards, undoing the previous 'what works' agenda.

Many of the interventions since the 1990s have adopted what had become an approach based mostly on received wisdom, with some variation. Naturally this both informed and created a general consensus of approach, obscuring any alternative way of doing things. Much of this ethos is based reasonably enough on ending harmful sexual abuse. The alternative to supposing that change was possible with the 'right' 'scientific' approach has a number of options, such as not to intervene as an unacceptably radically libertarian approach, a more draconian incapacitation and personal restrictions within institutional settings and imposing longer sentences, semi-institutional settings in supervised accommodation such as hostels, community control enhanced by the technology of electronic 'tagging' and legal measures to restrict personal liberty of movement, or community supervision constructed around a negotiated meaningful and structured enforceable skilled professional relationship. Currently, both external controls as well as rehabilitative programmes designed to promote internal change are used within the correctional services.

Alongside the treatment model has been a medicalized model that has previously seen the use of physiological methods of assessment such as the use of the PPG, a physical device put on the male penis that measures blood flow and provides a proxy of sexual arousal. Aligned to a classical behaviour modification approach, similarly, the polygraph for sexual offenders was formalized by the Offender Management Act 2007 on a voluntary basis for those already convicted of sexual offences (Marshall & Thomas, 2015). The polygraph was initially only used by the police but was later rolled out to be used in probation in a small number of areas. Despite some negative opinions on its use, it hopefully leads to greater disclosure by sexual offenders than those not using the polygraph, and enhances high-risk disclosures, motivates honesty, and encourages some greater personal reflection and truthfulness (Grubin, 2008, 2010; Spruin *et al.*, 2017). As an adjunct to treatment, however, it is controversial in its application. Currently, polygraph testing can be added to licence conditions on release from prison, although the results cannot be used as evidence in Court. The polygraph and more lately the use of functional magnetic resonance imaging (fMRI) to discover brain activity has been used within research on a small scale. Whilst clearly giving definitive results, many of the implications for social behaviour are interpretative, so, for instance, if part of the brain is apparently activated, or the penis becomes engorged, or the offender is proven to be a liar, does this mean that the person does not have personal agency, does not exercise choice, has no capacity for moral reflection, cannot exercise restraint and personal control, but still has the opportunity to commit abusive behaviour?

CONTROL, TREAT AND CORRECT

There are occasional public calls for a more punitive approach usually fuelled by particularly high-profile and unusual cases in the media and a shift in public opinion from the 1990s onwards, particularly in the US (Mancini & Mears, 2010, citing Garland, 2001). This 'mysterious' background for a more general and specific punitive 'get tough' approach arose from the late 20th century onwards, paradoxically at a time when the reporting of child sex crimes in particular was apparently reducing. This led to several states within the US extending the death penalty for homicides to include child sex crime. Mancini and Mears (2010) cite two surveys in 1997 (Time/CNN) and 2008 (Quinnipiac University) that stated that in the US '74 percent' of the public 'supported the death penalty for convicted murderers, 47 percent for convicted rapists, and 65 percent for those convicted of sexually molesting a child', and '63 percent of the public supported the death penalty for convicted murderers and 55 percent supported it for convicted child rapists' (p.960), based on beliefs about the nature of sex crime, although with some significant reported differences of opinion based on social groupings. In the UK the death penalty was abolished in 1965 (Murder (Abolition of the Death Penalty) Act 1965), with the debate between advocates of the death penalty for some crimes and abolitionists, the public expression supporting the reintroduction of the death penalty (Newburn, 2017, p.744) and an underlying sense of a collective consciousness of a supposed singular national identity (Kandola & Egan, 2014; Seal, 2014) that says it is what the public want. The issue of using harsh sentencing as a deterrent is controversial and has some considerable practical and moral issues when examined in detail (Walker, 1994).

Inevitably the issue of deterrence arises. Executing those found guilty of a sex offence clearly stops the person from committing another similar crime, and leaving aside the morality and sense of proportionality that has a long substantial history of debate, deterrence has tended to be the justification (Newburn, 2017, p.552). The debate on the general deterrent effect of imposing harsh penalties includes, for example, the issue of how harsh a penalty has to be to invoke a discernible deterrent to others, and how harsh can a sentence be when balanced against human rights, such as Article 2 'Right to Life' of the European Convention on Human Rights (ECHR) contained in the Human Rights Act 1998. But: 'To even put the words "human rights" and "sex offenders" in the same sentence is to risk a "dog whistle" response – that offenders' rights are being given priority over the rights of the community to live safely' (Erooga, 2008, p.171). The counter to the popularist view that capital punishment has a deterrent effect on other potential offenders is highly questionable (Durlauf, Fu & Navarro, 2012). The greatest deterrence appears to be the possibility of being detected and public shaming. Shaming can also confirm a person's status as somebody with a deviant identity, as a form of stigmatization, but respectful, educative, restorative 'reintegrative shaming' can be more effective (Braithwaite, 1989). Distinguished from a sense of guilt, shame can be more emotionally exposing but may also trigger a potentially angry 'turning outwards' and displacing of blame and responsibility as avoidance (Tangney, Stuewig & Hafez, 2011).

Allied to the view of the legal killing of sex offenders is that of reducing sex crime by reducing the sex drive of sex offenders using anti-libidinal drugs. Forsberg and Douglas (2017) examine the intended and unintended purpose of anti-libidinal pharmacological treatment, sometimes referred to as 'chemical castration', including the prescribing of anti-depressants, in California and in England and Wales. Accordingly it is unclear whether the use of these drugs is intended to treat, cure or control, or even whether they are solely for retributive or punishment purposes. Our experience of the use of anti-libidinal medication is that it can be useful when people are highly sexually preoccupied and need to make the transition from custody to the community. It allows these people a bit of space for transition into 'outside' life.

Approaches based on external control as opposed to treatment or encouraging internal personal change can be applied through legal incarceration or community restrictions. These are applied proportionately on the basis of reducing risks by reducing opportunities. It presumes that the person is inherently dangerous, and was once described by a police practitioner as 'a ticking time bomb'.

COGNITIVE BEHAVIOURAL APPROACHES

Some approaches, such as the cognitive-behavioural approach, take the view that those who sexually offend are presumed to have personal agency, and are able to think about and exercise rational choice of their behaviour. A range of authors cited by Briggs and Kennington (2006) (see, for example, Beech, Fisher & Beckett, 1998; Finkelhor, 1984; Hanson & Harris, 2000a; Malamuth, Heavey & Linz, 1993; Mann et al., 2002; Ryan et al., 1987; Thornton, 2000; Wolf, 1998) all point to 'thinking errors' referred to in various guises such as 'cognitive distortions' or 'deviant' thinking. As pointed out by Auburn (2005), sex offender treatment programmes since the 1990s have looked to explore and address the way in which sex offenders think about their offending behaviour and their victims and consequently habitually behave in a way that is contrary to normal social standards. Using a complex approach to narrative reflexivity to address cognitive distortions (Auburn, 2005), Ward (2009) has developed and outlined the 'extended mind theory (EMT)' (p.247) drawing on theories from cognitive science suggesting that there is an inter-relationship between the (inner) mind of the sex offender and their (external) social environment that may constitute cognitive distortions. These thinking errors are seen as falsehoods and deviations from normative social thinking, feelings and behaviours about sex that provide the rationalization, excuses, justifications or psychological schemas for harmful abuse that 'gives licence' to allow such behaviours.

The majority of people who sexually harm others are clearly aware and recognize that their behaviour is strongly socially disapproved of, to such an extent that they are seen as social pariahs. In prison, those convicted of sexual offences are viewed as legitimate targets requiring protection as vulnerable prisoners, where the terms 'nonce' or 'beast' are traditionally used as terms of condemnation, 'nonce' being originally ascribed to the practice of chalking on prison cell doors 'Not On Normal Communal Exercise'. Public hatred, anger and opprobrium of those viewed as 'sex offenders' is evident and creates subcultures and communities within institutions and community networks passing on information and 'intelligence' that rivals law enforcement agencies. As with all of us, to preserve their own sense of wellbeing, those who sexually harm others also provide their explanations and rationalization for their behaviours, described by those who treat them as 'cognitive distortions' (Abel et al., 1989) or faulty thinking consisting of beliefs and attitudes that provide rationalization for a sense of entitlement.

Examples of cognitive distortions commonly cited are things such as 'children are sexual beings who seek and encourage sex with adults', 'children enjoy sexual attention', 'sex with children enables early sexual education', 'sexual arousal is natural and uncontrollable', 'all women secretly desire to be raped', 'women like to be sexually dominated', 'sexual activity between men and young boys is entirely natural in other cultures', 'it happened to me and it did no harm', etc. A dominant target to treat and change sexual offenders in the past has been aimed at changing and reducing this thinking using exercises that explicitly reveal and provide detailed analysis of the stages in the 'roadmap', from arousal to harmful offending behaviour, based on Finkelhor's (1984) four-stage model, now mostly replaced within other treatment approaches. Despite the various controversies, a more or less normative approach has been in development through various phases of hope and 'hopes dashed' of finding a 'solution' in the UK, summarized by Briggs and Kennington (2006) and seen in several specific SOTPs, including treatment modules that aimed to motivate offenders to change.

Finkelhor's precondition model of child sexual abuse is one of the most enduring and influential descriptions of child sexual abuse, but has been critiqued for a lack of psychological and sociological theoretical underpinnings from research, conceptual problems, a vagueness, overlapping constructs and factors that require clarification (Ward & Hudson, 2001). Answering questions about sexual arousal as a precondition to sexually harmful behaviours has not been easy, and identifying causal distal or proximal factors, distinguished by the abuser's 'pre-dispositional (or) vulnerability... that emerge from both developmental experiences and genetic inheritance' (distal) or 'triggering processes or events' (proximal) (Ward & Hudson, 2001, pp.292–293). The basic issue of arousal and its causes is generally not well understood in this model but instead simply describes that it occurs, whether these causes are related to emotional congruence with children, opportunism or disinhibition. Now over 30 years old as a model, it continues to be influential in thinking about the process of abuse and the trajectory, modified and made to fit specific instances and examples of sexual abuse including the use of illegal online imagery. Whilst it remains a useful framework, it is generally lacking in subsequent sophistication of detailed evidence-based theory, and in many respects it incorporates many socially normative assumptions about sex and sexuality. Our experience is that it is effective when working with non-offending partners who find it useful to consider in their own context.

Remarkably robust, it tends to be a descriptive model rather than a theory, useful when analysing the steps that are presumed to be the precondition of sexually abusive behaviour. This has subsequently been adapted, incorporated within general practice and interpreted broadly as:

- Motivation for behaving in a certain way that might include sexual arousal and sexual interest in the case of a person who sexually abuses others and may include meeting emotional needs. (To highlight how this process works, in training we have used a number of non-sexual examples to help trainees think this through, such as eating cake, smoking and speeding.)
- Overcoming internal inhibitors that is about knowing that the act is wrong but finding ways to overcome this, e.g. self-talk about it not really doing any harm, etc. (It is often useful to consider how we use such permission giving processes in our own behaviour so that we can understand how others are able to do similarly.)
- Overcoming the external contextual inhibitors which might include 'grooming' a child and their family and putting oneself in a position in which abuse can take place. (In the case of eating cake, or speeding, choosing to avoid the scrutiny of others, or avoiding speed cameras.)
- And finally, overcoming the victim's reluctance to engage in sexual activity either through covert 'grooming' or direct coercion.

(adapted from Finkelhor, 1984)

In step 2, the previously commonly used term of 'cognitive distortion' is not without controversy and inconsistencies. It requires some caution, and lack of understanding can lead to ineffective muddled interventions. It is quite usual for everybody to rationalize and make excuses for their own desires and to provide justification for poor decisions (think about the desire to eat a doughnut, smoke a cigarette or have a quick gin and tonic after getting home from work), and the same is true for sex offenders. There is a tendency to view the processing of thoughts and behaviour as an unusual forensic cause and effect that, as Auburn (2005) points out, is given some special status within treatment for people who sexually offend. Abusers are often caught in a dilemma and admit that their 'faulty thinking' leads to harmful abuse, but they do not necessarily truly feel or think it, and are subsequently unresponsive to treatment that attempts to create personal change, re-socialization and correction.

As a route into accessing the underlying processes, examining cognitive distortion is useful but is also part of 'shared social practices', and rather than 'a psychological entity or process implicated in offending...[it is]...a lexicalized term that has acquired a specialist status within the professional arena of treatment and which is utilized to construct, in part, the lived experience of those populating the treatment setting, and to transact particular sorts of business or actions within that setting' (Auburn, 2010, p.106).

Linked to this is the overcoming of denial of the harmful impact of abuse, the denial or partial denial of responsibility and the impact, such as blaming the victim for the behaviour. For example, 'she led me on', 'she was dressed in a way that was provocative', 'he never complained so must have liked it', 'it wasn't as bad as it was described in Court', 'it was the alcohol', 'it was just a matter of the circumstances', etc., or even more outlandish excuses such as 'my penis just slipped in of its own accord', etc. Compared to the personally protective psychological function of denial, it is the practical legalistic aspect of denial that seeks to avoid culpability and hence guilt or a harsher sentence or allowing for earlier release on parole. Levenson and Morin (2001), cited by Briggs and Kennington (2006), describe five types of denial: of the facts, awareness, responsibility, impact or the need for treatment and to change personally.

The emerging trend of 'what works' morphed into 'evidence-based practice'. Subsequently a cognitive-behavioural framework of intervention largely became the standard approach applied to most different types of offending based within programmes addressing diverse types of sexual offending and sexual offences (Mair, 1997; McGuire, 1985; McGuire & Priestley, 1995).

As traditional psychodynamic, person-centred, non-directive 'talking therapy' approaches to sexual offending became less popular, so did elements of behaviourism. Although still used in particular contexts, such as therapeutic communities and secure hospital units, this was gradually overtaken within the general correctional services in favour of a broad formulation of practice intervention. According to Laws, Hudson and Ward (2000), in 1978 Janice Marques, a psychology intern in the US, expediently suggested that the cognitive-behavioural approach developed by Marlatt and Gordon (1985) should be used as an approach to poor outcomes of relapse prevention treatment (in Laws *et al.*, 2000b, p.3), an approach applied to other 'disorders of impulse control such as compulsive sexual behavior, compulsive gambling, some forms of sexual deviance, problem drinking, compulsive spending, shoplifting, or inter-personal violence' (p.4). Cognitive-behavioural approaches for the treatment of sex offenders increasingly predominated (Abel *et al.*, 1984, cited in Laws *et al.*, 2000b), despite cautioning about over-optimism. By the early 2000s, the design of standardized, accredited and approved programmes for sexual offending based on this cognitive-behavioural therapy (CBT) model became accepted as good practice, not without its critics and controversies (see Raynor, 2003). There was a sense of an underlying optimism that the solution to reducing re-offending had been found. Many commentators failed to recognize that the organizational and political context for promoting a 'what works' approach was purely political expediency to preserve the long-standing rehabilitative culture of the Probation Service, countering the political theme of 'prison works' promoted by the popularist right-wing Home Secretary Michael Howard (Mair, 1997). Caution about over-optimism has more recently been borne out when the core CBT-based SOTP in the UK was re-evaluated with some mixed results (Mews *et al.*, 2017).

PROGRAMM-IZATION

As a result, a more or less definitive 'what works' movement had been 'discovered', and a family of standardized curricula of 'programm-ized' approaches addressing a range of criminal behaviours became the standardized approach (Home office (2), 1998), derived, in part, from a complexity of issues and traditions of psychotherapy, cognitivism and behaviourism influenced by the major work of B.F. Skinner (1904–1990), Ivan Pavlov (1849–1936) and Aaron T. Beck (b.1921) (Chapman & Hough, 1998; McGuire, 2000; Chapter 1). Having overcome the professional cynicism of 'nothing works' to the hopeful 'something works', cognitive behavioural programmes based on Hall and Hirschman's Quadripartite model (Hall & Hirschman, 1991, 1992), Marshall and Barbaree's integrated theory (Marshall & Barbaree, 1990), Finkelhor's integrated theory of child abuse (Finkelhor, 1984, 1986), Wolf's multifactor model (Wolf, 1985) and Ward and Siegert's pathway model (Ward & Siegert (2), 2002) became influential in developing sex offender programmes (Brown, 2011). Sex offender treatment approaches incorporated elements of shame aversion therapy (Daniel, 1987), hetero-social skills training (Crawford & Allen, 1979; Perkins, 1987) and various behavioural approaches: aversion therapy using electric shock and olfactory techniques (Marshall, Anderson & Fernandez, 1999; McGuire, Carlisle & Young, 1964), covert sensitization (Marshall *et al.*, 1999), masturbatory reconditioning (Laws & Marshall, 1991; Kremsdorf *et al.*, 1980), verbal satiation (Laws, 1995) and antiandrogenic (Grubin & Beech, 2010) or selective serotonin reuptake inhibitor drugs (Kafka, 1997), etc., for treatment of paraphilias described in DSM-IV as reviewed by Beech and Harkins (2012). The most common method used has become cognitive-behavioural therapy. Whilst outcome studies have indicated that CBT combined with relapse prevention is effective for those who sexually abuse children and exhibitionists, other paraphilias such as rape are more equivocal (Beech & Harkins, 2012).

Using a wide range of research evidence, these standardized sex offender treatment programmes incorporated elements of social constructivism, personal attributions, social learning, self-regulation, theories of cognitive schema, environmental stressors, opportunities and triggers, classical conditioning and theories of cognitive dissonance, etc. Underlying the detailed prescribed elements of the programmes of cognitive behaviourism, sex offender programmes included social learning theory, theories of sexual deviance, sexual preoccupation, pro-offending attitudes, poor victim empathy, personal inadequacy, intimacy deficits, poor levels of self-esteem, social assertiveness, deficits in emotion recognition, emotional self-regulation and deficits in social perspective-taking (Allam, 2001; Faux, 2001). Along with the Northumbria community sex offender programme (Kennington, 1994) and the prison sex offender treatment programme (SOTP) (Beech, Fisher & Beckett, 1998), each of the sex offender programmes had a sophisticated management process of selection of workers, offenders and monitoring of programme compliance with a content and treatment ethos and approaches.

The process of creating a consistent CBT programme enabled a basic understanding of the relationship between thoughts, feelings and behaviour that was then cascaded down for use by practitioners by approved specialist trainers.

Not entirely redundant, the idea was that offences could be analysed in a step-by-step fashion to identify what a sexual offender was thinking, feeling and doing in an incremental ladder of stages. As a group process, each offender would be asked to think back to a primary index offence and describe the process of offending from start to finish, beginning with a basic description of what the offence was, when it took place, where specifically it took place, against whom (the victim) and how. Each stage of events was broken down in describing the behaviour, thought and feeling that then linked to the next step in the offence.

For example, the offender would be encouraged to disclose:

Stage 1: 'I sexually assaulted my niece; it was at a summer picnic; I arranged a "special" place. At the time I thought that my niece was sexually attractive and would like to have a sexual experience; I was feeling sexual anticipation and becoming aroused.'

Next stage: 'I invited her to lie next to me and began cuddling. I thought this would lead to more intimate contact; I was feeling increasingly sexually aroused.'

And so on, describing a step-by-step process that culminated in the offence immediately afterwards. At each step the offender is asked to disclose their thoughts and behaviours that are 'hidden' from view, known to the offender but not immediately known by others, using the simile of an iceberg where the top is visible above the water supported by a hidden part under the water.

The offender was then asked to review key stages of progression towards the offence, and what else they could have done to 'escape' from the sequence that led to the offence. At each stage, as a general descriptive adaption in practice of a CBT approach, the supporting thought and feeling is required to match the behaviour, displaying consonance between thought, feeling and behaviour. It is presumed that by introducing disparity or dissonance between the thought and feeling, this will cause a change in behaviour. In the example above, dissonance can be introduced by challenging the offender's thought that sexual contact with his niece was wrongly welcomed, by considering the substantial impact on the victim and her family, and encouraging the offender to take the victim's perspective through enhancing a sense of empathy (see below). Each of these presumptions is problematic, however.

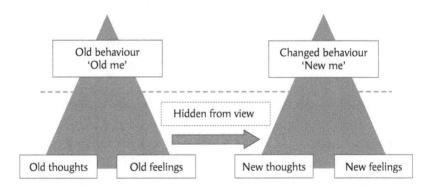

There are some issues in practice, such as the offender being able to distinguish between a thought and a feeling, the level of honesty of disclosures that can be partially substantiated by information used at Court for evidential purposes, and the skill of the group leader to motivate, engage and evoke honest and genuine responses. There are issues concerning denial of responsibility and victim blaming. Despite the drawback of implementation, however, the underlying model of a cognitive-behavioural framework has some validity.

Subsequent evaluation using outcome measures based on re-offending rates has not necessarily demonstrated the expected scale of positive change. The novel growth of the predominance of cognitive behaviourism arose out of some assumptions of previous treatment paradigms that led to a mantra of applying theory and research to practice through a doctrinal catechistic evidence-based treatment manual. Each individual session was carefully delivered and monitored within certain defined parameters by 'treatment managers' using a formulaic assessment of a treatment manager watching every fifth video recording of the programme as it was implemented.

The review of CBT-dominant approaches appears to display various weaknesses in the outcomes, and as a result, the range of processes has begun to encompass both 'old' and 'new', such as behaviour modification and aversion techniques, compulsive behaviour control (see above), thinking again about the place of ethical values, coping, affect regulation and the bio-social-psycho route to abusive behaviour. In 2017, a controversial evaluation of the prison core, initially presented as an internal evaluation in 2012, the SOTP, which had been delivered since 1992, produced some results on outcomes (Mews *et al.*, 2017) that did not differ enormously from previous results, demonstrating highly ambiguous treatment effects, but they were concerning enough for the programme to eventually be withdrawn by HM Prison and Probation Service. The evaluation claimed that there were approximately 180 more crimes over five years committed by 'treated' sex offenders than would otherwise have been the case. The report had been picked up by the media that focused on the negative conclusions, picking out certain aspects and leading to headlines about treatment making offenders worse. Subsequently reported as being tied in to issues about the employment status of the researcher, and counter-claims as to research rigour and potential bias (Casciani, 2017; Mews, Di Bella & Purver, 2017), this was enough to eventually facilitate the 'out with the old and in with the new' Horizon and Kaizen programmes, as had been previously rumoured for some time. Previous cautionary comments regarding the over-optimism about the effectiveness of SOTPs dating as far back as 2000 (Laws *et al.*, 2000b) appear to be justified. It does not reveal the extent to which effectiveness is due to design or less-than-perfect implementation. Our experience of working with men who have completed various SOTPs is that they have generally found some of the concepts useful.

The debate on the usefulness of a programm-ized CBT approach continues, with evaluations that cognitive behaviourism (Brown, 2011, pp.25–28) has previously indicated that this approach is effective as long as other conditions are also met, such as addressing precise criminogenic factors and ensuring that there is targeting of high-risk offenders with appropriate 'dosage'. Andrews (1989, cited in Brown, 2011) suggested that 'promising targets' should focus on:

> ...changing antisocial attitudes and feelings; reducing antisocial peer associations; promoting familial affection, communication, monitoring and supervision; promoting identification and association with anti-criminal role models; increasing self-control, self-management and problem-solving skills; replacing the skills of lying, stealing and aggression with more prosocial alternatives; reducing chemical dependencies; shifting the rewards and costs for criminal and non-criminal activities in familial, academic, vocational, recreational and other behavioural settings...etc. (Brown, 2011, p.37)

The formula for applying the CBT-dominant programme appears less effective than hoped for, failing to fit within a broader understanding of abusive sexual behaviour. These UK programmes are thought to reduce recidivism (Schmucker & Losel, 2017), but are based on weak-inferential studies (Walton, 2018).

It has been suggested that interventions should be targeted at the precise criminogenic factors in a specific individual offender's life, their dynamic thoughts, behaviour and circumstances. Placing emphasis on the 'risk principle', and on risk-needs-responsivity (RNR) (Andrews, 1989; Andrews & Dowden, 2007; Andrews, Bonta & Hoge, 1990), was later revisited and evaluated (Polaschek, 2012), both in general offending and in addressing sexual offending. Identifying and addressing individual risk factors has become more or less the norm in attempting to reduce re-offending. This includes such things as antisocial attitudes, changing social networks, increasing self-control and self-management, treatment readiness, preconditions for engagement in therapy and problem-solving skills.

The emphasis dynamic risk and criminogenic needs essentially focuses on replacing and modifying underlying emotions and attitudes that support offending. People naturally seek acquisition of social 'human goods' that meet their underlying desires and personal needs. In order to motivate offenders to pursue socially acceptable goals, it is necessary that they view the alternative personally meaningful ways of living valued by and valuable to them, without which the motivation to change will be reduced or lost – if it is felt by the abuser to be consciously or subconsciously that it is more advantageous to keep pursuing an abusing lifestyle and associated attitudes rather than a non-abusing lifestyle, abusers will continue to further abuse others (Ward & Brown, 2004). Importantly, offending and the desired-for change to pro-social behaviour take place within an influential personal social context and an effective skilled professional relationship (see Chapter 9).

The widespread adoption of CBT programmes has seen them adapted in a number of ways, for example with those with intellectual impairment. Acknowledging the wide disparity of terms, generally those with limited intellectual ability are frequently referred to as having a learning disability, and this became the more generally accepted term that is used with some variation of diagnosis in practice. Wilcox (2004) reviewed the literature on those with an intellectual disability, pointing out that the development of specific interventions has been slow, requiring knowledge of sexual offending and intellectual disability, however defined, but generally referring to those who have been assessed as having an IQ of less than 80 and Borderline Intellectual Functioning (IQ of 70–80). Whilst seen traditionally as a significant risk for delinquency and offending generally, more recent research indicates that the proportion of those who commit offences is not greater than in the general population but they are perhaps more likely to be apprehended. There are a number of standpoints that generally arise from the past, that those with a mental disability display 'childlike' naive exploratory behaviour, or face restrictions on privacy that would be available to most others, and hence sexual activity is more likely to be discovered and observed.

The limitations of using cognitive-behavioural approaches to treatment have been generally recognized, including recent evaluations of CBT-based programmes, but there has been a suggestion that 'adapted' CBT programmes are appropriate if suitably tailored to match limited intellectual abilities. However, the underlying theoretical presumptions within CBT-based programmes, such as presumed poor insight and abstract reasoning of those with limited intellectual abilities, have tended to err towards seeing that this is largely inapplicable, using instead a purely behavioural approach, a more direct approach to behaviour modification, social skills enhancement, sex education, impulse control, problem-solving, self-confidence and knowledge of legal and moral restrictions including increased knowledge of what is 'right and wrong'. Participative and therapeutic approaches require the adaption of materials and appropriate 'dosage' to maximize learning opportunities. The association between childhood trauma and sexual offending is increasingly becoming established, and those with an intellectual disability may be seen to be more prone to being victims of abuse because of their particular vulnerability.

A CBT approach was also adapted with the original 'internet offenders' programme for those men who accessed, downloaded and shared indecent imagery of children, aligned with the Finkelhor model that also had to be adapted. Overcoming the resistance of the children depicted was not necessary for the person accessing the indecent images, but was seen to have been pre-prepared by others who had taken the indecent image and made them available online.

In addition to a CBT element, programmes have incorporated relapse prevention strategies often as an additional or follow-up module. Influenced by the adoption of the model of the cycle of change (Krebs et al., 2019; Prochaska & DiClemente, 1982), it is used extensively in formulating targets for change of those who have experienced substance misuse and in other arenas, and who aim to change their substance-related behaviours. Described as a cycle of change, it consists of stages of beginning to think about change, becoming committed to change and achieving change (pre-contemplation, contemplation, preparation, action, maintenance and relapse). It is assumed that there are risks of relapse in behaviour for sexual offenders who may begin to think and plan to abuse others.

EMPATHY

Contributing to personal change, a common objective of treatment has previously been to increase victim awareness and empathy. Justifications and excuses act as a personal psychological protective mechanism. This can be interpreted as an avoidance strategy that in turn may be interpreted as those who sexually harm others lacking empathy for the victims of sexual abuse. This is controversial in at least two ways. Most sex offender programmes in the UK have contained a 'victim empathy' module, seeking to decrease the risk of re-offending by increasing acknowledgement of the long-term hurtful impact. It is thought that if the perpetrator vicariously feels the hurt of the victim, they are less likely to be hurtful. Perpetrators need to construct some reasoning or schema that allows them to justify their behaviour and defend their belief that it is acceptable to behave harmfully. Seen as an emotional deficit (Ward & Beech, 2006) that demonstrates a lack of ability to feel for others, a victim empathy component in treatment programmes began to be introduced in the 1980s (Murphy, Abel & Becker, 1980). This became more or less embedded in SOTPs, but was subsequently profoundly criticized as unscientific (Barnett & Mann, 2013). Subsequently it was downgraded and given far less emphasis within programme design, if not put to one side. Victim empathy began to be seen as a barrier to other interventions designed to explore the emotional functional purpose of sex and sexual abuse. But victim empathy continues to have some focus in research on establishing effective approaches, such as with young people (Coetzee, 2019) or those with intellectual disabilities (Michie & Lindsay, 2012), etc. Whilst apparently sensible and rational to include a victim empathy module to address victim empathy deficits (Farrington, 2007; Marshall *et al.*, 1998), as far back as the 1990s concerns were raised for a number of reasons as to the efficacy of including this (Polaschek, 2003, pp.182–183). Walker and Brown (2013) identified that not only sex offenders have empathy deficits, but other people in the general population also have empathy deficits when thinking about infidelity within relationships and the process of rationalizing with lack of remorse and self-interest. Our experience is that working to increase victim empathy tends to be a treatment 'red herring', and one that people can get a bit 'stuck' on once they begin to fully realize the harm they have done. It is only by allowing a person to have the opportunity to fully understand themselves and their own behaviour that they can begin to create a safer future.

Several issues arise in the conceptual underpinning and assumption that increasing victim empathy will decrease the risk of hurting another person. The personal context of sex offending is important to consider, and that no two people's circumstances are exactly the same within the total heterogeneous group of sex offenders, although similarities may exist. The perpetrator may have always perpetrated hurtful abusive behaviours within a context of their personal psychosocial history, and that history will involve some factors that relate to both the triggering of sexually abusive behaviours and desistance factors of continuing to abuse once triggered. Such a trajectory mirrors stage 1 of the Finkelhor model (1984), in that sexual arousal is experienced; it mirrors the biosocial model of arousal that occurs within the brain, triggering an endocrinal reaction; and it mirrors the conceptual model that sexually motivated behaviours can be restructured, ameliorated and remodelled within the conscious reflective processes of the higher brain. But if the amount of 'hurt' experienced by the perpetrator and the need to compensate for that hurt is greater than the hurt that is being perpetrated, the influence of victim empathy is likely to be ameliorated downwards, with a lesser impact on desistance.

This leads to asking questions about the relationship between a perpetrator's abusive behaviour and their own experience of abuse, early trauma, negative childhood experience, revenge for perceived psychological slighting, and poor mental health and wellbeing. If the perpetrator's experience of their own abuse is more impactful than their painful recognition of the hurtful abuse they are perpetrating, the abuse is likely to happen or continue. If the self-salving of their prior hurting lessens their emotional pain and the need is greater than the painful impact of empathizing with their victim's pain, abuse may continue. It is an emotional cost–benefit calculation of weighing up the bio-psycho-social impact on the perpetrator against the pain of the abuse victim experienced vicariously and empathically. A person hurt by their past, if unresolved, is likely to hurt others.

ADVERSE CHILDHOOD EXPERIENCES AND DESISTANCE

Adverse childhood experiences include childhood abuse and poor environmental factors, such as poverty deprivation and/or peer victimization. Between 9 and 14 per cent of children experience four or more such experiences in the UK. This can lead to an enhanced risk of antisocial behaviour (Boullier & Blair, 2018).

The original study on adverse childhood experiences (CDC-Kaiser Permanante Study 1995–97) provides detailed descriptions of individual, family and community risk factors and protective factors. The emphasis of the original study and much of the subsequent interest focuses naturally on the implications for the child, who is far more vulnerable to abuse and neglect as a result of these factors.

In the subsequent life of the adult, adverse childhood experiences have been linked to adult alcohol abuse (Loudermilk *et al.*, 2018), suicide (Rytilä-Manninen *et al.*, 2018), impulsivity (Shin, McDonald & Conley, 2018) and interpersonal difficulties in adulthood (Poole, Dobson & Pusch, 2018), in addition to other factors.

The relationship between adverse childhood experiences and sexual offences committed later as an adult is open to further detailed questioning. That some link exists between offending generally and adverse childhood experiences appears to be strongly suggested (Craig *et al.*, 2016), but whilst the risk increases for delinquency and criminal behaviour, dependent on frequency and accumulation of several events, protective factors are also at play such as increased positive social bonds. There is some evidence that adverse childhood experiences are related to sexual homicide, with the conclusion that those most at risk of committing such an offence were those with more extensive histories of having been abused as a child, an effect that was elevated when considering 'childhood enuresis, cruelty to animals, parental abandonment, deviant sexual behaviours, poor self-image, and sexual problems', and that the 'adverse childhood experiences framework is salient to forensic populations and the most extreme forms of antisocial conduct, namely sexual homicide' (DeLisi & Beauregard, 2017, p.487). A number of methodological issues have to be taken into account, such as the threshold for an event or events measured by frequency and intensity, that is then recorded as an adverse childhood experience, that exposure to sexual abuse as a child did not automatically lead to sexual homicide as an adult, that therapy addressing prior trauma is useful to reduce future risk and will affect subsequent outcomes, etc., and this indicates the complexity of the relationship between childhood experiences and sexual homicide, but there are indications that suggest there is a link with an accumulation of four or more childhood experiences. Specifically, whilst there is some early evidence of a relationship between disclosure of sexual abuse as a child and post-traumatic stress disorder (PTSD) (McTavish *et al.*, 2019), there is controversial evidence that child sexual abuse correlates with later sexual offending, and some recent evidence that child sexual abuse is a unique feature illustrating the sexually abused→sexual abuser hypothesis (Drury, Elbert & DeLisi, 2019).

Critiquing the risk management paradigm and having become influenced by the desistance literature and positive psychology, the more recent GLM focuses on the acquisition of sufficient social capital that supports a non-offending lifestyle. This would generally include socially and economically rewarding work, pro-social leisure activities, social networks and support, emotionally and practically. Developed by Tony Ward, the GLM is for working with sexual offenders (Ward & Marshall, 2004). It is a strengths-based model with the premise that sexual offenders, similarly to non-offenders, seek 'primary goods' that are beneficial to human beings (Ward & Brown, 2004). Maslow's theory (1943) is sometimes too simplistically interpreted as a proxy for indicating level of social need rather than the original idea of being a motivational theory. Widely adapted to purely describe a hierarchy of needs, the theory says that people are motivated by striving to gain essential needs that begins with the basic physiological need for food and shelter, and progress through the various levels of safety, love/belonging, esteem, and eventually self-actualization, but it contains some important caveats. Whilst needs were originally seen as in a hierarchy, with one need usually resting on the prior satisfaction of a previous need, 'no need or drive can be treated as if it were isolated or discrete and every drive is related to the state of satisfaction or dissatisfaction of other drives' (Maslow, 1943, p.370). Subsequently, whilst it is usually assumed that the basic levels must be satiated before any of the higher levels, it can be viewed more as a series of overlapping waves rather than a strict motivational and hierarchical ladder (Deckers, 2018).

The focus is on increasing strengths rather than focusing on deficits. Whilst the GLM seems anecdotally popular with practitioners, it is yet to fully penetrate mainstream policy in England and Wales. It appears to have moved further forward in Scotland with the Moving Forward Making Changes (MFMC) programme (Safer Communities Directive, 2018).

The Healthy Sex Programme (HSP), a revised version of the accredited Healthy Sexual Functioning Programme (HSFP) (NOMS, 2013), has just evolved into its latest iteration. Described as 'bio-psycho-social' in its methodology, it incorporates a combination of behavioural, cognitive-behavioural and psychodynamic techniques as well as some contemporary elements such as mindfulness and compassion-focused techniques. It also relies heavily on traditional approaches derived from psychotherapy.

Despite the scepticism of the significance of empathy within treatment programmes, the role of empathy has been implicated in psychotherapy, substantially influenced by the work of Carl Rogers (1951, 1957, 1961, 1963), and the suggestion that the therapist may be deliberately aware of and sensitive to understanding the patient's thoughts and feelings from the client's point of view, seeing the world through the other person's eyes and eliciting the meanings that the other person attributes to their experiences as they feel these happen.

However, there has been a lack of a consensual definition of empathy, although this has received a boost in exploring the identification of so-called 'mirror neurons' in the motor cortex of macaque monkeys, which has then contributed to a broader understanding of human empathy (Decety & Ickes, 2009 and Decety & Lamm, 2009, both cited in Elliott *et al.*, 2011). This suggests that watching another being gain satisfaction from a positive experience such as eating replicates and excites an area of the brain of the being that watches the other one eating. It is subsequently thought that there are three major neuro-anatomical sub-processes of: an *emotional simulation* process that mirrors another person's brain activity in the limbic system; a *perspective-taking* process; and an *emotion-regulation* process that helps mobilize compassion and helping behaviour.

The HSP is quite a different programme to the others. Those delivering the programme are called 'therapists' rather than 'facilitators', denoting the style of delivery. It is delivered on a one-to-one basis rather than in a group, and this allows for much deeper exploration of the person's way of seeing the world and their harmful behaviour. Whilst it is quite different in approach from the other programmes, the language of the HSP is still very much in line with the RNR principles of the 'what works' agenda (NOMS, 2013), and it is still time-limited and audited in the usual way. Because it is so resource-intensive, it is a programme reserved for those who demonstrate high sexual deviance and/or preoccupation. Our experience of being a therapist on this programme is that it is usually delivered to men who have committed very serious offences and who have completed the previous 'suite' of SOTP programmes, usually delivered within a year of release or eligibility for parole and for those for whom there are still concerns about their ability to manage safely within the community.

Within other disciplines, the emergence of the importance of the development of a therapeutic alliance is seen as critical to the possibility of personal change (see Chapter 9). A complex influential area, the complexity of the relationship of design, implementation, style of engagement, the relationship between worker and offender and the encouragement of motivation to change are all pivotal to success.

New programmes and the worker's committed belief in the efficacy of a novel approach as a trailblazer is an under-researched area where new programmes with newly trained workers tend to show much promise. When the programme 'goes to scale' and is then cascaded to workers further down in an informal hierarchy of expertise, both the original intention, understanding of underlying theory and approach, and mutual commitment between worker and offender to engage and seek change, can become diluted, the programme becomes 'tired', and the essential novel optimism becomes a routine expectation.

The complexity of the understanding of the context and the intra and inter processes embedded within the context defy attempts at any single approach. Understanding is a fluid, recursive and reflexive process applied differently to each unique case but with some common understanding of theory.

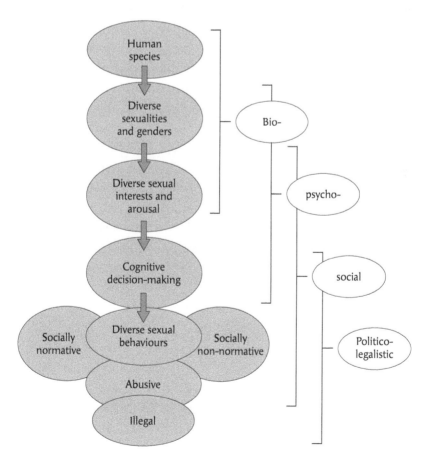

As a result of the evaluation of the 'old' programmes and in light of 'new' knowledge, Kaizen and Horizon programmes were put in place. Kaizen is aimed at higher-risk offenders and takes a more holistic view of the offender, incorporating biological, psychological and social factors, using strengths-based and desistance-focused approaches. Horizon is for those assessed as lower risk and takes the view that sex offenders are much like any other offender, addressing self-regulation, problem-solving and difficulties in relationships (McCartan & Prescott, 2017). A selling point of this programme is that it is also designed to work with men who deny their offending behaviour. Whilst this is, of course, welcome, we would state that it has always been entirely possible to work with 'deniers' on previous programmes, and indeed, this was frequently the case on the CSOGP.

In the community, older models of the sex offender programme are currently being phased out, with Horizon as the replacement for all levels of risk; Kaizen is currently being piloted in particular areas. The future for community-based programmes is uncertain, and it is too early for any published evaluations; statutory services rely on a conviction and a commensurate sentence that allows time for a person to complete a programme.

Other services, such as the NSPCC, have worked with men who are not necessarily convicted. Their assessment process, Assessing the Risk, Protecting the Child (ARPC) (Belton, 2017), has taken a whole-family approach in considering risk management in situations in which a man might be deemed a risk but who is not subject to the criminal justice process. Following a recent evaluation, this programme, which was focused on assessment and risk management in order to assist Court proceedings, has been withdrawn. It is not known whether the NSPCC will offer further interventions for adult perpetrators.

Prevention is gathering currency in the practice of work with sexual offending: there is a helpline for men who feel at risk of sexual offending, Stop It Now! (Lucy Faithfull Foundation, n.d.), a prevention committee situated within NOTA (NOTA (3), n.d.) and a new prevention project in Circles South West (Radford, n.d.) that seeks to replicate existing European innovations such as Dunkelfeld (Beier *et al.*, 2014) within the English and Welsh context. The Lucy Faithfull Foundation has also devised 'Inform' training for those who commit sexual offences on the internet; it is delivered by local partners, such as Circles South West in the South West of England.

In contrast to the tendency towards the punitiveness of the criminal justice system, Circles of Support and Accountability began to develop in the UK from 1999. This involves lay members of the community effectively forming a 'circle' around a sexual offender in order to reduce social isolation and increase support, with the view that this, in turn, reduces risk. Initially developed in Canada in the Mennonite church, Nick McGeorge, a former psychologist and member of the Quaker Society of Friends, alongside Helen Drewery, Assistant Secretary of Quaker Social Responsibility and Education, began to consider whether this could be developed in the UK (Nellis, 2009). Carol Kellas, Head of the Dangerous Offenders Unit of the Home Office, with Paddy Doyle, a seconded probation officer from Northumbria, identified pilot areas to test out the scheme and it was later rolled out. Mike Nellis (2009), in his enlightening account of how Circles developed, emphasizes the fact that Circles progressed almost against all odds; the Home Office had previously actively discouraged volunteers from working with sexual offenders as well as being committed to accredited and evidence-based intervention (Nellis, 2009). Nellis (2009) attributes this success to the particular group of individuals involved in its inception and implementation. Circles in the UK is slightly different from the original Canadian model in that in the UK it is firmly embedded within the MAPPA process but has continued and developed using volunteers, seemingly reasonably successfully (Thomas, Thompson & Karstedt, 2014; Thompson, Thomas & Karstedt, 2017). The umbrella organization is Circles UK, which approves and audits independent local projects. Unfortunately, due to recent cuts in statutory funding, a number of projects have ceased to run. Those that remain are tasked with finding innovative ways to attract a number of income streams in order to survive and to draw from a reducing number of funding opportunities. Because it relies on volunteers to assist in the reintegration of high-risk sexual offenders in the community, it locates itself within the paradigm of restorative justice.

Our overall experience, which is beginning to be borne out by research, is that it is the therapeutic relationship that has the power to make a difference. This seems to be most effective in a one-to-one setting where the offender and practitioner have a chance to get to establish a genuine, warm and reciprocal professional relationship. In our experience, most people who sexually harm others would not wish to be like that, and approaching the work from a starting point of compassion is crucial for a relationship with the power to transform lives. The creation of a therapeutic alliance between worker and client (in this case the abuser), whilst not without controversy and uncertainty of effect, based on empathic understanding, is significant in attempting to achieve a successful impactful outcome and positive change (Doran, 2016; Horvath, 2018; Nienhuis *et al.*, 2018; Sandhu & Rose, 2012). A confrontational style is, in our experience, less likely to achieve the same positive effect (Marshall *et al.*, 2003) and is important within a Good Lives Model for a positive non-offending future (Ward & Brown, 2004). This is not about minimizing the terrible harm that someone has caused, but to understand that what led to that harm is generally a human who is suffering. Our basic premise is that we are all doing our best to get through life and we all adopt different strategies for doing so. Unfortunately, some people create dreadful harm and devastation for all affected by the abuse, but trying to understand the function and meaning of that behaviour is the origin of stopping it happening again.

CHAPTER 9

The Reflective Professional

PROMOTING POSITIVE CHANGE TO REDUCE THE RISK OF FUTURE HARM

Working effectively with people who sexually abuse others is emotionally and intellectually challenging and complex. It involves levels of uncertainty in every sphere, uncertainty of information, of motivation, and of behaviours, reasons and theory. To cope with uncertainty there is a tendency to seek certainty through some 'technical rationality' (Schön, 1991, cited in Hood, 2018, p.12; Schön, 2016), a sense of a linear view of causality where the sequential adding together of several known factors leads to a conclusion. Total technical rationality requires total expertise and knowledge about sexual behaviours, and knowing all that there is to be known about every individual, overcoming contradictions and conflicts of views and evidence.

The authors of this book have particular professional backgrounds that emphasize the optimistic belief that a positive change in people's lives is possible. The basis of this book is that it is possible to encourage personal change in the lives of those who cause harm to occur, a transformation from one state of being to another, from an abusive pattern of behaviour to non-abusive behaviour. The authors recognize that the community must be protected from a small number of highly dangerous people, either by being incarcerated, closely restricted or controlled. For others who are in the community, whilst the risk of harm can be reduced, this cannot be ultimately guaranteed, even under the most preventive conditions. The authors believe that a change in personal behaviour reduces the risk of further abuse and future harm. If the influence of the 'risk society' has had a tendency to bolster proceduralism and the 'new managerialism', then, antithetically, practice wisdom, 'multiple' intelligences and intuitive thinking (Dane, Rockman & Pratt, 2012; Gardner, 1993; Sheppard, 1995; Zander *et al.*, 2015) have had a tendency to create a retrenchment towards and defence of a value-based practice paradigm (Ward, 2007).

Whilst well-established risk assessment tools seek to establish greater certainty in an uncertain social world, the reflective process requires an informed professional scepticism, and without some doubt, we are unlikely, if ever, to be truly reflective and come to some conclusion about the truth of the matter. This uncertainty suggests that in seeking expert certainty, the accepted inter-subjective knowledge held and shared by people becomes normalized as 'true', with the inference that there are some things that are subjugated as 'not true' or un-thinkable. This is reliant on the social standpoint that we presume to take, and the power associated with that standpoint. The exercise of power in this sense is a complex social function and a social technique, allowing the formation of some discourses and belief systems, disallowing others, influencing what is seen as right or wrong, normal or deviant. Challenging the idea of 'realist', objective knowledge independent of 'the knower', blurs the boundaries between rational independent scientific enquiry and more subjective areas of enquiry such as politics and art.

PROFESSIONAL VALUES AND PERSONAL CHANGE

Thinking about personal and professional values is essential when working with people who sexually abuse others. Briggs and Kennington (2006) explicitly state their value base (p.12), believing in the uniqueness of each person, that abusers have the potential for change and a non-abusing lifestyle, that many professions can contribute to the change process, that those who work with abusers should not abuse the abusers and that those who work with abusers have some personal responsibility to ensure that their own wellbeing is satisfactorily cared for. Furthermore, to achieve successful, authentic, genuine and meaningful personal realizations that make clear explicit and uncomfortable truths about the harm of abuse, this comes necessarily with high support, and it is through 'nurturance' (Briggs & Kennington, 2006, p.15) and the development of self-worth, not forgetting and fully acknowledging the harmfulness of abusive behaviour.

Hackett (2000) has developed a fulcrum model (cited in Briggs & Kennington, 2006, p.63) balancing overly liberal approaches of over-identifying with the abuser, colluding with their behaviours and the reasons they provide that excuse their behaviour, over-simplification and optimism balanced against a pathological pessimistic labelling, not acknowledging the positives in an abuser, and lack of recognition of the possibility of personal change. This is developed further in the GLM (Lindsay *et al.*, 2007; Ward & Marshall, 2004; Ward & Stewart, 2003).

The process of personal change is not easy to articulate. It is not necessarily well understood, is difficult to accomplish, and it takes a long time. Change is hard and not easily achieved through intervention. Wholesale sudden epiphany happens infrequently. For those who are in a cycle of abuse, when faced with the challenge of difficult personal change, the retreat back into abuse is comfortable, comforting and familiar. But having achieved change, people talk about becoming another person who is different to the 'old' person, to become a 'new me'. This does not happen quickly or easily, and can be a process of small changes that are met with relapse, only to begin again. However, most people eventually change, partly because of intervention, partly because of changing life circumstances, and partly simply because of increasing age.

Personal transformation and change from an abusive to a non-abusing attitude is often constrained by defensive and understandable agency decisions on the basis of what is seen as the safest decision. This needs to be managed and negotiated, and rationally defensive decision-making that allows opportunities for personal change to be balanced against professionally organizational defensive decisions that protect the agency from criticism if the perpetrator harms again and the level of trauma that needs to be addressed. This is a decision made on different kinds of risk. For example, it may be safer not to release an offender on parole, or it may be a safer option in the short term not to allow an abusive parent to have contact with a family, but may not be optimal for personal redemption, rehabilitation and reintegration in the longer term.

An emphasis on risk, engendered by fear of the rare high-impact cases such as child homicides, can distort the traditional purpose and practice of professional interventions (Macdonald & Macdonald, 2010). The assumption about people who sexually abuse as a class of individuals as being especially dangerous in society leads to organizational responses that overwhelmingly demonstrate 'risk-averse' defensive practice, potentially limiting opportunities for positive change, personal growth and social development.

Abusive behaviours operate within a place of negative emotions of the perpetrator of fear, shame, guilt, anger, disgust, self-hatred and low self-esteem, lacking self-compassion, etc. There is a lack of positive emotions 'as markers of flourishing, or optimal well-being...such as joy, interest, contentment, love, and the like' (Fredrickson, 2001, p.219). Most people are motivated by wanting to live a better life. Most people who abuse others eventually come to the realization that they wish to change. The cycle of change (Prochaska & DiClemente, 1982) is a reasonable model of a stage of personal change that is underwritten by an understanding that people are fundamentally motivated to seek an improved sense of personal wellbeing, not dissimilar to the engine of motivational desire within Maslow's hierarchy of needs (1943) that can be powerfully linked to motivational interviewing techniques (Miller & Rollnick, 2002, 2013).

We consider this helpful as a starting point to assess the motivation of the individual as this will impact on how you choose to work with a person. If someone is in the precontemplative stage, they perhaps do not acknowledge that they have perpetrated any sexual harm at all. This can sometimes feel like the most challenging and frustrating issue to work with; it is easy to get stuck in an unproductive line of enquiry. The most productive approach in this instance is to work with where the individual is at. Pushing too hard or being confrontational or combative is unhelpful, as with all of us, the tendency would be to become defensive and further withdraw. It is important to understand why this particular individual is adopting the stance that he is and the meaning this has for him. It is useful to acknowledge how much devastation their behaviour has wrought on everybody's life.

Even when a person is 'in denial' it is possible to work with them, but using a slightly different approach. This 'rolling with resistance' (Miller & Rollnick, 2002, 2013) is a technique that allows them to explore how things are without having to admit culpability whilst introducing elements of cognitive dissonance, and allowing the perpetrator to reflect using the 'one step removed' approach; for example, 'If a person harmed somebody sexually, what might people say about them, for instance a child's social worker?' This kind of 'one step removed' questioning allows the person to explore the issues without them having to admit anything. For taking more personal responsibility, a question such as 'How do you make sense of finding yourself in this situation?' enables the practitioner to get a sense of how much responsibility the person is prepared to own at this stage.

As professionals, it is our responsibility to allow service users to make progress at every available opportunity. The use of 'cognitive dissonance' (Festinger, 1957) is a helpful motivational technique to allow a person the opportunity of doing so. This is generally when someone is perhaps wavering between the precontemplation and contemplation stages, that is, they are beginning to think about undertaking personal change, so that they are not admitting anything but are perhaps starting to realize that things are not as they would wish; for example, 'What do you think it will take to improve the situation you find yourself in?' This allows for a person to begin to explore dissonance, the 'sweet spot' of progress and change. Gentle encouragement and probing here can allow the person to consider moving forward. The goal is not to force someone to admit to the harm they have caused, but our experience has shown us that, in using this approach, this does occasionally happen, and in that instance, the practitioner has to be prepared to hear it and contain the situation appropriately. This can just be about exploring what it was like to say whatever he did out loud, and to provide some positive reinforcement for taking responsibility.

Using cognitive dissonance is a way of encouraging people to take further responsibility for their life and their actions, and is an important part of work with sex offenders. People will only generally do this in a positive way if they feel supported and understood. An example of an opportunity to give someone more responsibility in this situation might be: 'You say you haven't done this, but yet you're here, prepared to talk to me; what does it say about you that you feel able to do that?'

If the individual is taking responsibility for their harmful sexual behaviour, this is also a good opportunity for taking further responsibility and for making progress towards an offence-free life. All of us usually get an intuitive sense of whom we feel able to trust and who is really prepared to listen; we also know who is not. We, as practitioners, always strive to be the person with whom an individual can feel as safe as possible to disclose as much as they feel prepared to share. A useful technique for doing so conveys the sense that you are prepared to hear what a person has to say and to make sure that that is really the case. One way of doing this is to ask assumptive questions that imply that you know a piece of behaviour is likely to have occurred and are checking the detail; for example, 'How many times a day would you masturbate to the thought of...?' This removes the first obstacle in a person disclosing something potentially very embarrassing by making the assumption that this occurred. If the assumption is wrong, it is very likely to be corrected or challenged and the question can be reframed or withdrawn.

The desire for self-esteem and a sense of worthiness is innate, but not everybody is at a stage of readiness to begin taking steps towards change. There is evidence that positive emotions enable personal change, and countering negative emotions increases resilience and enhances a personal sense of emotional wellbeing (Fredrickson, 2001). According to Seligman and Csikszentmihalyi (2000), psychology is not just about identifying deficits; it is also about nurturing wellbeing (Moneta, 2014).

Difficult to articulate, the underlying driver for changed behaviour can be described as a change of underlying attitude, from an abusive to a non-abusing attitude. It is surprising how little this is explicitly mentioned. Various definitions of attitude have been proposed (Maio *et al.*, 2019), but 'attitude' generally has three components of: beliefs and thoughts, feelings and emotions, and behaviours and experiences (pp.31–32). Changing behaviour reduces the risk of future abuse, and is the key to change.

The theory of reasoned action (Ajzen & Fishbein, 1977, 1980, cited in Maio *et al.*, 2019) suggests a link between attitude and behaviour due to an element of intentionality. This is combined with some 'subjective norm' that is, in turn, seen to be the product of 'how people who are important to the individual expect him or her to act and the individual's motivation to comply with these expectations' (Maio *et al.*, 2019, p.89).

In a non-specialist role, it is unlikely that a professional would have to provide any specific intervention with someone who has sexually harmed others. The interaction is likely to be just part of working within the wider family network. This does not mean that there cannot be value in the contact, however. It is our view that, as professionals, every contact should provide the opportunity for the service user to make progress. This is the difference between having a 'chat' with someone and actively engaging in the process of change. The key to personal change is through an effective and influential professional relationship between the perpetrator and the worker. The organizational over-emphasis on risk, engendered by fear of the rare high-impact cases, can distort the traditional purpose and practice of professional activities (Macdonald & Macdonald, 2010). It can distort and reduce the effectiveness of practice relationships. Relationship-based approaches are pivotal (Dix, Hollinrake & Meade, 2019; Hollinrake, 2019; Howells, 2019) and essential to addressing the underlying reasons for abusive behaviours and reducing the risk of future abuse.

Under pressure for social intervention organizations not to be seen to fail, the organizational formalization of approaches to case management, risk and risk management has tended to display a bureaucratic-instrumental bias. For some aspects of practice, in particular criminal justice social work, risk assessment has become central and critical to the core work. In re-considering original research within the equivalent of serious case reviews, it was apparent that some cases that have been 'properly' assessed as low risk (that is, rated as not high or very high) result in the offender committing a serious further offence (SFO), and that the majority of SFOs arise from low-risk cases (Wills, 2008). This can be seen as the failure of organizational bureaucratic-instrumentalist approaches, which may be ameliorated by the use of informal logic and re-stating of practice as a humane, value-based enterprise (Akademikerförbundet SSR, 2018; Broadhurst *et al.*, 2010; Ward, 2007).

A PERSON-CENTRED APPROACH

Person-centred theory and practice, influenced by Carl Rogers (1951, 1957, 1961, 1963), subsequently adapted and developed into humanistic practice (Egan, 2007; Payne, 2011), and is not infrequently linked to Maslow's motivational 'fusion' (1943, p.371) theory of the hierarchy of needs. A person-centred approach is based on addressing social difficulties through empowering people as self-determining individuals as an 'actualizing tendency' (Rogers, 1961, 1963, cited in Murphy, Duggan & Joseph, 2012, p.707), mediated by the social environment. The 'actualizing tendency' will develop if the social environment conditions are optimal and allow it to occur (Deckers, 2018).

It is important to have an awareness of research and theoretical knowledge and frameworks about work with people who sexually harm others. These are likely to be different depending on the profession of the practitioner. Those who might routinely come across and have to work directly with people who sexually abuse, such as psychologists, social workers and probation officers, as well as practitioners in other professions, have overlapping but diverse ways of approaching things. Cross-discipline working across other professional 'knowledges' and disciplines is an effective way of working and learning. Each discipline will have specific organizational and professional approaches, and each will have differences in types of knowing.

Factual static and descriptive knowledge is referred to as declarative knowledge. Much of the research on the causes of sexual abuse is declarative knowledge (see Chapter 3). Knowing how something can be achieved is generally referred to as procedural knowledge or processual knowledge. The overall aim of this book is to encourage skilled practice by moving from solely declarative knowledge to incorporating procedural knowledge, a difficult task that involves self-reflective critical thinking skills.

THINKING CRITICALLY ABOUT COMPLEX BEHAVIOURS

Critical thinking is a habit that can be learnt (Cotterell, 2017). In applying critical thinking skills we need to consider the worldview that each professional may have and the worldview that the perpetrator holds. The worldview is a set of beliefs, social constructs, cognitive thinking frameworks and psychological affect that provide the reasoning for why the abuse has taken place. There will be different competing viewpoints about the same event. We also need to understand the point of view of the perpetrator, the way in which they make sense of things and establish meanings. In synthesizing these viewpoints sceptically, we bring some logic and linked reasoning into play that enables practitioners to make some judgement. A jarring inconsistency within a person's narrative of events may raise a sense that 'something does not quite fit'. Being self-aware of the moment when there is a lack of 'flow' and incoherent detail is an essential cue and clue to sceptically explore and review flaws in reasoning.

To think about the complexities of sexual offending is challenging. So instead we replace this almost impossibly difficult task with a simplifying heuristic, replacing the difficult issue with a simpler question and resulting explanation. The heuristic process takes something that is unfamiliar and replaces it with something that is familiar, understandable and predictable, and about which we have had some prior experience.

The process of replacing a complex issue or question with a simpler one, known as representativeness, tends to guide us towards holding assumptions about a particular group and assumes that members of the group have the same characteristics. If we assume that all people are sexually aroused by the same things, this can be misleading, so, for example, some people have specific paraphilias that they pursue because they are sexually aroused by specific things. There a number of considerably wrong assumptions that 'lump together' all sex offenders, but as has been repeatedly stated, there is considerable heterogeneity. This also relates to 'conjunction fallacy', or the simple rule that two events occurring together are less likely than one of the events occurring on its own (Greetham, 2016, pp.17–18).

It is simplistic and axiomatic that thinking about sexual abuse requires thought, but the concept and process of thinking requires itself to be thought about, that is, thinking deeply about thinking, and a personal meta-analysis of how we think as individuals (Minda, 2015). 'Thinking' simply expressed involves mental representation, planning and behaviours in different contexts, and is generally different from the calculative reasoning of, for example, playing chess, but is also considered to be part of thinking. Reasoning alone involving the logical induction of deductive steps does not necessarily involve all aspects of thinking – it is possible to take a series of valid logical steps mechanistically but not to think about the ideas being used in taking those steps (Greetham, 2016, p.25).

Greetham (2016) suggests an extended practical sense of thinking that includes and extends the rational approach of formal logical reasoning that at the same time allows the process of reflective imaginative discovery, speculation and creativity. It involves the meta-cognitive abilities of thinking-about-thinking as it happens, and counter-intuitively thinking-the-unthinkable to generate novel perspectives.

Whilst any judgement must be contingent on what we know and think at any one time, we must make our own decision based on multiple perspectives and our professional judgement using both declarative and processual knowledge. This reflective approach is continually learnt and applied by the novice and experienced practitioner alike. This broader practical concept of thinking involves not just reasoning but also 'Smart Thinking' (Greetham, 2016).

Each perpetrator is an individual with different life circumstances, ways of being, feeling and thinking and establishing meaning. The most important aspect of being effective is to try to understand their world from their particular viewpoint. It is only when people feel understood that they begin to feel safe enough to make the significant and life-changing transformations needed in order to live a different kind of life.

This requires trust and openness. People do not always tell 'the truth', but listening actively to what is being told and how it is being told is as important as 'finding facts'. There are many 'truths' to any given situation. Relaxing into the intervention is therefore helpful, without the worry that as a practitioner you, too, are being 'groomed' or 'manipulated'. Adopting a position of 'respectful curiosity' is an effective way of making sense of how someone perceives their situation.

Our experience is that most people have not had the opportunity to develop fluency of emotional language. The 'onion' analogy is generally appropriate – gently and sensitively giving space without forcefully pushing, and allowing the peeling back of layers of emotional expression for people to reveal to themselves their core vulnerabilities that are at the heart of the harmful behaviour. It is important to recognize they may need additional support to manage the impact of personal vulnerability.

LOOKING AFTER OURSELVES

Supervision for practitioners is extremely important. For assisting with the work, this can be about challenging the practitioner's view of the work they are doing. Knowing one's own strengths and tendencies is important so that a supervisor can assist in raising other factors – for example, if a practitioner is strongly academic and a theorist, another person may be able to raise issues of emotionality. Supervision is also important, of course, to ensure staff wellbeing and support where needed. The work is impactful and requires understanding.

The negative psychological impact of burnout, compassion fatigue, emotional fatigue and vicarious trauma has been described in some considerable background literature (Figley, 1995; Kadambi & Truscott, 2003, 2004; Maslach, 1976; Maslach & Jackson, 1981, 1986; Pearlman & Saakvitne, 1995). There are some methodological issues within specific areas of research and some ambiguity within the interplay of complex issues. Clarke (2011), in reviewing the literature as it relates to working with sex offenders, states that whilst there may be prevalence of 'deleterious effects' (p.335), there is also cause for optimism, and a sense that the work can be professionally rewarding. Whether people are susceptible to burnout appears debatable, but there is also evidence of high levels of satisfaction combined with low levels of compassion fatigue and vicarious trauma if the necessary organizational support is available, reflecting the common theme that good levels and quality supervision are entirely necessary (Hatcher & Noakes, 2010).

Practitioners knowing themselves is also important for the work. Being aware of what is going on in the room between a practitioner and a person being worked with is crucial to working reflexively. The dynamics in between are likely to be a tangle of both people's 'stuff', and it is worth pondering on this. It is also worth acknowledging this and checking out whether the stuff that is being 'picked up' is accurate or not. Demonstrating naming feelings by the practitioner can also be the beginning of emotional articulation for the person who is being worked with, underpinned by practice acknowledgement of the place of emotional literacy (Steiner, 1997).

Most importantly, it is okay to feel whatever is felt about the person and what they have done; it is totally healthy to feel anger, outrage, sadness and disgust about a situation where someone has harmed someone else so fundamentally. Usually these feelings become manageable once there is a better understanding of the perpetrator, although they may be there in the background. It is time to seek support if these feelings become pervasive or unmanageable or adversely impact on personal life. Also important is the understanding that practitioners cannot get everything 'right' and cannot take responsibility for the behaviour of others. Sometimes people are not in a position to make the necessary changes to live a safer life, and effectiveness is limited in these cases, which might mean greater exertion of external controls that are necessary to protect people from future harm.

Whatever the intervention, in our view there is a professional duty to allow a person to make some progress towards feeling heard and understood and to begin to question their own way of seeing the world. People will often give cues and clues that are worthy of further exploration or as a way of exploiting 'cognitive dissonance'. With this in mind, we find the 'motivational cycle of change' (Prochaska & DiClemente, 1982) a useful point of reference to locate the person and use appropriate strategies. There is little point in trying to push someone towards 'taking action' towards personal change when they are still thinking about whether they should be taking action and are in the 'precontemplation' stage. Working with someone requires patience and understanding that is authentic and effective.

The authors begin work with people from a place of optimism in the belief that people can go on to live safe and healthy lives in which they learn to care for themselves, and that this then extends to others. We believe wholeheartedly in the potential for people to change and to become better versions of themselves. This does not come from a place of naivety, but from fully immersing ourselves in the inner world of the perpetrator; only then can we really understand the risk that they pose and how to safely manage it.

References

Abel, G.G. (1999) 'Assessing and Treating Sex Offenders.' Paper presented at the Specialised Services Conference Presentation on Assessing and Treating Sex Offenders, August, Chicago, IL.

Abel, G.G., Gore, D.K., Holland, C.L., Camp, N., Becker, J.V. and Rathner, J. (1989) 'The measurement of the cognitive distortions of child molesters.' *Annals of Sex Research 2*, 135–153.

Agnew, R. (2013) 'When criminal coping is likely: An extension of general strain theory.' *Deviant Behavior 34*, 653–670.

Aigner, M., Eher, R., Fruehwald, S., Frottier, P., *et al.* (2000) 'Brain abnormalities and violent behavior.' *Journal of Psychology & Human Sexuality 11*, 3, 57–64.

Ajzen, I. & Fishbein, M. (1977) 'Attitude-behaviour relations: A theoretical analysis and review of empirical research.' *Psychological Bulletin 84*, 888–918.

Ajzen, I. & Fishbein, M. (1980) *Understanding Attitudes and Predicting Social Behaviour.* Englewood Cliffs, NJ: Prentice Hall.

Akademikerförbundet SSR (2018) *Ethical Values and Norms for Social Work.* Stockholm: Akademikerförbundet SSR. Available at https://akademssr.se/sites/default/files/files/ethics_in_social_work_0.pdf, accessed on 20 May 2018.

Alexandros, K.A. & Akrivos, D. (2017) *The Rise of Extreme Pornography: Legal and Criminological Perspectives on Extreme Pornography in England & Wales.* Basingstoke: Palgrave Macmillan.

Allam, J. (2001) *Community Sex Offender Groupwork Programme (C-SOGP) Theory Manual.* Birmingham: National Probation Service (West Midlands).

Alvesson, M. (2002) *Understanding Organisational Culture.* London: Sage.

Andrews, D.A. (1989) 'Recidivism is predictable and can be influenced: Using risk assessments to reduce recidivism.' *Forum of Correction Research Online 1*, 2, 11–18.

Andrews, D.A. & Bonta, J. (1994) *The Psychology of Criminal Conduct.* Cincinnati, OH: Anderson.

Andrews, D.A., Bonta, J. & Hoge, R.D. (1990) 'Classification for effective rehabilitation: Rediscovering psychology.' *Criminal Justice and Behavior 17*, 19–52.

Andrews, D.A. & Dowden, C. (2007) 'The risk-need-responsivity model of assessment and human service in prevention and corrections: Crime-prevention jurisprudence.' *Canadian Journal of Criminology and Criminal Justice 49*, 4, 439–464.

APA (American Psychiatric Association) (1980) *Diagnostic and Statistical Manual of Mental Disorders*, 3rd edition. Available at https://dsm.psychiatryonline.org/doi/pdf/10.1176/appi.books.9780521315289.dsm-iii, accessed on 18 December 2019.

APA (2013) *Diagnostic and Statistical Manual of Mental Disorders*, 5th edition (DSM-5). Available at https://Doi.org/10.1176/appi.books.9780890425596, accessed on 15 November 2019.

Attwood, F. (ed.) (2009) *Mainstreaming Sex: The Sexualisation of Western Culture.* London: J.B. Tauris.

Attwood, F. (2018) 'Women's Pornography.' In K. Harrison & C. Ogden (eds) *Pornographies 2018: Critical Positions* (pp.49–69). Chester: University of Chester Press.

Auburn, T. (2005) 'Narrative reflexivity as a repair device for discounting "cognitive" distortions in sex offender treatment.' *Discourse & Society 16*, 5, 697–718.

Auburn, T. (2010) 'Cognitive distortions as social practices: an examination of cognitive distortions in sex offender treatment from a discursive psychology perspective.' *Psychology, Crime & Law, 16*, 1–2, 103–123.

Aven, T. (2011) 'On different types of uncertainties in the context of the uncertainty principle.' *Risk Analysis 31*, 10, 1515–1525. doi:10.1111/j.1539-6924.2011.01612.x.

Babchishin, K.M., Hanson, R.K. & Hermann, C.A. (2011) 'The characteristics of online sex offenders: A meta-analysis.' *Sexual Abuse 23*, 1, 92–123. Available at https://Doi.org/10.1177/1079063210370708, accessed on 22 October 2019.

Bailey, J.M., Vasey, P.L., Diamond, L.M., Breedlove, S.M., Vilain, E. & Epprecht, M. (2016) 'Sexual orientation, controversy and science.' *Association for Psychological Science 17*, 2, 45–101. Available at www.psychologicalscience.org/publications/sexual_orientation.html, accessed on 24 June 2019.

Barbaree, H.E., Seto, M.C., Langton, C.M. & Peacock, E.J. (2001) 'Evaluating the predictive accuracy of six risk assessment instruments for adult sex offenders.' *Criminal Justice and Behavior 28*, 490–521. Available at www.researchgate.net/publication/247744837_Evaluating_the_Predictive_Accuracy_of_Six_Risk_Assessment_Instruments_for_Adult_Sex_Offenders, accessed on 30 October 2019.

Barnett, G. & Mann, R.E. (2013) 'Empathy deficits and sexual offending: A model of obstacles to empathy.' *Aggression and Violent Behavior 18*, 228–239. Available at https://psycnet.apa.org/record/2012-34038-001, accessed on 30 October 2019.

Bateman, T. (2017) *The State of Youth Justice 2017: An Overview of Trends and Developments*. Bedford: National Association for Youth Justice/Justice for Children in Trouble. Available at http://uobrep.openrepository.com/uobrep/handle/10547/622241, accessed on 20 December 2019.

Bateman, T. & Neal, H. (2014) *Beyond Youth Custody: Youth Justice Timeline*. Salford and Bedford: Beyond Youth Custody Partnership. Available at www.beyondyouthcustody.net/wp-content/uploads/youth-justice-timeline.pdf, accessed on 20 December 2019.

BBC News (1) (2018) 'Dark web paedophile Matthew Falder jailed for 32 years.' 19 February. Available at www.bbc.co.uk/news/uk-england-43114471, accessed on 19 February 2018.

BBC News (2) (2018) '"Devil incarnate" Barry Bennell sentenced to 31 years.' 19 February. Available at www.bbc.co.uk/news/uk-43118069, accessed on 19 February 2018.

BBC News (3) (2018) 'Banned Georgian sex manual reveals strange beliefs.' 13 February. Available at www.bbc.co.uk/news/uk-england-43044066, accessed on 19 February 2018.

BBC News (4) (2018) 'Equal pay: What is the extent of the problem?' 8 January. Available at www.bbc.co.uk/news/uk-42611725, accessed on 7 March 2018.

BBC News (5) (2018) 'International women's day: "Without women the world stops."' 6 March. Available at www.bbc.co.uk/news/av/world-europe-43326040/international-women-s-day-without-women-the-world-stops, accessed on 8 March 2018.

Bear, M., Connors, B.W. & Paradiso, M.A. (2016) *Neuroscience: Exploring the Brain.* 4th edition. Philadelphia, PA: Walters Kluwer.

Beck, U. (1992) *Risk Society: Towards a New Modernity.* London: Sage.

Beech, A.R. & Harkins, L. (2012) 'DSM-IV paraphilia: Descriptions, demographics and treatment intervention.' *Aggression and Violent Behavior 17*, 6, 527–539.

Beech, A.R. & Ward, T. (2004) 'The integration of etiology and risk in sexual offenders: A theoretical framework.' *Aggression and Violent Behavior 10*, 31–63.

Beech, A., Fisher, D. & Beckett, R. (1998) *STEP 3: An Evaluation of the Prison Sex Offender Treatment Programme. A Report for the Home Office by the STEP Team.* London: Home Office.

Beevor, A. (2014) *The Second World War.* London: Weidenfeld & Nicolson.

Beier, K.M., Grundmann, D., Kuhle, L.F., Scherner, G., Konrad, A. & Amelung, T. (2014) 'The German Dunkelfeld project: A pilot study to prevent child sexual abuse and the use of child abusive images.' *The Journal of Sexual Medicine 12*, 2, 529–542.

Belton, E. (2017) *Assessing the risk, protecting the child: final evaluation report.* London: NSPCC. Available at http://learning.nspcc.org.uk/research-resources/2017/assessing-the-risk-protecting-the-child-final-evaluation, accessed 9 June 2020.

Bentley, H., Burrows, A., Hafizi, M., Kumari, P., *et al.* (2017) *How Safe Are Our Children?* London: NSPCC. Available at www.nspcc.org.uk/globalassets/documents/research-reports/how-safe-children-2017-report.pdf, accessed on 16 May 2018.

Berlin, F.S. (2014) 'Pedophilia and DSM-5: The importance of clearly defining the nature of pedophilic disorder.' *Journal of the American Academy of Psychiatry and the Law 42*, 404–407.

Biollat, C., Schwab, N., Stutz, M., Pflueger, M.O., Graf, M. & Rosburg, T. (2017) 'Neuroticism as a risk factor for child abuse in victims of childhood sexual abuse.' *Child Abuse & Neglect 68*, 44–54.

Blackburn, R. (2000) 'Risk Assessment and Prediction.' In J. McGuire, T. Mason & A. O'Kane (eds) *Behaviour, Crime and Legal Processes: A Guide for Forensic Practitioners* (Chapter 9). London: Wiley.

Blastland, M. & Spiegelhalter, D. (2013) *The Norm Chronicles.* London: Profile Books.

Boucher, F. (c.1754). *Venus playing with two doves* [pastel on paper]. In B. Hughes (2019) *Venus & Aphrodite: History of a goddess.* London: Weidenfeld & Nicolson.

Boullier, M. & Blair, M. (2018) 'Adverse childhood experiences.' *Paediatrics and Child Health 28*, 3, 132–137.

Boyarin, D. & Castelli, E.A. (2001) 'Introduction. Foucault's "The History of Sexuality": The further volume, or a field left fallow for others to till.' *Journal of the History of Sexuality 10*, 3/4, 357–374.

Boyer-Kassem, T. (2017) 'Is the precautionary principle really incoherent?' *Risk Analysis 37*, 11, 2026–2034. doi:10.1111/risa.12774. Available at https://onlinelibrary-wiley-com.plymouth.idm.oclc.org/Doi/full/10.1111/risa.12774, accessed on 18 October 2019.

Bradley, H. (2012) *Gender* (2nd edn). Cambridge: Polity Press.

Braithwaite, J. (1989) 'Reintegrative Shaming.' In J. Braithwaite (ed.) *Crime, Shame and Reintegration*. Melbourne, VIC: Cambridge University Press.

Briggs, D. & Kennington, R. (2006) *Managing Men Who Sexually Abuse*. London: Jessica Kingsley Publishers.

Broadhurst, K., Hall, C., Wastell, D., White, S. & Pithouse, A. (2010) 'Risk, instrumentalism and the humane project in social work: Identifying the informal logics of risk management in children's statutory services.' *British Journal of Social Work 40*, 1046–1064.

Bronfenbrenner, U. (1979) *The Ecology of Human Development: Experiments by Nature and Design*. Cambridge, MA: Harvard University Press.

Brown, M. (2019) 'Gareth Thomas revealing HIV status will "tackle stigma": Terrence Higgins Trust say rugby legend's decision will have "massive impact".' *The Guardian*, 15 September. Available at www.theguardian.com/sport/2019/sep/15/gareth-thomas-revealing-hiv-status-will-tackle-stigma, accessed on 15 November 2019.

Brown, S. (2011) *Treating Sex Offenders: An Introduction to Sex Offender Treatment Programmes*. Abingdon: Routledge.

Brownmiller, S. (1975) *Against Our Will: Men, Women and Rape*. London: Bantam.

Bryson, V. (2016) *Feminist Political Theory*. London: Palgrave.

Burgess, A.W., Commons, M.L., Safarik, M.E., Looper, R.R. & Ross, S.N. (2007) 'Sex offenders of the elderly: Classification by motive, typology, and predictors of severity of crime.' *Aggression and Violent Behavior 12*, 582–597. Available at www.dareassociation.org/documents/BurgessEtAl2007.pdf, accessed on 30 October 2019.

Burgess, E.W. (1928) 'Factors Determining Success or Failure on Parole.' In A.A. Bruce (ed.) *The Workings of the Indeterminate Sentence Law and the Parole System in Illinois*. Springfield, IL: Illinois Committee on Indeterminate-Sentence Law and Parole.

Campbell, R. & O'Neill, M. (2006) *Sex Work Now*. Cullompton: Willan.

Carr, H. & Goosey, D. (2019) *Law for Social Workers*. 15th edition. Oxford: Oxford University Press.

Carr, J. (2012) 'The unbelievable truth about child pornography in the UK.' HuffPost. Available at www.huffingtonpost.co.uk/john-carr/child-pornography-the-unbelievable-truth-ab_b_1970969.html?guccounter=1&guce_referrer_us=aHR0cHM6Ly93d3cuYmluZy5jb20vc2VhcmNoNoP3E9Y2VvVccCtzdGF0XN0aWNzZK2ZvcisyMDE3K2NoaWxkK3Bvcm5vZ3JhcGh5KzZx cz1uJmZvcm09UUJSRSZzcD0tMSZ wcT1jZW9wK3N0YXRpc3RpY3MgRpY3R pY3Mg, accessed on 28 December 2018.

Carter, B. (2014) 'Can 10,000 hours of practice make you an expert?' BBC News, 1 March. Available at www.bbc.co.uk/news/magazine-26384712, accessed on 19 August 2019.

Casciani, D. (2017) 'Sex offender treatment in prison led to more offending.' BBC News, 30 June. Available at www.bbc.co.uk/news/uk-40460637, accessed on 10 February 2020.

Chapman, T. & Hough, M. (1998) *Evidence-Based Practice: A Guide to Effective Practice. Her Majesty's Inspectorate of Probation*. Available at https://www.academia.edu/25849973/A_Guide_to_Effective_Practice, accessed on 5 June 2020.

Children's Hearings Scotland (2019) *Children's Hearings Scotland*. Available at http://www.chscotland.gov.uk/about-chs, accessed on 11 June 2020.

Clarke, J. (2011) 'Working with sex offenders: Best practice in enhancing practitioner resilience.' *Journal of Sexual Aggression 17*, 3, 335–355.

Circles South West (n.d.) 'Sara Radford.' Available at https://circles-southwest.org.uk/staffandtrust/sara-radford, accessed on 12 June 2020.

Clements, H., Dawson, D. & Das Nair, R. (2014) 'Female-perpetrated sexual abuse: A review of victim and professional perspectives.' *Journal of Sexual Aggression 20*, 2, 197–215.

Cobley, C. (2005) *Sex Offenders: Law, Policy and Practice*. Bristol: Jordan Publishing.

Cockbain, E., Brayley, H. & Sullivan, J. (2013) 'Towards a common framework for assessing the activity and associations of groups who sexually abuse children.' *Journal of Sexual Aggression 20*, 2, 156–171. doi:10.1080/13552600.2013.791730.

Coetzee, L. (2019) 'Victim empathy in young sex offenders in the emergent adulthood developmental phase.' *Journal of Sexual Aggression*, 1–12. doi:10.1080/13552600.2019.1618931.

Comfort, A. (1972) *The Joy of Sex: A Gourmet Guide*. London: Crown Publishers.

Cooke, L. (2019) 'The power of deceit.' BBC Sounds, broadcast 6 August. Available at www.bbc.co.uk/sounds/play/m0007bck, accessed on 11 August 2019.

Copelon, R. (1995) 'Gendered War Crimes: Reconceptualising Rape in Time of War.' In J.S. Peters & A. Wolper (eds) *Women's Right, Human Rights: International Feminist Perspectives*. London: Routledge.

Cortoni, F., Hanson, R.K. & Coache, M.E. (2010) 'The recidivism rates of female sexual offenders are low: A meta-analysis.' *Sexual Abuse 22*, 387–401.

Costopoulos, J.S. & Juni, S. (2018) 'Psychoanalytic understanding of the origins of sexual violence.' *Journal of Forensic Psychology Research and Practice 18*, 1, 57–76. doi:10.1080/24732850.2018.1430936.

Cotterell, S. (2017) *Critical Thinking Skills: Effective Analysis, Argument and Reflection*. London: Palgrave Macmillan.

CPS (Crown Prosecution Service) (n.d.) *Domestic Abuse*. Available at http://cps.gov.uk/publication/domestic-abuse, accessed on 14 October 2019.

CPS (1) (2019) 'Rape and Sexual Offences – Chapter 2: Sexual Offences Act 2003 – Principal Offences, and Sexual Offences Act 1956 – Most commonly charged offences', 12 April. Available at www.cps.gov.uk/legal-guidance/rape-and-sexual-offences-chapter-2-sexual-offences-act-2003-principal-offences-and, accessed on 4 January 2020.

CPS (2) (2019) 'Rape and Sexual Offences – Chapter 3: Consent.' Available at www.cps.gov.uk/legal-guidance/rape-and-sexual-offences-chapter-3-consent, accessed on 4 January 2020.

CPS (3) (2019) 'CPS takes action to tackle childlike sex dolls.' Available at www.cps.gov.uk/cps/news/cps-takes-action-tackle-childlike-sex-dolls, accessed on 13 October 2019.

CPS (4) (2019) *Obscene Publications: Evidential Consideration*. Available at www.cps.gov.uk/legal-guidance/obscene-publications, accessed on 3 February 2020.

CQC (Care Quality Commission) (2011) *CQC report on Winterbourne View confirms its owners failed to protect people from abuse*. Newcastle upon Tyne: CQC. Available at https://www.cqc.org.uk/news/releases/cqc-report-winterbourne-view-confirms-its-owners-failed-protect-people-abuse, accessed 9 June 2020.

Craig, J.M., Baglivio, M.T., Wolff, K.T., Piquero, A.R. & Epps, N. (2016) 'Do social bonds buffer the impact of adverse childhood experiences on reoffending?' *Youth Violence and Juvenile Justice 15*, 1, 3–20. doi.org/10.1177%2F1541204016630033.

Crawford, D.A. & Allen, J.V. (1979) 'A Social Skills Training Programme with Sex Offenders.' In M. Cook & G. Wilson (eds) *Love and Attraction*. Oxford: Pergamon Press.

Crawford, K. (2013) 'The Good, the Bad and the Textual: Approaches to the Study of the Body and Sexuality, 1500–1750.' In S. Toulalan & K. Fisher (eds) *The Routledge History of Sex and the Body: 1500 to the Present* (Chapter 1). Abingdon: Routledge.

Craig, L. & Beech, A. (2012) 'Psychometric Assessment of Sexual Deviance.' In *Assessment and Treatment of Sex Offenders: A Handbook* (pp.89–107). doi:10.1002/9780470714362.ch6.

Criminal Justice Act 2003, c.44. London: HMSO.

Criminal Justice and Immigration Act 2008. Available at www.legislation.gov.uk/ukpga/2008/4/contents, accessed on 26 December 2018.

Da Vinci, L. (circa 1492) *Studies of the Sexual Act and Male Sexual Organ*. London: Royal Library.

Dabhoiwala, F. (2013) *The Origins of Sex: A History of the First Sexual Revolution*. London: Penguin.

Dane, E., Rockman, K.W. & Pratt, M.G. (2012) 'When should I trust my gut? Linking domain expertise to intuitive decision-making effectiveness.' *Organizational Behavior and Human Decision Processes 119*, 2, 187–194. Available at https://Doi.org/10.1016/j.obhdp.2012.07.009, accessed on 28 November 2019.

Daniel, B. (2010) 'Concepts of adversity, risk, vulnerability and resilience: A discussion in the context of the "child protection system".' *Social Policy & Society 9*, 2, 231–241. doi:1017/S1474746409990364.

Daniel, C.J. (1987) 'Shame Aversion Therapy and Social Skills Training in Indecent Exposure.' In B.J. McGurk, D.M. Thornton & M. Williams (eds) *Applying Psychology to Imprisonment: Theory and Practice*. London: HMSO.

Darling, A., Hackett, S. & Jamie, K. (2018) 'Female sex offenders who abuse children whilst working in organisational settings: Offending, conviction and sentencing.' *Journal of Sexual Aggression 24*, 2, 195–213.

Davies, G., Bull, R. & Milne, R. (2016) 'Analyzing and Improving the Testimony of Vulnerable Witnesses Interviewed under the "Achieving Best Evidence" Protocol.' In P. Radcliffe, G. Gudjonsson, A. Heaton-Armstrong & D. Wolchover (eds) *Witness Testimony in Sexual Cases: Evidential, Investigative and Scientific Perspectives*. Oxford: Oxford University Press.

Dawkins, R. (1976) *The Selfish Gene*. Oxford: Oxford University Press.

Deal, T. & Kennedy, A. (1982) *Corporate Cultures*. Reading, MA: Addison Wesley.

Decety, J. & Ickes, W. (eds) (2009) *The Social Neuroscience of Empathy*. Cambridge, MA: MIT Press.

Decety, J. & Lamm, C. (2009) 'Empathy versus Personal Distress: Recent Evidence from Social Neuroscience.' In J. Decety & W. Ickes (eds) *The Social Neuroscience of Empathy*. Cambridge, MA: MIT Press.

Deckers, L. (2018) *Motivation: Biological, Psychological, and Environmental*. London: Routledge.

DeLisi, M. & Beauregard, E. (2017) 'Adverse childhood experiences and criminal extremity: New evidence for sexual homicide.' *Journal of Forensic Sciences 63*, 2, 484–489. doi.org/10.1111/1556-4029.13584.

Denov, M.S. (2001) 'A culture of denial: Exploring professional perspectives on female sex offending.' *Canadian Journal of Criminology 43*, 3, 303–329.

De Orio, S. (2017) 'The invention of bad gay sex: Texas and the creation of a criminal underclass of gay people.' *Journal of the History of Sexuality 26*, 1, 53–87.

DfE (Department for Education) (2013) *Working Together to Safeguard Children: A Guide to Inter-Agency Working to Safeguard and Promote the Welfare of Children*. London: The Stationery Office.

DfE (2017) *Child Sexual Exploitation: Definition and a Guide for Practitioners, Local Leaders and Decision-Makers Working to Protect Children from Child Sexual Exploitation*. Available at https://assets.publishing.service.gov.uk/government/uploads/system/uploads/attachment_data/file/591903/CSE_Guidance_Core_Document_13.02.2017.pdf, accessed on 9 October 2019.

DH (2017) *Strengths-Based Social Work Practice with Adults: Roundtable Report*. London: DH. Available at https://assets.publishing.service.gov.uk/government/uploads/system/uploads/attachment_data/file/652773/Strengths-based_social_work_practice_with_adults.pdf, accessed on 17 March 2019.

Dix, H., Hollinrake, S. & Meade, J. (eds) (2019) *Relationship-Based Social Work with Adults*. Plymouth: Critical Publishing.

Donat, P.L.N. & D'Emilio, J. (1997) 'A Feminist Redefinition of Rape and Sexual Assault: Historical Foundations and Change.' In J. Clay-Warner & M.E. Odem (eds) *Confronting Rape and Sexual Assault*. New York: Rowman & Littlefield.

Doran, J.M. (2016) 'The working alliance: Where have we been, where are we going?' *Psychotherapy Research 26*, 2, 146–163. doi:10.1080/10503307.2014.954153.

Douglas, K. & Hart, S.D. (1996) 'Major Mental Disorder and Violent Behavior: A Meta-Analysis of Study Characteristics and Substantive Factors Influencing Effect Size.' Paper presented at the Biennial Meeting of the American Psychology-Law Society (APA Div. 41), Hilton Head, South Carolina.

Douglas, M. (1992) *Risk and Blame: Essays in Cultural Theory*. London: Routledge.

Drury, A.J., Elbert, M.J. & DeLisi, M. (2019) 'Childhood sexual abuse is significantly associated with subsequent sexual offending: New evidence among federal correctional clients.' *Child Abuse & Neglect*, 1–10. doi.org/10.1016/j.chiabu.2019.104035.

Duggan, C. & Dennis, J. (2014) 'The place of evidence in the treatment of sex offenders.' *Criminal Behaviour and Mental Health 24*, 3, 153–164.

Duménil, G. & Lévy, D. (2005) 'The Neoliberal (Counter-)Revolution.' In A. Saad-Filho & D. Johnston (eds) *Neoliberalism: A Critical Reader* (Chapter 1). London: Pluto.

Durlauf, S., Fu, C. & Navarro, S. (2012) 'Assumptions matter: Model uncertainty and the deterrent effect of capital punishment.' *The American Economic Review 102*, 3, 487–492. Available at www.jstor.org.plymouth.idm.oclc.org/stable/23245580, accessed on 31 October 2019.

Dworkin, A. (1983) *Right-Wing Women: The Politics of Domesticated Females*. London: Women's Press.

Egan, G. (2007) *The Skilled Helper: A Problem-Management and Opportunity-Development Approach to Helping.* Belmont, CA: Brooks Cole.

Eher, R., Matthes, A., Schilling, F., Haubner-Maclean, T. & Rettenberger, M. (2012) 'Dynamic risk assessment in sexual offenders using STABLE-2000 and the STABLE-2007: An investigation of predictive and incremental validity.' *Sexual Abuse: A Journal of Research and Treatment 24*, 1, 5–28.

Eldridge, H.J. & Wyre, R. (1998) 'The Lucy Faithfull Foundation's Residential Program for Sexual Offenders.' In W.L. Marshall, S.M. Hudson, T. Ward & Y.M. Fernandez (eds) *Sourcebook of Treatment Programs for Sexual Offenders.* New York: Plenum.

Elliott, R., Bohart, A.C., Watson, J.C. & Greenberg, L.S. (2011) 'Empathy.' *Psychotherapy 48*, 1, 43–49. doi:10.1037/a0022187.

Endrass, J. & Rosseger, A. (2010) 'Child pornography as a risk factor for hands on sex offending.' *European Psychiatry 25*, 1, 676.

Ericsson, K.A., Krampe, R.T. & Tesch-Romer, C. (1993) 'The role of deliberate practice in the acquisition of expert performance.' *Psychological Review 100*, 3, 363–406.

Erooga, M. (2008) 'A human rights-based approach to sex offender management: The key to effective public protection?' *Journal of Sexual Aggression 14*, 3, 171–183. doi:10.1080/13552600802413247.

Family Rights Group (2018) *Care Crisis Review – Options for Change.* London: Nuffield Foundation. Available at www.frg.org.uk/images/Care_Crisis/CCR-FINAL.pdf, accessed on 4 January 2020.

Farrington, D.P. (2007) 'Advancing knowledge about desistance.' *Journal of Contemporary Criminal Justice 23*, 125. Available at https://doi.org/10.1177/1043986206298954, accessed on 4 June 2020.

Faux, M. (2001) *Thames Valley Management Manual.* London: National Probation Service.

Festinger, L. (1957) *A Theory of Cognitive Dissonance.* Stanford, CA: Stanford University Press.

Figley, C.R. (1995) *Compassion Fatigue: Coping with Secondary Traumatic Stress Disorder in Those Who Treat the Traumatized.* Levittown, PA: Brunner/Mazel.

Finkelhor, D. (1984) *Child Sexual Abuse: New Theory and Research.* New York: Free Press.

Finkelhor, D. (1986) *A Sourcebook on Child Sexual Abuse.* Beverly Hills, CA: Sage.

Forsberg, L. & Douglas, T. (2017) 'Anti-libidinal interventions in sex offenders: Medical or correctional?' *Medical Law Review 24*, 4, 453–473. Available at https://Doi-org.plymouth.idm.oclc.org/10.1093/medlaw/fww003, accessed on 28 November 2019.

Foucault, M. (1976) *The Will to Knowledge.* Translated by R. Hurley. London: Penguin.

Franke, I. & Graf, M. (2016) 'Kinderpornografie.' *Forensische Psychiatrie, Psychologie, Kriminologie 10*, 2, 87.

Fredrickson, B.L. (2001) 'The role of positive emotions in positive psychology: The broaden-and-build theory of positive emotions.' *American Psychologist 56*, 3, 218–226. doi:10.1037/0003-066X.56.3.218.

Friendship, C. & Beech, A.R. (2005) 'Reconviction of sexual offenders in England and Wales: An overview of research.' *Journal of Sexual Aggression 11*, 1, 1–15.

Furedi, F. (1997) *Culture of Fear: Risk-Taking and the Morality of Low Expectation*. London: Cassell.

Furlong, M.W. (2008) 'The multiple relationships between the discipline of social work and the contributions of Michael White.' *Australian Social Work 61*, 4, 403–420. doi:10.1080/03124070802428530.

Gannon, T.A. & Rose, M.R. (2008) 'Female child sex offenders: Towards integrating theory and practice.' *Aggression and Violent Behavior 13*, 6, 442–461.

Gardner, H. (1993) *Multiple Intelligences: The Theory in Practice*. New York: Basic Books.

Garland, D. (2001) *The Culture of Control: Crime and Social Order in Contemporary Society*. Chicago, IL: University of Chicago Press.

Garrett, T. (2017) 'Working with Sexual Offenders with Mental Health Issues.' In D.T. Wilcox, M.L. Donathy, R. Gray & C. Baim (eds) *Working with Sex Offenders: A Guide for Practitioners* (Chapter 13). London: Routledge.

George, M. (2015) 'The harmless psychopath: Legal debates promoting the decriminalization of sodomy in the United States.' *Journal of History of Sexuality 24*, 2, 225–261.

Gerwinn, H., Weiß, S., Tenbergen, G., Amelung, T., *et al.* (2018) 'Clinical characteristics associated with paedophilia and child sex offending – Differentiating sexual preference from offence status.' *European Psychiatry 51*, 74–85. Available at http://dx.Doi.org/10.1016/j.eurpsy.2018.02.002, accessed on 28 November 2019.

Giddens, A. (1990) *The Consequences of Modernity*. Cambridge: Polity Press.

Gill, R. (2012) 'The sexualisation of culture?' *Social and Personality Compass 6/7*, 483–498.

Gillespie, A. & Weare, S. (2019) *The English Legal System*. Oxford: Oxford University Press.

Göbbels, S., Ward, T. & Willis, G.M. (2012) 'An integrative theory of desistance from sex offending.' *Aggression and Violent Behavior 17*, 453–462.

Gottfredson, S.D. & Gottfredson, D.M. (1994) 'Behavioral prediction and the problem of incapacitation.' *Criminology 32*, 441–475.

Gray, D. & Watt, P. (2013) *Giving Victims a Voice: Joint Report into Sexual Allegations Made against Jimmy Savile*. London: Metropolitan Police/NSPCC. Available at www.nspcc.org.uk/globalassets/documents/research-reports/yewtree-report-giving-victims-voice-jimmy-savile.pdf, accessed on 15 August 2019.

Greenall, P.V. & Wright, M. (2019) 'Stranger sexual homicide: An exploratory behavioural analysis of offender crime scene actions.' *Journal of Sexual Aggression*. doi:10.1080/13552600.2019.1606948. Available at www.tandfonline.com/doi/abs/10.1080/13552600.2019.1606948, accessed on 31 October 2019.

Greetham, B. (2016) *Smart Thinking: How to Think Conceptually, Design Solutions, and Make Decisions*. London: Palgrave Macmillan.

Grove, W.M. & Meehl, P.E. (1996) 'Comparative efficiency of informal (subjective, impressionistic) and formal (mechanical, algorithmic) prediction procedures: The clinical-statistical controversy.' *Psychology, Public Policy, and Law 2*, 2, 293–323.

Grubin, D. (1994) 'Sexual murder.' *British Journal of Psychiatry 165*, 624–629.

Grubin, D. (2008) 'The case for polygraph testing of sex offenders.' *Legal and Criminal Psychology 13*, 177–189.

Grubin, D. (2010) 'A trial of voluntary polygraphy testing in 10 English probation areas.' *Sexual Abuse: A Journal of Research and Treatment 22*, 266–278. doi:10.1177/1079063210369012.

Grubin, D. & Beech, A.R. (2010) 'Chemical castration for sex offenders.' *British Medical Journal 340*. doi:10.1136/bmj.c74.

Grubin, D. & Mason, D. (2007) 'Medical Models and Interventions in Sexual Deviance.' In D.R. Laws & W.T. O'Donohue (eds) *Sexual Deviance: Theory, Assessment and Treatment*. London: Guilford Press.

Gunst, E. (2012) 'Experiential psychotherapy with sex offenders: Experiencing as a way to change, to live more fulfilling lives, to desist from offending.' *Person-Centered & Experiential Psychotherapies 11*, 321–334. doi:10.1080/14779757.2012.740324.

Hackett, S. (2000) 'Sexual aggression, diversity and the challenge of anti-oppressive practice.' *Journal of Sexual Aggression 5*, 1, 4–20.

Hacking, I. (1975) *The Emergence of Probability: A Philosophical Study of the Early Ideas about Probability, Induction and Statistical Inference*. Cambridge: Cambridge University Press.

Hall, G.C.N. & Hirschman, R. (1991) 'Toward a theory of sexual aggression: A quadripartite model.' *Journal of Consulting and Clinical Psychology 59*, 662–669.

Hall, G.C.N. & Hirschman, R. (1992) 'Sexual aggression against children: A conceptual perspective of etiology.' *Criminal Justice and Behavior 19*, 1, 8–23. doi:10.1177/0093854892019001003.

Hammer, E.F. & Glueck, B.B. (1957) 'Psychodynamic patterns in sex offenders: A four-factor theory.' *Psychiatric Quarterly 31*, 1–4, 325–345.

Hanson, R.K. & Bussière, M.T. (1996) *Predictors of Sexual Offender Recidivism: A Meta-Analysis. User Report 96-04*. Ottawa, ON: Department of the Solicitor General of Canada. Available at www.publicsafety.gc.ca/cnt/rsrcs/pblctns/prdctrs-sxl-ffnd/index-en.aspx, accessed on 31 October 2018.

Hanson, R.K. & Bussière, M.T. (1998) 'Predicting relapse: A meta-analysis of sexual offender recidivism studies.' *Journal of Consulting and Clinical Psychology 66*, 2, 348–362.

Hanson, R.K. & Harris, A.J.R. (2000a) *Sex Offender Needs Assessment Rating (SONAR)*. Ottawa, ON: Department of the Solicitor General of Canada.

Hanson, R.K. & Harris, A.J.R. (2000b) 'Where should we intervene? Dynamic predictors of sexual offence recidivism.' *Criminal Justice and Behavior 27*, 6–35.

Hanson, R.K., Harris, A.J.R., Scott, T.-L. & Helmus, L. (2007) *Assessing the Risk of Sexual Offenders on Community Supervision: The Dynamic Supervision Project*. Ottawa: Public Safety Canada. Available at www.publicsafety.gc.ca/cnt/rsrcs/pblctns/ssssng-rsk-sxl-ffndrs/index-eng.aspx, accessed on 20 June 2018.

Hare, R.D. (1991) *The Hare Psychopathy Checklist – Revised*. Toronto, ON: Multi-Health Systems.

Hare, R.D. (2003) *The Hare Psychopathy Checklist – Revised*. 2nd edition. Toronto, ON: Multi-Health Systems.

Hare, R.D. (2016) 'Psychopathy, the PCL-R, and criminal justice: Some new findings and current issues.' *Canadian Psychology 57*, 1, 21–34. doi:10.1037/cap0000041.

Harris, A.J.R. & Hanson, R.K. (2010) 'Clinical, actuarial, and dynamic risk assessment of sexual offenders: Why do things keep changing?' *Journal of Sexual Aggression 16*, 3, 296–310. doi.org/10.1080/13552600.2010.494772.

Harrison, L.E., Clayton-Smith, J. & Bailey, S. (2001) 'Exploring the complex relationship between adolescent sexual offending and sex chromosome abnormality.' *Psychiatric Genetics 11*, 1, 5–10.

Hart, S.D., Laws, R., Kropp, P.R. & Klaver, J. (2003) 'The risk for sexual violence protocol (RSVP): Structured professional guidelines for assessing risk of sexual violence.' Burnaby: Simon Fraser University.

Hart, S.D., Laws, R., Kropp, P.R. & Klaver, J. (2003) 'The risk for sexual violence protocol (RSVP): Structured professional guidelines for assessing risk of sexual violence.' In Watt, K.A. (ed.) *Mental Health, Law & Policy Institute/Pacific Psychological Assessment Corporation/The British Columbia Institute Against Family Violence*. Burnaby: Simon Fraser University.

Hatcher, R. & Noakes, S. (2010) 'Working with sex offenders: The impact on Australian treatment providers.' *Psychology, Crime & Law 16*, 1–2, 145–167.

Heath, D. (2010) *Purifying Empire: Obscenity and the Politics of Moral Regulation in Britain, India and Australia*. Cambridge: Cambridge University Press.

Heffernan, R. & Ward, T. (2017) 'A comprehensive theory of dynamic risk and protective factors' *Aggression and Violent Behavior, 37*, pp.129–141. Available at http://dx.doi.org/10.1016/j.avb.2017.10.003, accessed on 9 June 2020.

Henggeler, S.W., Schoenwald, S.K., Borduin, C.M., Rowland, M.D. & Cunningham, P.B. (2009) *Multisystemic Therapy for Antisocial Behavior in Children and Adolescents*. 2nd edition. New York: Guilford Press.

Herman, J.L. (1990) 'Sex Offenders: A Feminist Perspective.' In W.L. Marshall, D.R. Laws & H.E. Barbaree (eds) *Handbook of Sexual Assault*. New York: Springer.

HM Prison & Probation Service (2012) *Multi-Agency Public Protection Arrangements (MAPPA)*, v.4.5. London: Ministry of Justice. Available at www.gov.uk/government/publications/multi-agency-public-protection-arrangements-mappa--2, accessed on 3 January 2020.

Hollinrake, S. (2019) 'Theoretical Perspectives for Relationship-Based Practice with Adults.' In H. Dix, S. Hollinrake & J. Meade (eds) *Relationship-Based Social Work with Adults*. Plymouth: Critical Publishing.

Holmes, M. (2007) *What is Gender? Sociological Approaches*. London: Sage.

Holmes, R.M. (1998) 'Stalking in America: Types and Methods of Criminal Stalkers.' In R.M. Holmes & S.T. Holmes (eds) *Contemporary Perspectives on Serial Murder*. Thousand Oaks, CA: Sage.

Holt, K. & Kelly, N. (2019) 'Care in crisis – is there a solution? Reflections on the care crisis review 2018.' *Child & Family Social Work*, 1–7. doi:rg.plymouth.idm. oclc.org/10.1111/cfs.12644.

Home Office (1) (1998) *Effective Practice Initiative: A National Implementation Plan for the Supervision of Offenders*. Probation Circular 35/1998. London: Home Office.

Home Office (2) (1998) *Reducing Offending: An Assessment of Research Evidence on Ways of Dealing with Offending Behaviour*. Home Office Research Study No. 187. London: Home Office.

Home Office (2012) *Sexual Offences Act 2003 (Notification Requirements) (England and Wales) Regulations 2012*. Available at www.gov.uk/government/publications/sexual-offences-act-2003-notification-requirements-england-and-wales-regulations-2012, accessed on 24 September 2019.

Home Office (2016) *Report of the Inter-Departmental Ministerial Group on Modern Slavery 2016*. London: Home Office. Available at www.gov.uk/government/publications/report-of-the-inter-departmental-ministerial-group-on-modern-slavery-2016, accessed on 13 March 2019.

Hood, R. (2016) 'Assessment for Social Work Practice.' In K. Davies & R. Jones (eds) *Skills for Social Work Practice* (Chapter 5). London: Sage.

Hood, R. (2018) *Complexity in Social Work*. London: Sage.

Horvath, A.G. (2018) 'Research on the alliance: Knowledge in search of a theory.' *Psychotherapy Research 28*, 4, 499–516. doi:10.1080/10503307.2017.1373204.

House of Commons Library (2019) *Sentences of Imprisonment for Public Protection*. 6 June. Available at https://researchbriefings.parliament.uk/ResearchBriefing/Summary/SN06086, accessed on 4 January 2020.

Howard, M. (1993) 'Prison works.' Available at www.michaelhoward.org, accessed on 6 February 2020.

Howells, A. (2019) 'The IDEAS Model.' In H. Dix, S. Hollinrake & J. Meade (eds) *Relationship-Based Social Work with Adults*. Plymouth: Critical Publishing.

Howells, K. (1984) 'Coercive Sexual Behaviour.' In K. Howells (ed.) *The Psychology of Sexual Diversity*. Oxford: Blackwell.

Hucker, S.J. & Bain, J. (1990) 'Androgenic Hormones and Sexual Assault.' In W.L. Marshall, D.R. Laws & H.E. Barbaree (eds) *Handbook of Sexual Assault: Issues, Theories and Treatment of the Offender* (pp.93–102). New York: Plenum.

Hughes, B. (2019) *Venus and Aphrodite: History of a Goddess*. London: Weidenfeld & Nicolson.

Human Rights Act 1998, c.42. Available at www.legislation.gov.uk/ukpga/1998/42/contents, accessed on 26 September 2018.

Hunt, L. (ed.) (1996) *The Invention of Pornography*. Cambridge, MA: MIT Press.

Hutton, L. & Whyte, B. (2006) 'Children and young people with harmful sexual behaviours: First analysis of data from a Scottish sample.' *Journal of Sexual Aggression 12*, 2, 115–125.

IDAS (2018) *Myths about Rape*. Available at www.idas.org.uk/our-services/sexual-violence/myths-about-rape, accessed on 5 November 2018.

Illich, I. (1983) *Gender*. London: Marion Boyars.

Ingram, M. (2017) *Carnal Knowledge: Regulating Sex in England, 1470–1600*. Cambridge: Cambridge University Press.

International Women's Day (2018) *Press for Progress*. Available at www.internationalwomensday.com, accessed on 8 March 2018.

Itzin, C. (ed.) (2000) *Home Truths about Child Sexual Abuse: Influencing Policy and Practice. A Reader*. London: Routledge.

Iversen, M.H., Kilvik, A. & Malmedal, W. (2015a) 'Sexual abuse of older residents in nursing homes: A focus group interview of nursing home staff.' *Nursing Research and Practice 2015*. Available at www.ncbi.nlm.nih.gov/pmc/articles/PMC4442408, accessed on 9 August 2019.

Iversen, M.H., Kilvik, A. & Malmedal, W. (2015b) 'Sexual abuse of older nursing home residents: A literature review.' *Nursing Research and Practice 2015*. Available at www.hindawi.com/journals/nrp/2015/902515, accessed on 9 August 2019.

James, K. (2011) 'Purity and Pollution: Sex as Moral Discourse.' In S. Seidman, N. Fischer & C. Meeks (eds) *Introducing the New Sexuality Studies*. 2nd edition. Abingdon: Routledge.

Jenkins, H. (2004) 'Foreword: So You Want to Teach Pornography?' In P.C. Gibson (ed.) *More Dirty Looks: Gender, Pornography and Power*. London: British Film Institute.

Josselson, R. & Harway, M. (2012) 'The Challenges of Multiple Identity.' In R. Josselson & M. Harway (eds) *Navigating Multiple Identities: Race, Gender, Culture, Nationality, and Roles* (Chapter 1). Oxford: Oxford Scholarship Online. doi:10.1093/ acprof:oso/9780199732074.003.0001.

Kadambi, M.A. & Truscott, D. (2003) 'Vicarious trauma and burnout among therapists working with sex offenders.' *Traumatology 9*, 4, 216–230. doi:10.1177/153476560300900404.

Kadambi, M.A. & Truscott, D. (2004) 'Vicarious trauma among therapists working with sexual violence, cancer, and general practice.' *Canadian Journal of Counselling 38*, 4, 260–276.

Kafka, M.P. (1997) 'A monoamine hypothesis for the pathophysiology of paraphilic disorders.' *Annals of the New York Academy of Sciences 989*, 1, 86–94. doi:10.1111/j.1749-6632.2003.tb07295.x.

Kahneman, D. (2011) *Thinking, Fast and Slow: The Quick Intuitive Assessment Versus the Slower Rational/Logical Assessment*. London: Allen Lane.

Kahneman, D. & Tversky, A. (1982) 'The psychology of preferences.' *Scientific American 246*, 1, 160–173.

Kandola, S.S. & Egan, V. (2014) 'Individual differences underlying attitudes to the death penalty.' *Personality and Individual Differences 66*, 48–53. Available at http://dx.Doi.org/10.1016/j.paid.2014.03.005, accessed on 31 October 2019.

Keenan, M. (2012) *Child Sexual Abuse and the Catholic Church*. Oxford: Oxford University Press.

Kemshall, H. (2010) 'Risk rationalities in contemporary social work policy and practice.' *British Journal of Social Work 40*, 1247–1262.

Kendrick, D.T. (2006) 'A Dynamical Evolutionary View of Love.' In R.J. Sternberg & K. Weis, *The New Psychology of Love*. New Haven, CT: Yale University Press.

Kennington, R. (1994) 'Northumbria's sex offender team.' *Probation Journal 2*, 81–85.

Keynes, J.M. (1921 [1973]) *The Collected Writings of John Maynard Keynes, Volume VIII: A Treatise on Probability*. 2nd edition. London: Macmillan.

Kilpatrick, D.G., Veronen, J.L. & Best, C.L. (1985) 'Factors Predicting Psychological Distress among Rape Victims.' In C.R. Fidgley (ed.) *Trauma and its Wake* (Chapter 7). New York: Brunner/Mazel Press.

Kinsey, A.C., Pomeroy, W.B. & Martin, C.E. (1948) *Sexual Behavior in the Human Male*. Philadelphia, PA: W.B. Saunders.

Kinsey, A.C., Pomeroy, W.B., Martin, C.E. & Gebhard, P. (1953) *Sexual Behavior in the Human Female*. Philadelphia, PA: W.B. Saunders.

Kjellgren, C. (2019) 'Perspectives of young adult males who displayed harmful sexual behaviour during adolescence on motive and treatment.' *Journal of Sexual Aggression 25*, 2, 116–130. doi:10.1080/13552600.2018.1563647.

Klebin, H., Chesin, M.S., Jeglic, E.L. & Mercado, C.C. (2012) 'An exploration of crossover sexual offending.' *Sexual Abuse 5*, 5, 427–443. Available at https:// Doi.org/10.1177/1079063212464397, accessed on 28 November 2019.

Kraus, S.W., Voon, V., Kor, A. & Potenza, M.N. (2016) 'Searching for clarity in muddy water: Future considerations for classifying compulsive sexual behavior as an addiction.' *Addiction 111*, 12, 2113–2114.

Krebs, P., Norcross, J.C., Nicholson, J. & Prochaska, J. (2019) 'Stages of Change.' In J.C. Norcross (ed.) *Psychotherapy Relationships that Work: Evidence-Based Responsiveness*. New York: Oxford University Press. Available at www.researchgate.net/publication/333500063_Stages_of_Change, accessed on 18 December 2019.

Kremsdorf, R.B., Holmen, M.L. & Laws, D.R. (1980) 'Orgasmic reconditioning without deviant imagery: A case report with a pedophile.' *Behaviour Research and Therapy 18*, 3, 203–207. doi:10.1016/0005-7967(80)90037-6.

Krug, E.G., Dahlberg, L.L., Mercy, J.A., Zwi, A.B. & Lozano, R. (eds) (2002) *World Report on Violence and Health*. Geneva: World Health Organization. Available at https://apps.who.int/iris/bitstream/handle/10665/42495/9241545615_eng.pdf;jsessionid=182DAA6CEF8A4DA2255CFAB7276F6959?sequence=1, accessed on 31 October 2019.

Lambert, B. (2018) *A Student's Guide to Bayesian Statistics*. London: Sage.

Lang, B., Damousi, J. & Lewis, A. (2017) *A History of the Case Study: Sexology, Psychoanalysis, Literature*. Manchester: Manchester University Press.

Laqueur, T. (1990) *Making Sex. Body and Gender: From Greeks to Freud*. Boston, MA: Harvard University Press.

Lash, S. & Wynne, B. (1992) 'Introduction.' In U. Beck, *Risk Society: Towards a New Modernity* (pp.1–6). Translated by M. Ritter. London: Sage.

Laws, D.R. (1965) 'Verbal satiation: Notes on procedure, with speculations on its mechanism of effect.' *Sexual Abuse: A Journal of Research and Treatment 7*, 155–166.

Laws, D.R. & Marshall, W.L. (1991) 'Masturbatory reconditioning with sexual deviates: An evaluative review.' *Advances in Behaviour Research and Therapy 13*, 1, 13–25.

Laws, R. & Ward, T. (2011) *Desistance from Sex Offending: Alternatives to Throwing away the Key*. New York: Guilford Press.

Laws, R., Hudson, S.M. & Ward, T. (2000) 'The Original Model of Relapse Prevention with Sex Offenders: Promises Unfulfilled.' In R. Laws, S.M. Hudson & T. Ward (eds) *Remaking Relapse Prevention with Sex Offenders: A Source Book*. London: Sage.

Laycock, G. (1979) 'Behaviour modification in prisons.' *British Journal of Criminology 19*, 400–415.

Levenson, J.S. & Morin, J.W. (2001) *Connections Workbook*. London: Sage.

LGA (Local Government Association) (2018) 'LGA: Biggest increase in children on child protection plans in four years.' News, 25 October. Available at www.local.gov.uk/about/news/lga-biggest-increase-children-child-protection-plans-four-years, accessed on 4 January 2020.

Liberty (n.d.) *Human Rights Law: Truth and Illusion*. Available at www.libertyhumanrights.org.uk/human-rights-law-truth-and-illusion, accessed on 23 September 2019.

Lindsay, W.R., Ward, T., Morgan, T. & Wilson, I. (2007) 'Self-regulation of sex offending, future pathways and the Good Lives Model: Applications and problems.' *Journal of Sexual Aggression 13*, 1, 37–50. doi:10.1080/13552600701365613.

Lobert, A. (2017) *Fallen: Out of the Sex Industry and into the Arms of the Savior*. Nashville, TN: Worthy.

Loudermilk, E., Loudermilk, K., Obenauer, J. & Quinn, M. (2018) 'Impact of adverse childhood experiences (ACEs) on adult alcohol consumption behaviors.' *Child Abuse & Neglect*, 368–374. doi.org/10.1016/j.chiabu.2018.08.006.

Lloyd, J. (2019) 'Response and interventions into harmful sexual behaviour in schools.' *Child Abuse & Neglect 94*, 104037. doi:10.1016/j.chiabu.2019.104037.

Luo, L. (2016) *Principles of Neurobiology*. London: Garland Science.

MacCulloch, M.J., Snowden, P.R., Wood, P.J. & Mills, H.E. (1983) 'Sadistic fantasy, sadistic behavior and offending.' *British Journal of Psychiatry 143*, 1–20. doi:10.1192/bjp.143.1.20.

Macdonald, G. & Macdonald, K. (2010) 'Safeguarding: A case for intelligent risk management.' *British Journal of Social Work 40*, 1174–1191.

MacKinnon, C.A. (1989) 'Sexuality, pornography, and method: Pleasure under patriarchy.' *Ethics 99*, 2, 314–346. Available at https://Doi.org/10.1086/293068, accessed on 28 November 2019.

Macneil, C.A., Hasty, M.K., Conus, P. & Berk, M. (2012) 'Is diagnosis enough to guide interventions in mental health? Using case formulation in clinical practice.' *BMC Medicine 10*, 111. Available at https://bmcmedicine.biomedcentral.com/track/pdf/10.1186/1741-7015-10-111, accessed on 23 October 2019.

Maio, G.R., Haddock, G. & Verplanken, B. (2019) *The Psychology of Attitudes and Attitude Change*. 3rd edition. London: Sage.

Mair, G. (1997) 'Community Penalties and Probation.' In M. Maguire, R. Morgan & R. Reiner (eds) *Oxford Handbook of Criminology* (pp.1195–1232). Oxford: Oxford University Press.

Maitlis, E. (2018) 'Chippendales: Do male strippers feel objectified?' BBC News, 19 February. Available at www.bbc.co.uk/news/world-us-canada-43111120, accessed on 19 February 2018.

Malamuth, N.M., Heavey, C.L. & Linz, D. (1993) 'Predicting Men's Anti-Social Behaviour against Women: The Interaction Model of Sexual Aggression.' In G.C.N. Hall, R. Hirshman, J.R. Graham & M.S. Zaragoza (eds) *Sexual Aggression: Issues in Aetiology, Assessment and Treatment* (Chapter 5). Washington, DC: Taylor & Francis.

Mancini, C. & Mears, D.P. (2010) 'To execute or not to execute? Examining public support for capital punishment of sex offenders.' *Journal of Criminal Justice 38*, 959–968.

Mandeville-Norden, R., Beech, A. & Hayes, E. (2008) 'Examining the effectiveness of a UK community-based sexual offender treatment programme for child abusers.' *Psychology, Crime & Law 14*, 6, 493–512.

Manet, E. (1863) 'Olympia.' Paris: Musee d'Orsay.

Mann, R.E., O'Brien, M., Thornton, D., Rallings, M. & Webster, S. (2002) *Structured Assessment of Risk and Need*. London: HM Prison Service.

Maras, M. & Shapiro, L.R. (2017) 'Child sex dolls and robots: More than just an uncanny valley.' *Journal of Internet Law*, December, 3–21.

Marchbank, J. & Letherby, G. (2007) *Introduction to Gender: Social Science Perspective*. Harlow: Pearson.

Marlatt, G.A. & Gordon, J.R. (eds) (1985) *Relapse Prevention*. New York: Guilford Press.

Marques, J.K., Wiederanders, M., Day, D.M., Nelson, C. & van Ommeren, A. (2005) 'Effects of a relapse prevention program on sexual recidivism: Final results from

California's sex offender treatment and evaluation project (SOTEP).' *Sexual Abuse 17*, 1, 79–107.

Marriot, E. (2008) 'Ray Wyre: Trailblazing therapist with a unique approach to sex offenders.' *The Guardian*, 8 August. Available at www.theguardian.com/science/2008/aug/08/psychology.ukcrime, accessed on 18 April 2019.

Marshall, D. & Thomas, T. (2015) 'Polygraphs and sex offenders: The truth is out there.' *Probation Journal 62*, 2.

Marshall, W.L. & Hollin, C. (2015) 'Historical developments in sex offender treatment.' *Journal of Sexual Aggression 21*, 2, 125–135. doi:10.1080/1355260 0.2014.980339.

Marshall, W.L., Anderson, D. & Fernandez, Y. (1999) *Cognitive Behavioural Treatment of Sexual Offenders*. Chichester: Wiley.

Marshall, W.L., Fernandez, Y.M., Hudson, S.M. & Ward, T. (eds) (1998) *Sourcebook of Treatment Programs for Sexual Offenders*. New York: Plenum Press.

Marshall, W.L., Serran, G.A., Fernandez, Y.M., Mulloy, R., Mann, E. & Thornton, D. (2003) 'Therapist characteristics in the treatment of sexual offenders: Tentative data on their relationship with indices of behaviour change.' *Journal of Sexual Aggression 9*, 1, 25–30. doi:10.1080/355260031000137940.

Martinson, R. (1974) 'What works? Questions and answers about prison reform.' *The Public Interest*, 22–54.

Maslach, C. (1976) 'Burnout.' *Human Behaviour 5*, 16–22.

Maslach, C. & Jackson, S.E. (1981) 'The measurement of experienced burnout.' *Journal of Occupational Behaviour 2*, 99–113.

Maslach, C. & Jackson, S.E. (1986) *The Maslach Burnout Inventory Manual*. 2nd edition. Palo Alto, CA: Consulting Psychologists Press.

Maslow, A.H. (1943) 'A theory of human motivation.' *Psychological Review 50*, 4, 370–396. doi:10.1037/h0054346.

Masson, H. & Hackett, S. (2003) 'A decade on from the NCH report (1992): Adolescent sexual aggression policy, practice and service delivery across the UK and Republic of Ireland.' *Journal of Sexual Aggression 9*, 2, 109–124. doi:10.1080/13552600310001632084.

Mathew, H.C.G. & Harrison, B. (2004) *Oxford Dictionary of National Biography: From the Earliest Times to the Year 2000*. Oxford: Oxford University Press.

Mathews, C. (2018) 'The day an out-of-control Land Rover plunged 150ft through a roof next to Doc Martin's picturesque Port Isaac cottage.' CornwallLive, 17 March. Available at www.cornwalllive.com/news/cornwall-news/day-out-control-land-rover-1342289, accessed on 18 October 2019.

Mayes, R. & Horwitz, A.V. (2005) 'DSM-lll and the revolution on the classification of mental illness.' *Journal of the History of the Behavioral Sciences 41*, 3, 249–267. Available at https://facultystaff.richmond.edu/~bmayes/pdf/dsmiii.pdf, accessed on 20 December 2019.

McAlinden, A. (2011) 'The Reintegration of Sexual Offenders: From a Risks- to Strength-Based Model of Offender Resettlement.' In S. Farrall, M. Hough, S. Maruna & R. Sparks (eds) *Escape Routes: Contemporary Perspectives on Life after Punishment* (Chapter 6). Abingdon: Routledge.

McCartan, K. & Prescott, D. (2017) 'Bring me the Horizon! (and Kaizen).' NOTA Prevention Blog, 29 June.

McClurg, G. & Craissati, J. (1999) 'A descriptive study of alleged child sexual abusers known to social services.' *Journal of Sexual Aggression 4*, 1, 22–30. doi:10.1080/13552609908413280.

McCrory, E. (2010) *A Treatment Manual for Adolescents Displaying Harmful Sexual Behaviour: Change for Good*. London: Jessica Kingsley Publishers.

McDermott, C. (2018) 'An Examination of the Child Sex Offender Disclosure Scheme in One Police Service Area.' Masters thesis. University of Huddersfield.

McGuire, J. (ed.) (1995) *What Works: Reducing Reoffending*. Chichester: Wiley.

McGuire, J. (2000) *Cognitive-Behavioural Approaches: An Introduction to Theory and Research*. London: Home Office, Her Majesty's Inspectorate of Probation.

McGuire, J. & Priestley, P. (1985) *Offending Behaviour: Skills and Stratagems for Going Straight*. London: Batsford.

McGuire, J. & Priestley, P. (1995) *Reviewing 'What Works' Past, Present and Future*. Chichester: Wiley.

McGuire, R.J., Carlisle, J.M. & Young, B.G. (1964) 'Sexual deviations as conditioned behavior: A hypothesis.' *Behaviour Research and Therapy 2*, 2–4, 185–190. doi:10.1016/0005-7967(64)90014-2.

McKenna, K. (1999) 'The brain is the master organ in sexual functions: Central nervous system control of male and female function.' *International Journal of Impotence Research 11*, Suppl. 1, S48–S55.

McTague, T. (2014) 'Police struggling to cope with soaring number of child abuse images circulating online warns NSPCC.' *Daily Mail*, 3 October. Available at www.dailymail.co.uk/news/article-2779459/Police-struggling-soaring-number-child-abuse-images-online-warns-NSPCC.html, accessed on 4 February 2020.

McTavish, J.R., Sverdlichhenko, I., MacMillan, H.L. & Wekerle, C. (2019) 'Child sexual abuse, disclosure and PTSD: A systematic and critical review.' *Child Abuse & Neglect 92*, 196–208. Available at https://doi.org/10.1016/j.chiabu.2019.04.006, accessed on 13 January 2020.

Meehl, P.E. (1954) *Clinical Versus Statistical Prediction: A Theoretical Analysis and Review of the Evidence*. Minneapolis, MN: University of Minneapolis Press.

Merdian, H.L., Curtis, C., Thakker, J., Wilson, N. & Boer, D.P. (2011) 'The three dimensions of online child pornography offending.' *Journal of Sexual Aggression 19*, 1, 121–132.

Mews, A., Di Bella, L. & Purver, M. (2017) *Impact Evaluation of the Prison-Based Core Sex Offender Treatment Programme*. London: Ministry of Justice. Available at https://assets.publishing.service.gov.uk/government/uploads/system/uploads/attachment_data/file/623876/sotp-report-web-.pdf, accessed on 13 April 2019.

Michie, A. & Lindsay, W. (2012) 'A treatment component designed to enhance empathy in sex offenders with an intellectual disability.' *The British Journal of Forensic Practice 14*, 1, 40–48. doi.org/10.1108/14636641211204450.

Miller, W.R. & Rollnick, S. (2002) *Motivational Interviewing: Preparing People to Change*. New York: Guilford Press.

Miller, W.R. & Rollnick, S. (2013) *Motivational Interviewing: Helping People to Change*. 3rd edition. New York: Guilford Press.

Millet, K. (1970) *Sexual Politics*. New York: Avon.

Minda, J.P. (2015) *The Psychology of Thinking: Reasoning, Decision-Making and Problem-Solving*. London: Sage.

Ministry of Justice NOMS (National Offender Management Service) (2019) *MAPPA Guidance 2012*, v.4.4. Available at https://mappa.justice.gov.uk/connect.ti/MAPPA/view?objectId=41211397, accessed on 3 January 2020.

Ministry of Justice and the Rt Hon Sir Mike Penning MP (2014) *New Support for Male Rape and Sexual Violence Victims.* Press release 11 December. Available at www.gov.uk/government/news/new-support-for-male-rape-and-sexual-violence-victims, accessed on 28 November 2019.

Monahan, J., Steadman, H.J., Silver, E., Appelbaum, P.S., *et al.* (2001) *Rethinking Risk Assessment: The MacArthur Study of Mental Disorder and Violence.* Oxford: Oxford University Press.

Moneta, G.B. (2014) *Positive Psychology: A Critical Introduction.* Basingstoke: Palgrave.

Morgan, R.K., Hart, A., Freeman, C., Coutts, B., Colwill, D. & Hughes, A. (2012) 'Practitioners, professional cultures, and perceptions of impact assessment.' *Environmental Impact Assessment Review 32*, 11–24.

Moulton, I.F. (2013) 'Erotic Representation 1500–1750.' In S. Toulalan & K. Fisher (eds) *The Routledge History of Sex and the Body 1500 to the Present* (Chapter 6). London: Routledge.

Munro, E. (2011) *The Munro Review of Child Protection: A Child Centred System. Final Report.* London: Department of Education. Available at https://assets. publishing.service.gov.uk/government/uploads/system/uploads/attachment_data/file/175391/Munro-Review.pdf, accessed on 21 October 2019.

Munro, E. & Hubbard, A. (2011) 'A systems approach to evaluating organisational change in children's social care.' *British Journal of Social Work 41*, 726–743. doi:1093/bjsw/bcr074.

Murphy, D., Duggan, M. & Joseph, S. (2012) 'Relationship-based social work and its compatibility with person-centred approach: Principle versus instrumental perspectives.' *British Journal of Social Work 43*, 703–719.

Murphy, W.D., Abel, G.G., Becker, J.V. (1980). 'Future research issues.' In Cox, D. J., Daitzman, R. J. (eds) *Exhibitionism: Description, assessment and treatment* (pp.339-392). New York, NY: Springer.

Murray, C.J.L., Lopez, A.D., Mathers, C.D. & Stein, C. (2001) *The Global Burden of Disease 2000 Project: Aims, Methods and Data Sources.* Geneva: World Health Organization (GPE Discussion Paper No. 36).

Nanda, S. (2014) 'Multiple Genders among North American Indians.' In J.A. Spade & C.G. Valentine (eds) *The Kaleidoscope of Gender: Prisms, Patterns and Possibilities.* 4th edition. Thousand Oaks, CA: Sage.

National Archives (n.d.) 'Records created or inherited by the National Offender Management Service/NOMS.' Available at https://discovery.nationalarchives. gov.uk/details/r/C401, accessed on 6 February 2020.

National Probation Service (NPS)(2007) *PC17/2007-Assessment and Management of Sex Offenders.* London: National Probation Service. Available at https:// webarchive.nationalarchives.gov.uk/20100809180919/http://www.probation. homeoffice.gov.uk/files/pdf/PC17%202007.pdf, accessed on 9 June 2020. Nellis, M. (2009) 'Circles of support and accountability for sex offenders in England and Wales: Their origins and implementation between 1999–2005.' *British Journal of Community Justice 7*, 1, 23–44.

Newburn, T. (2007) '"Tough on crime": Penal policy in England and Wales.' *Crime and Justice 36*, 1, 425–470.

Newburn, T. (ed.) (2017) *Criminology*. Abingdon: Routledge.

Newman, J. & Nutley, S. (2003) 'Transforming the probation service: "What works", organisational change and professional identity.' *Policy & Politics 31*, 4, 547–563. doi:10.1332/030557303322439407.

Nienhuis, J.B., Owen, J., Valentine, J.C., Winkeljohn Black, S., *et al.* (2018) 'Therapeutic alliance, empathy, and genuineness in individual adult psychotherapy: A meta-analytic review.' *Psychotherapy Research 28*, 4, 593–605. doi:10.1080/1050330 7.2016.1204023.

NOMS (2013) 'Conduct and discipline.' Available at www.justice.gov.uk/downloads/ offenders/psipso/psi-2010/psi_2010_06_conduct_and_discipline.doc, accessed on 24 September 2019.

North, N. & Thompson, S. (2016) 'Neurological Memory Disorders.' In P. Radcliffe, G.H. Gudjonsson, A. Heaton-Armstrong & D. Wolchover (eds) *Witness Testimony in Sexual Cases: Evidential, Investigative and Scientific Perspectives.* Oxford: Oxford University Press.

NOTA (1) (n.d.) 'Prevention committee/prevention committee plan 2018/19.' Available at www.nota.co.uk, accessed on 4 February 2020.

NOTA (2) (n.d.) 'Supporting professionals to prevent sexual abuse.' Available at www.nota.co.uk, accessed on 4 February 2020.

NOTA (3) (n.d.) *Prevention Committee.* Available at http://nota.co.uk/?s=prevention, accessed on 3 June 2020.

NSPCC (National Society for the Protection of Children) (2018) 'Statistics on child abuse.' Available at https://learning.nspcc.org.uk/statistics-child-abuse, accessed on 16 May 2018.

Nursing Home Abuse Center (n.d.) 'Sexual abuse of the elderly.' Available at www. nursinghomeabusecenter.com/elder-abuse/types/sexual-abuse, accessed on 9 August 2019.

Obscene Publications Act 1857 (repealed) 1952. *Journal of Criminal Law 16*, 3, 279–284.

Obscene Publications Act 1959. Available at www.legislation.gov.uk/ukpga/Eliz2/7-8/66, accessed on 26 December 2018.

Obscene Publications Act 1964. Available at www.legislation.gov.uk/ukpga/1964/74, accessed on 26 December 2018.

Onfray, M. (2015) *A Hedonist Manifesto: The Power to Exist.* New York: Columbia University Press.

ONS (Office for National Statistics) (2018) 'Population estimates for the UK, England and Wales, Scotland and Northern Ireland: Mid-2018.' Available at www.ons.gov.uk/peoplepopulationandcommunity/populationandmigration/ populationestimates/bulletins/annualmidyearpopulationestimates/mid2018, accessed on 9 August 2019.

Oxburgh, G.E. & Hynes, I. (2016) 'Investigative Practice.' In P. Radcliffe, G. Gudjonsson, A. Heaton-Armstrong & D. Wolchover (eds) *Witness Testimony in Sexual Cases: Evidential, Investigative and Scientific Perspectives.* Oxford: Oxford University Press.

Payne, M. (2011) *Humanistic Social Work: Core Principles in Practice.* Basingstoke: Palgrave Macmillan.

Parole Board (n.d.) *The parole board: working with others to protect the public/About us.* Available at https://www.gov.uk/government/organisations/parole-board/ about, accessed on 9 June 2020.

Pearlman, L.A. and Saakvitne, K.W. (1995) *Trauma and the Therapist: Countertransference and Vicarious Traumatization in Psychotherapy with Incest Survivors*. New York: Norton.

Pegg, S. & Davies, A. (2016) *Sexual Offences: Law and Context*. Abingdon: Routledge.

Perkins, D.E. (1982) 'The Treatment of Sex Offenders.' In M.P. Feldman (ed.) *Developments in the Study in the Criminal Behaviour. Vol. 1: The Prevention of Control and Offending* (pp.191–217). Chichester: John Wiley & Sons.

Perkins, D.E. (1987) 'Psychological Treatment Programme for Sex Offenders.' In B. McGurk, D. Thornton & M. Williams (eds) *Applying Psychology to Imprisonment* (pp.191–217). London: HMSO.

Peterson, M. (2006) 'The precautionary principle is incoherent.' *Risk Analysis 26*, 3, 595–601.

Pickford, J. (2012) 'The Laws and Sentencing Framework of Contemporary Youth Justice Practice.' In J. Pickford & P. Dugmore (eds) *Youth Justice and Social Work*. London: Sage.

PlymouthLive (2019) 'Pictures of Vanessa George laughing and enjoying her freedom are an insult to her victims.' Available at www.plymouthherald.co.uk/news/plymouth-news/pictures-vanessa-george-laughing-enjoying-3403096, accessed on 10 October 2019.

Polaschek, D.L.L. (2003) 'Relapse prevention, offense process models, and the treatment of sexual offenders.' *Professional Psychology: Practice and Research 34*, 361–367.

Polaschek, D.L. (2012) 'An appraisal of the risk-need-responsivity (RNR) model of offender rehabilitation and its application in correctional treatment.' *Legal and Criminological Psychology*, 1–17. doi:10.1111/j.2044-8333.2011.02038.x.

Poole, J.C., Dobson, K.S. & Pusch, D. (2018) 'Do childhood experiences predict adult interpersonal difficulties? The role of emotional dysregulation.' *Child Abuse & Neglect*, 123–133. doi.org/10.1016/j.chiabu.2018.03.006.

Prentky, R. & Barbaree, H. (2011) 'Commentary: Hebephilia – A would-be paraphilia caught in the twilight zone between prepubescence and adulthood.' *The Journal of the American Academy of Psychiatry and the Law 39*, 4, 506–510.

Prentky, R.A., Barbaree, H.E. & Janus, E.S. (2015) *Sexual Predators: Society, Risk and the Law*. London: Routledge.

Preves, S.E. (2014) 'Beyond Pink and Blue.' In J.A. Spade & C.G. Valentine (eds) *The Kaleidoscope of Gender: Prisms, Patterns and Possibilities*. 4th edition. Thousand Oaks, CA: Sage.

Prins, H. (1980) *Offenders, Deviants or Patients?* London: Tavistock.

Prochaska, J.O. & DiClemente, C.C. (1982) 'Transtheoretical therapy: Towards a more integrative model of change.' *Psychotherapy: Theory, Research & Practice 19*, 3, 276–288. https://doi.org/10.1037/h0088437.

Quayle, E. (2008) 'The COPINE Project.' *Irish Probation Journal 5*, 65–83.

Quinsey, V.L., Harris, G.T., Rice, M.E. & Cormier, C.A. (1998) *Violent Offenders: Appraising and Managing the Risk*. Washington, DC: American Psychological Association.

Radcliffe, P. & Gudjonsson, G.H. (2016) 'Witness Testimony: Vulnerabilities, Context, and Issues.' In P. Radcliffe, G. Gudjonsson, A. Heaton-Armstrong & D. Wolchover (eds) *Witness Testimony in Sexual Cases: Evidential, Investigative and Scientific Perspectives*. Oxford: Oxford University Press.

Raynor, P. (2003) 'Evidence-based probation and its critics.' *Probation Journal 50*, 4, 334–345.

Reiner, R. (2008) 'Success or statistics? New Labour and crime control.' *Criminal Justice Matters 67*, 1, 4–37. doi:10.1080/09627250708553198.

Rhen, T. & Crews, D. (2007) 'Why Are There Two Sexes?' In J.B. Becker, K.J. Berkley, N. Geary, E. Hampson, *et al.* (eds) *Sex Differences in the Brain: From Genes to Behaviour* (Chapter 1). Oxford: Oxford Scholarship Online. Available at www.oxfordscholarship.com/view/10.1093/acprof:oso/9780195311587.001.0001/acprof-9780195311587, accessed on 27 November 2019.

Ridley, M. (2004) *Evolution*. 3rd edition. Chichester: John Wiley.

Rogers, C. (1951) *Client-Centred Therapy: Its Current Practice, Implications and Theory*. Boston, MA: Houghton Mifflin.

Rogers, C. (1957) 'The necessary and sufficient conditions of therapeutic personality change.' *Journal of Consulting and Clinical Psychology 60*, 6, 827–832 (reprinted December 1992). doi:10.1037/0022-006X.60.6.827.

Rogers, C. (1961) *On Becoming a Person*. Boston, MA: Houghton Mifflin.

Rogers, C. (1963) 'The Actualising Tendency in Relation to "Motives" and to Consciousness.' In M.R. Jones (ed.) *Nebraska Symposium on Motivation*, vol. 11. Lincoln, NE: University of Nebraska Press.

Rook, P. & Ward, R. (2016) *Sexual offences: law and practice*. 5th edition. London: Sweet & Maxwell.

Ross, R.R., Fabiano, E.A. & Ewles, C.D. (1988) 'Reasoning and rehabilitation.' *International Journal of Offender Therapy and Comparative Criminology 32*, 1, 29–36.

Ryan, G., Lane, S.R., Davis, J.M. & Isaac, C.B. (1987) 'Juvenile sex offenders: Development and correction.' *Child Abuse & Neglect 2*, 385–395.

Rytilä-Manninen, M., Haravuori, H., Fröjd, S., Marttunen, M. & Lindberg, N. (2018) 'Mediators between adverse childhood experiences and suicidality.' *Child Abuse & Neglect*, 99–109. doi.org/10.1016/j.chiabu.2017.12.007.

Saad-Filho, A. & Johnston, D. (2005) 'Introduction.' In A. Saad-Filho & D. Johnston (eds) *Neoliberalism: A Critical Reader* (pp.1–5). London: Pluto.

Safer Communities Directorate (2018) *Moving Forward Making Changes: Evaluation of a Group-Based Treatment for Sex Offenders – Summary (MFMC)*. Edinburgh: Scottish Government. Available at www.gov.scot/publications/moving-forward-making-changes-evaluation-group-based-treatment-sex-offenders-9781788519908, accessed on 10 January 2020.

Saleeby, D. (2013) *The Strengths Perspective in Social Work Practice*. 6th edition. London: Pearson.

Sampson, R.J. & Laub, J.H. (2003) 'Life-course desisters? Trajectories of crime among delinquent boys followed to age 70.' *Criminology 41*, 3, 555–592.

Sandhu, D.K. & Rose, J. (2012) 'How do therapists contribute to therapeutic change in sex offender treatment? An integration of the literature.' *Journal of Sexual Aggression 18*, 3, 269–283. doi:10.1080/13552600.2011.566633.

Sandler, J.C. & Freeman, N.J. (2009) 'Female sex offender recidivism: A large-scale empirical analysis.' *Sexual Abuse: A Journal of Research and Treatment 21*, 4, 445–473.

Sarre, R. (2001) 'Beyond what works? A 25 year jubilee retrospective of Robert Martinson's famous article.' *Australian & New Zealand Journal of Criminology 34*, 1, 38–46. doi:10.1177%2F000486580103400103.

Schmucker, M. & Losel, F. (2017) 'Sexual offender treatment for reducing recidivism among convicted sex offenders: A systematic review and meta-analysis.' *Campbell Systematic Reviews 13*, 1. doi:10.4073/csr.2017.8.

Schön, D.A. (1987) *Educating the Reflective Practitioner.* San Francisco, CA: Jossey Bass.

Schön, D.A. (1991) *The Reflective Practitioner: How Professionals Think in Action.* Aldershot: Avebury.

Schor, J.B. (2014) *Born to Buy: The Commercialised Child and the New Consumer Cult.* New York: Scribner.

Scottish Government (2002) *Stalking and Harassment in Scotland.* Available at www2.gov.scot/Publications/2002/11/15756/13116, accessed on 10 October 2019.

Scully, P. (1995) 'Rape, race, and colonial culture: The sexual politics of identity in the nineteenth century Cape Colony, South Africa.' *The American Historical Review 100*, 2, 335–359.

Seal, L. (2014) 'Imagined communities and the death penalty in Britain, 1930–65.' *The British Journal of Criminology 54*, 5, 908–927. Available at https://Doi-org.plymouth.idm.oclc.org/10.1093/bjc/azu045, accessed on 27 November 2019.

Segal, L. (2004) 'Only the Literal: The Contradictions of Anti-Pornography Feminism.' In P.C. Gibson (ed.) *More Dirty Looks: Gender, Pornography and Power* (Chapter 5). London: British Film Institute.

Seidman, S. (2011) 'Sex as a Social Fact: Theoretical Perspectives.' In S. Seidman, N. Fischer & C. Meeks (eds) *Introducing the New Sexuality Studies.* 2nd edition. Abingdon: Routledge.

Self, W. (2019) 'A point of view: Against theory.' BBC Radio 4, broadcast 18 August, 08:45. Available at www.bbc.co.uk/programmes/m000712h, accessed on 18 August 2019.

Seligman, M.E.P. & Csikszentmihalyi, M. (2000) 'Positive psychology: An introduction.' *American Psychologist 55*, 5–14.

Seto, M.C., Hanson, K. & Babchishin, K.M. (2011) 'Contact sexual offending by men with online sexual offenses.' *Sexual Abuse 23*, 1, 124–145. Available at https://Doi.org/10.1177/1079063210369013, accessed on 27 November 2019.

Sexual Offences Act 2003, c.42. Available at www.legislation.gov.uk/ukpga/2003/42/contents, accessed on 25 September 2003.

Sheppard, M. (1995) 'Social work, social science and practice wisdom.' *British Journal of Social Work 25*, 265–293.

Shin, S.H., McDonald, S.E. & Conley, D. (2018) 'Profiles of adverse childhood experiences and impulsivity.' *Child Abuse & Neglect*, 118–126. doi.org/10.1016/j.chiabu.2018.07.028.

Skye, S., Newman, J.E., Cantor, J.M. & Seto, M.C. (2017) 'The Static-99R predicts sexual and violent recidivism for individuals with low intellectual functioning.' *Journal of Sexual Aggression 24*, 1, 1–11. doi:10.1080/13552600.2017.1372936.

Slovic, P. & Peters, E. (2006) 'Risk perception and affect.' *Current Directions in Psychological Science 15*, 6, 322–325.

Smallbone, S. & Cale, J. (in press) 'Situational Theories.' In T. Ward & A.R. Beech (eds) *Theories of Sexual Offending.* Oxford: Wiley-Blackwell.

Smith, C., Allardyce, S., Hackett, S., Bradbury-Jones, C., Lazenbatt, A. & Taylor, J. (2014) 'Practice and policy in the UK with children and young people who display harmful sexual behaviours: An analysis and critical review.' *Journal of Sexual Aggression 20*, 3, 267–280. doi:10.1080/13552600.2014.927010.

Sorrentino, R. (2016) 'DSM-5 and paraphilias: What psychiatrists need to know.' *Psychiatric Times*, 28 November.

Spade, J.A. & Valentine, C.G. (2014) *The Kaleidoscope of Gender: Prisms, Patterns and Possibilities*. 4th edition. Thousand Oaks, CA: Sage.

Spruin, E., Wood, J.L., Gannon, T.A. & Tyler, N. (2017) 'Sexual offenders' experiences of polygraph testing: A thematic study in three probation trusts.' *Journal of Sexual Aggression 24*, 1, 12–24. doi:10.1080/13552600.2017.1378025.

Stalking Protection Act 2019. Available at www.legislation.gov.uk/ukpga/2019/9/enacted, accessed on 10 October 2019.

Stanford, S. (2008) 'Taking a stand or playing it safe? Resisting the moral conservatism of risk in social work practice.' *European Journal of Social Work 11*, 3, 209–220.

Steiner, C. (1997) *Achieving Emotional Literacy*. London: Bloomsbury.

Stephens, S. & Seto, M.C. (2015) 'Hebephilia.' In P. Whelehan & A. Bolin (eds) *The Encyclopedia of Human Sexuality*. Chichester: Wiley-Blackwell.

Stephens, S. & Seto, M.C. (2016) 'Hebephilic Sexual Offending.' In A. Phenix & H.M. Hoberman (eds) *Sexual Offending: Predisposing Antecedents, Assessments and Management*. New York: Springer.

Sternberg, R.J. & Weis, K. (2006) *The New Psychology of Love*. New Haven, CT: Yale University Press.

Stevens, P., Hutchin, K., French, L. & Craissati, J. (2013) 'Developmental and offence-related characteristics of different types of adolescent sex offender: A community sample.' *Journal of Sexual Aggression 19*, 2, 138–157.

Strachan, R. & Tallant, C. (1997) 'Improving Judgement and Appreciating Biases within the Risk Assessment Process.' In J. Pritchard and H. Kemshall (eds) *Good Practice in Risk Assessment and Risk Management 2*. London: Jessica Kingsley Publishers.

Strickland, P. (2015) *Sentences of imprisonment for public protection: briefing paper 06086*. London: House of Commons library. Available at https://www.insidetime.org/download/research_&_reports/house_of_commons_briefings/HoC-Briefing_IPP-Sentences.pdf, accessed 9 June 2020.

Tangney, J.P., Stuewig, J. & Hafez, L. (2011) 'Shame, guilt, and remorse: Implications for offender populations.' *The Journal of Forensic Psychiatry & Psychology 22*, 5, 706–723. doi:10.1080/14789949.2011.617541.

Taylor, M. and Quayle, E. (2003) *Child Pornography: An Internet Crime*. Hove: Brunner–Routledge.

Taylor, M., Holland, G. & Quayle, E. (2001) 'Typology of paedophile picture collections.' *Police Journal: Theory, Practice and Principles*, 74. doi.org/10.1177/0032258X0107400202.

Terry, K. (2017) 'What Is Sex Crime?' In T. Sanders (ed.) *The Oxford Handbook of Sex Offences and Sex Offenders*. Oxford: Oxford University Press.

The Lucy Faithfull Foundation (n.d.) *Stop it now!: helping prevent child sexual abuse*. Available at http://stopitnow.org.uk, accessed on 3 June 2020.

Thomas, T., Thompson, D. & Karstedt, K. (2014) *Assessing the Impact of Circles of Support and Accountability on the Reintegration of Adults Convicted of Sexual Offences in the Community*. Leeds: Centre for Criminal Justice Studies, School of Law, University of Leeds.

Thompson, D., Thomas, T. & Karstedt, S. (2017) *The Resettlement of Sex Offenders after Custody: Circles of Support and Accountability*. Routledge Studies in Crime and Society. London: Taylor & Francis.

Thompson, N. (2005) *Understanding Social Work: Preparing for Practice*. London: Palgrave.

Thornhill, R. & Palmer, C.T. (2000) *Rape: A Natural History*. Cambridge, MA: MIT Press.

Thornton, D. (2000) 'Risk matrix 2000.' Presentation at Association for Treatment of Sexual Abusers Conference. San Antonio.

Thornton, D. (2007) 'Scoring guide for risk matrix 2000.9/SVC.' Available at www. birmingham.ac.uk/documents/college-les/psych/rm2000scoringinstructions. pdf, accessed on 21 May 2018.

Toulalan, S. & Fisher, K. (eds) (2013) *The Routledge History of Sex and the Body: 1500 to the Present*. Abingdon: Routledge.

Travis, C.B. (2003) *Evolution, Gender, and Rape*. Cambridge, MA: MIT Press.

Tversky, A. & Kahneman, D. (1973) 'Availability: A heuristic for judging frequency and probability.' *Cognitive Psychology 5*, 2, 207–232.

UN (United Nations) (n.d.) 'Ageing.' Available at www.un.org/en/sections/issues-depth/ageing, accessed on 9 August 2019.

UN Human Rights Office of the Commissioner (n.d.) 'Rape: Weapon of war.' Available at www.ohchr.org/EN/NewsEvents/Pages/RapeWeaponWar.aspx, accessed on 26 August 2019.

UNCED (United Nations Conference on Environment and Development) (1992) 'Rio Declaration on Environment and Development.' Rio de Janeiro, 3–14 June.

Vizard, E. (2013) 'Practitioner review: The victims and juvenile perpetrators of child sexual abuse – assessment and intervention.' *Journal of Child Psychology and Psychiatry 54*, 5, 503–515.

von Krafft-Ebing, R. & Chaddock, C.G. (1892) *Psychopathia Sexualis: With Special Reference to Contrary Sexual Instinct. A Medico-Legal Study*. London & Philadelphia: F.A. Davis Co. Available at www.gender.amdigital.co.uk.plymouth. idm.oclc.org/Documents/Details/Psychopathia%20Sexualis0, accessed on 10 January 2020.

Walker, G. (2013) 'Rape, acquittal and culpability in popular crime reports in England, c.1670–c.1750.' *Past and Present 220*, 115–142.

Walker, K. & Brown, S.J. (2013) 'Non-sex offenders display distorted thinking and have empathy deficits too: A thematic analysis of cognitions and the application of empathy.' *Journal of Sexual Aggression 19*, 10, 81–101. doi:10.1080/1355260 0.2011.618276.

Walker, N. (1994) 'Reductivism and Deterrence.' In A. Duff & D. Garland (eds) *A Reader on Punishment* (pp.210–217). Oxford: Oxford University Press.

Wallace, C., Mullen, P.E., Burgess, P. & Palmer, S. (1998) 'Serious criminal offending and mental disorder: Case linkage study.' *British Journal of Psychiatry 172*, 6, 477–484.

Walton, J. (2018) 'Random assignment in sexual offending programme evaluation: The missing method.' *The Journal of Forensic Practice 20*, 1, 1–9. doi:10.1108/ JFP-08-2017-0032.

Ward, T. (2007) 'On a clear day you can see forever: Integrating values and skills in sex offender treatment.' *Journal of Sexual Aggression 13*, 3, 187–201. doi:10.1080/13552600701794036.

Ward, T. (2009) 'The extended mid theory of cognitive distortions in sex offenders.' *Journal of Sexual Aggression 15*, 3, 247–259. doi:10.1080/13552600903263087.

Ward, T. (2014) 'The explanation of sexual offending: From single factor theories to integrative pluralism.' *Journal of Sexual Aggression 20*, 2, 130–141. doi:1010 80/13552600.2013.870242.

Ward, T. & Beech, T. (2017) 'The Explanation of Sexual Offending.' In T. Sanders (ed.) *The Oxford Handbook of Sex Offences and Sex Offenders.* Oxford: Oxford University Press.

Ward, T. & Brown, M. (2004) 'The Good Lives Model and conceptual issues in offender rehabilitation.' *Psychology, Crime & Law 10*, 3, 243–257. doi:10.1080/ 10683160410001662744.

Ward, T. & Hudson, S.M. (2001) 'Finkelhor's precondition model of child sexual abuse: A critique.' *Psychology, Crime & Law 7*, 291–307.

Ward, T. & Marshall, W.L. (2004) 'Good lives, etiology and the rehabilitation of sex offenders: A bridging theory.' *Journal of Sexual Aggression 10*, 153–169.

Ward, T. & Siegert, R. (1) (2002) 'Rape and evolutionary psychology: A critique of Thornhill and Palmer's theory.' *Aggression and Violent Behavior 7*, 2, 145–168.

Ward, T. & Siegert, R. (2) (2002) 'Towards a comprehensive theory of child sexual abuse: A theory knitting perspective.' *Psychology, Crime and Law 8*, 4, 319–351.

Ward, T. & Sorbello, L. (2003) 'Explaining Child Sexual Abuse: Integration and Elaboration.' In T. Ward, D.R. Laws and S.M. Hudson (eds) *Sexual Deviance: Issues and Controversies.* London: Sage.

Ward, T. & Stewart, C.A. (2003) 'The treatment of sex offenders: Risk management and good lives.' *Professional Psychology: Research & Practice 34*, 353–360.

Warrell, I. (2012) *Turner's Secret Sketches.* London: Tate Publishing.

Webb, S.A. (2006) *Social Work in a Risk Society: Social and Political Perspectives.* Basingstoke: Palgrave Macmillan.

Weeks, J. (2005) 'Remembering Foucault.' *Journal of the History of Sexuality 14*, 1/2, 186–236.

Weitzer, R.J. (2010) *Sex for Sale: Prostitution, Pornography, and the Sex Industry.* 2nd edition. New York: Routledge.

West, D. (1996) 'Sexual Molesters.' In N. Walker (ed.) *Dangerous People* (pp.51–69). London: Blackstone.

Whittaker, A. & Havard, T. (2016) 'Defensive practice as "fear-based" practice: Social work's open question?' *British Journal of Social Work 46*, 5, 1158–1174. doi:10.1093/bjsw/bcv048.

WHO (World Health Organization) (2016) *International Classification of Diseases (ICD-10).* 11th edition. Available at www.who.int/classifications/icd/ icdonlineversions/en, accessed on 28 April 2019.

Wijkman, M. (2011) 'Female sex offenders: Specialists, generalists and once only offenders.' *Journal of Sexual Aggression 17*, 1, 34–45. Available at www-tandfonline-com.plymouth.idm.oclc.org/Doi/full/10.1080/13552600.2010.54 0679, accessed on 15 June 2018.

Wilcox, D.T. (2004) 'Treatment of intellectually disabled individuals who have committed sexual offences: A review of the literature.' *Journal of Sexual Aggression 10*, 1, 85–100. doi:10.1080/13552600410001670955.

Wilcox, D.T., Foss, C.M. & Donathy, M.L. (2005) 'A case study of a male sex offender with zoosexual interests and behaviours.' *Journal of Sexual Aggression 11*, 3, 305–317. doi:10.1080/13552600500333804.

Willemsen, J., Says, V., Gunst, E. & Desmet, M. (2016) '"Simply speaking your mind, from the depths of your soul": Therapeutic factors in experiential group psychotherapy for sex offenders.' *Journal of Forensic Psychology Practice 16*, 3, 151–168.

Williams, M.W.M., Blackwood, K., van Rensburg, J.B.J., Jones, D.T. & Calvert, S.W. (2016) 'From known to stranger crossover: A retrospective study of child sex offenders released into the community.' *Sexual Offender Treatment 11*, 1, 1–14. Available at www.sexual-offender-treatment.org/152.html, accessed on 27 April 2019.

Wills, A.R. (2008) 'Low-Risk Offenders Who Re-Offend Seriously – Some Implications for Risk Analysis in Probation Practice.' Unpublished PhD thesis. Anglia Ruskin University.

Wolf, S. (1998) 'A model of sexual aggression/addiction.' *Journal of Social Work and Human Sexuality 7*, 1.

Wolf, S.C. (1985) 'A multifactor model of deviant sexuality.' *Victimology: An International Journal 10*, 359–374.

Wolfenden, J. (1957) *Report of the Committee on Homosexual Offences and Prostitution (Wolfenden Report)*. London: HMSO. Available at www.parliament.uk/about/living-heritage/transformingsociety/private-lives/relationships/collections1/sexual-offences-act-1967/wolfenden-report-, accessed on 24 December 2018.

World Economic Forum (2017) *The Global Gender Gap Report 2017*. Available at www.wherewomenwork.com/Career/640/Global-Gender-Gap-WorldEconomic Forum, accessed on 8 March 2018.

Yates, P., Allardyce, S. & MacQueen, S. (2012) 'Children who display harmful sexual behaviour: Assessing the risks of boys abusing at home, in the community or across both settings.' *Journal of Sexual Aggression 18*, 1, 23–35. doi:10.1080/13 552600.2011.634527.

Zander, T., Horr, N.K., Bolte, A. & Volz, K.G. (2015) 'Intuitive decision-making as a gradual process: Investigating semantic intuition-based and priming-based decisions with fMRI.' *Brain and Behavior 6*, 1. doi:10.1002/brb3.42.

List of Sexual Offences (Sexual Offences Act 2003) and Recorded Number of Sexual Offences (2019)

SEXUAL OFFENCES ACT 2003[1]

Section 1 Rape

Section 2 Assault by penetration

Section 3 Sexual assault

Section 4 Causing a person to engage in a sexual activity without consent

Section 5 Rape of a child under 13

Section 6 Sexual assault of a child under 13 by penetration

Section 7 Sexual assault of a child under 13

Section 8 Causing a child under 13 to engage in sexual activity

Section 9 Sexual activity with a child

Section 10 Causing or inciting a child to engage in sexual activity

---

1   Sexual Offences Act 2003, c.42. Available at: www.legislation.gov.uk/ ukpga/2003/42/contents

Section 11 Engaging in sexual activity in the presence of a child

Section 12 Causing a child to watch a sexual act

Section 13 Child sex offences committed by a child

Section 14 Arranging or facilitating commission of a child sex offence

Section 15 Meeting a child following sexual grooming etc.

Section 15A Sexual communication with a child

Abuse of position of trust

Section 16 Abuse of position of trust: sexual activity with a child

Section 17 Abuse of position of trust: causing or inciting a child to engage in sexual activity

Section 18 Abuse of position of trust: sexual activity in the presence of a child

Section 19 Abuse of position of trust: causing a child to watch a sexual act

Section 20 Abuse of position of trust: acts done in Scotland

Section 21 Positions of trust

Section 22 Positions of trust: interpretation

Section 23 Sections 16–19: exception for spouses and civil partners

Section 24 Sections 16–19: sexual relationships which pre-date position of trust

Familial child sex offences

Section 25 Sexual activity with a child family member

Section 26 Inciting a child family member to engage in sexual activity

Section 27 Family relationships

Section 28 Sections 25 and 26: exception for spouses and civil partners

Section 29 Sections 25 and 26: sexual relationships which pre-date family relationships

Offences against persons with a mental disorder impeding choice

Section 30 Sexual activity with a person with a mental disorder impeding choice

Section 31 Causing or inciting a person, with a mental disorder impeding choice, to engage in sexual activity

Section 32 Engaging in sexual activity in the presence of a person with a mental disorder impeding choice

Section 33 Causing a person, with a mental disorder impeding choice, to watch a sexual act

Inducements etc. to persons with a mental disorder

Section 34 Inducement, threat or deception to procure sexual activity with a person with a mental disorder

Section 35 Causing a person with a mental disorder to engage in or agree to engage in sexual activity by inducement, threat or deception

Section 36 Engaging in sexual activity in the presence, procured by inducement, threat or deception, of a person with a mental disorder

Section 37 Causing a person with a mental disorder to watch a sexual act by inducement, threat or deception

Care workers for persons with a mental disorder

Section 38 Care workers: sexual activity with a person with a mental disorder

Section 39 Care workers: causing or inciting sexual activity

Section 40 Care workers: sexual activity in the presence of a person with a mental disorder

Section 41 Care workers: causing a person with a mental disorder to watch a sexual act

Section 42 Care workers: interpretation

Section 43 Sections 38–41: exception for spouses and civil partners

Section 44 Sections 38–41: sexual relationships which pre-date care relationships

Indecent photographs of children

Section 45 Indecent photographs of persons aged 16 or 17

Section 46 Criminal proceedings, investigations etc.

Sexual exploitation of children

Section 47 Paying for sexual services of a child

Section 48 Causing or inciting sexual exploitation of a child

Section 49 Controlling a child in relation to sexual exploitation

Section 50 Arranging or facilitating sexual exploitation of a child

Section 51 Sections 48–50: interpretation

Prostitution

Section 51A Soliciting

Section 52 Causing or inciting prostitution for gain

Section 53 Controlling prostitution for gain

Section 53A Paying for sexual services of a prostitute subjected to force etc.

Section 54 Sections 51A–53A: interpretation

Amendments relating to prostitution

Section 55 Penalties for keeping a brothel used for prostitution

Section 56 Extension of gender-specific prostitution offences

Trafficking

Section 57 Trafficking into the UK for sexual exploitation

Section 58 Trafficking within the UK for sexual exploitation

Section 58A Trafficking outside the UK for sexual exploitation

Section 59 Trafficking out of the UK for sexual exploitation

Section 59A Trafficking people for sexual exploitation

Section 60 Section 59A: interpretation

Section 60A Forfeiture of land vehicle, ship or aircraft

Section 60B Detention of land vehicle, ship or aircraft

Section 60C Sections 60A and 60B: interpretation

Preparatory offences

Section 61 Administering a substance with intent

Section 62 Committing an offence with intent to commit a sexual offence

Section 63 Trespass with intent to commit a sexual offence

Sex with an adult relative

Section 64 Sex with an adult relative: penetration

Section 65 Sex with an adult relative: consenting to penetration

Other offences

Section 66 Exposure

Section 67 Voyeurism

Section 67A Voyeurism: additional offences

Section 68 Voyeurism: interpretation

Section 69 Intercourse with an animal

Section 70 Sexual penetration of a corpse

Section 71 Sexual activity in a public lavatory

RECORDED NUMBER OF SEXUAL OFFENCES (2019)[2]

Statistics for the number of sexual offences based on two principal datasets of the Crime Survey for England and Wales and police

---

2   NAO (National Audit Office) (2019) 'Crime and justice figures on crime levels and trends for England and Wales based primarily on two sets of statistics: The Crime Survey for England and Wales (CSEW) and police recorded crime data/Crime in England and Wales. Appendix tables.' Available at: www. ons.gov.uk/peoplepopulationandcommunity/crimeandjustice/datasets/ crimeinenglandandwalesappendixtables.

recorded crime data indicate the total number of recorded sexual offences up to year ending June 2019. This shows the following:

- The total number of sexual offences was 163,076, an increase of 5 per cent on the previous year (in 2009 there were 50,185).
- The total number of rapes was 58,947, an increase of 7 per cent, of which 16,488 were the rape of a child under 16.
- Adding together the recorded figures, the total number of crimes against a child was 83,979, including sexual assault on a male and female child, both those aged under and those over 13; unlawful sexual intercourse with a girl, both those over and those under 16; and sexual activity involving a child under 16.
- Additionally there were 878 crimes involving incest or family, and 962 crimes involving abuse of children through sexual exploitation.

Subject Index

Author Index

203ۆ

Elliott, R. 142
Endrass, J. 60
Ericsson, K.A. 76
Erooga, M. 123
Ewles, C.D. 119

Fabiano, E.A. 119
Family Rights Group 111
Farrington, D.P. 137
Faux, M. 46, 131
Fernandez, Y. 130
Festinger, L. 151
Figley, C.R. 158
Finkelhor, D. 12, 124, 126, 127, 130, 138
Fishbein, M. 153
Fisher, D. 124, 131
Fisher, K. 24
Forsberg, L. 124
Foss, C.M. 55
Foucault, M. 24, 26, 27, 28, 33
Franke, I. 60
Fredrickson, B.L. 150, 152
Freeman, N.J. 65
Friendship, C. 93
Fu, C. 123
Furedi, F. 75
Furlong, M.W. 38

Gannon, T.A. 65
Gardner, H. 148
Garland, D. 122
Garrett, T. 67
George, M. 29
Gerwinn, H. 99
Giddens, A. 73, 74
Gill, R. 19
Gillespie, A. 7
Glueck, B.B. 40, 41
Göbbels, S. 47, 48, 50
Goosey, D. 110, 111
Gordon, J.R. 129
Gottfredson, D.M. 87
Gottfredson, S.D. 87
Gov.uk 64

Graf, M. 60
Gray, D. 76
Greenall, P.V. 68
Greetham, B. 156
Grove, W.M. 96
Grubin, D. 15, 16, 68, 122, 130
Gudjonsson, G.H. 113
Gunst, E. 40

Hackett, S. 65, 69, 70, 149
Hacking, I. 78
Haddock, G. 18
Hafez, L. 123
Hall, G.C.N. 12, 130
Hammer, E.F. 40, 41
Hanson, K. 89
Hanson, R.K. 43, 60, 65, 67, 97, 124
Hare, R.D. 67
Harkins, L. 130
Harris, A.J.R. 67, 97, 124
Harrison, B. 116
Harrison, L.E. 41
Hart, S.D. 67, 76, 100
Harway, M. 22
Hatcher, R. 158
Havard, T. 94
Hayes, E. 46
Heath, D. 33
Heavey, C.L. 124
Heffernan, R. 100
Henggeler, S.W. 71
Herman, J.L. 42
Hermann, C.A. 60
Hirschman, R. 12, 130
HM Prison & Probation Service 97
Hoge, R.D. 134
Holland, G. 34
Hollin, C. 118
Hollinrake, S. 153
Holmes, M. 23
Holmes, R.M. 66
Holt, K. 111
Home Office 19, 120, 129
Hood, R. 38, 81, 111, 147
Horvath, A.G. 146

Tallant, C. 77
Tangney, J.P. 123
Taylor, M. 34
Terry, K. 9
Tesch-Romer, C. 76
Thomas, T. 121, 145
Thompson, D. 145
Thompson, N. 46
Thompson, S. 114
Thornhill, R. 17
Thornton, D. 82, 96, 97, 100, 124
Toulalan, S. 24
Travis, C.B. 41
Truscott, D. 158
Tversky, A. 90

UN Human Rights Office of
the Commissioner 64
UN (United Nations) 72
UNCED (United Nations
Conference on Environment
and Development) 83

Valentine, C.G. 22
Veronen, J.L. 39
Verplanken, B. 18
Vizard, E. 71
von Krafft-Ebing, R. 39, 72

Walker, G. 18
Walker, K. 138
Walker, N. 123
Wallace, C. 67
Walton, J. 134

Ward, R. 105
Ward, T. 12, 17, 39, 42, 43, 45,
46, 47, 48, 50, 100, 125,
126, 129, 130, 135, 137,
140, 146, 148, 149, 154
Warrell, I. 32
Watt, P. 76
Weare, S. 7
Webb, S.A. 83
Weeks, J. 17, 29, 33
Weis, K. 25
Weitzer, R.J. 19
West, D. 9, 118, 119
Whittaker, A. 94
WHO (World Health
Organization) 72
Whyte, B. 68
Wijkman, M. 65
Wilcox, D.T. 55, 135
Willemsen, J. 40
Williams, M.W.M. 54
Willis, G.M. 47
Wills, A.R. 95, 154
Wolf, S. 124, 130
Wolfenden, J. 34
World Economic Forum 22
Wright, M. 68
Wynne, B. 73, 91
Wyre, R. 119

Yates, P. 70
Young, B.G. 130

Zander, T. 148